ALSO BY BILL MURPHY JR.

*In a Time of War: The Proud and Perilous Journey of
West Point's Class of 2002*

THE INTELLIGENT ENTREPRENEUR

THE
INTELLIGENT
ENTREPRENEUR

HOW THREE HARVARD BUSINESS SCHOOL
GRADUATES LEARNED THE 10 RULES OF
SUCCESSFUL ENTREPRENEURSHIP

BILL MURPHY JR.

HENRY HOLT AND COMPANY   NEW YORK

Henry Holt and Company, LLC
Publishers since 1866
175 Fifth Avenue
New York, New York 10010
www.henryholt.com

Henry Holt® and 📖® are registered trademarks of
Henry Holt and Company, LLC.

Library of Congress Cataloging-in-Publication Data
Murphy, Bill, Jr.
    The intelligent entrepreneur: how three Harvard Business School graduates
learned the 10 rules of successful entrepreneurship / Bill Murphy Jr.
        p. cm.
    ISBN 978-0-8050-9166-3
    1. Entrepreneurship.   2. Success in business.   I. Title.
    HB615.M87 2010
    658.4'21—dc22   2010008915

Henry Holt books are available for special promotions and
premiums. For details contact: Director, Special Markets.

First Edition 2010

Designed by Kelly S. Too

Printed in the United States of America
1   3   5   7   9   10   8   6   4   2

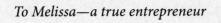

To Melissa—a true entrepreneur

CONTENTS

THE INTELLIGENT ENTREPRENEUR

INTRODUCTION

WONDERFUL NEWS:
MOST NEW BUSINESSES FAIL

Let me guess. If you're reading this book, it's probably because you hope to become a truly successful entrepreneur. You want to build something dynamic, useful, and great, and maybe even get rich in the process. If that's the case, then allow me to give you the good news right up front:

Most new ventures fail—usually for good reasons.

They fail because their founders launch without being truly committed to their success. They fail because a would-be entrepreneur becomes convinced that a lousy business idea is brilliant, or because he doesn't understand the market he's targeting. They fail because their leaders don't hire the right people or offer the best people a good reason to join the venture. They fail because the founders don't have enough capital, don't know how to communicate effectively, or don't adapt to take advantage of new opportunities. Sometimes they fail because of bad luck. But more often—and this is key—unsuccessful entrepreneurs blame bad luck because they don't understand what actually caused their failure.

How can all this amount to good news for aspiring entrepreneurs? Simple: it opens up a world of opportunity. Since most founders don't learn from their successes and failures (let alone those of their predecessors), anyone who is willing and eager to learn the rules of successful entrepreneurship can enjoy a great advantage.

We live in a culture that claims to value entrepreneurship. We've made household names of the founders of some of our most successful companies. If you're standing in the business section at Barnes & Noble as you read this, or browsing through this book on Amazon, chances are you'll see the memoirs of several of those founders nearby.

But in recent years much of the success that many entrepreneurs supposedly achieved was revealed as illusory. Market after market collapsed. Companies that were once worth a great deal of money on paper shut their doors. More recently, a new body of research has shown that much of what we think we know about entrepreneurship is wrong. We think of startups as exciting new ventures, incorporating spectacular innovation and great new ideas. We imagine businesses operating in emerging fields, led by founders with big dreams for growth. But the truth is quite different.

- Most new businesses launch in unattractive, static fields.
- Most startups offer no innovation or competitive advantage, cannot articulate growth plans, employ only the founders, and generate revenues of less than $100,000 a year.
- Only a third of new businesses last seven years.
- The typical startup begins with less than $25,000 in capital, acquired from the founder's savings (or run up on his or her personal credit cards).

Sounds daunting, doesn't it? But for the committed founder, the one who is truly determined to dare mighty things and succeed, all that entrepreneurial carnage can be a blessing. Here's why.

First, there is rarely any reason to reinvent the wheel in entrepreneurship. Some successful founder, somewhere, has addressed the same issues that just about every founder or aspiring entrepreneur faces today. By studying their examples and outcomes, the intelligent entrepreneur can dramatically improve his or her odds of success. The answers are out there, if only you know where to look.

Second, the doomed-to-fail entrepreneur doesn't have to be you. He or she can be—should be—your competition. Remember General George Patton's wise advice about the nobility of sacrificing one's life in combat: "No bastard ever won a war by dying for his country. He won it by making the other poor dumb bastard die for *his* country."

MODELING SUCCESS

Easy enough, right? Just identify the best examples and follow them. As it turns out, though, these lessons can be difficult to find. Even at a place like Harvard Business School (HBS), where they investigate successful enterprises for a living, there is a wealth of academic research on how to manage and grow big corporations—but nowhere near as much data-driven research on early-stage companies.

"Even knowing what questions to ask is difficult," explains Noam Wasserman, an HBS professor who specializes in entrepreneurship. "Moreover, these are private companies. And that means that inherently there are no data. I have to go out and collect all of my own data."

True, Wasserman continues, when companies prepare for an initial public offering, they have to reveal themselves to the Securities and Exchange Commission (SEC) and the world. But when academics study these companies, Wasserman points out, they are almost never able to study founders, because at that point few of them are still around. "Until recently, we weren't able to really draw any real conclusions about the types of issues and decisions that founders face."

I know that other authors have tried to tackle this problem. But this book is different from others, most of which choose between providing a dry analysis of founders and startups, or using made-up examples, anonymous anecdotes, and composite stories to illustrate their theories. Instead, *The Intelligent Entrepreneur* tells the true stories of three entrepreneurs from the Harvard Business School class of 1998 who started four successful businesses within ten years of graduating. Over the course of that decade, these HBS graduates also learned ten key rules of intelligent entrepreneurship, and this book examines the rules in detail, allowing every reader to discover what it takes to start a new business and make it a big success.

Chances are, you don't know this trio of entrepreneurs unless you happen to have been a client or competitor of one of their companies. But by following them over roughly a decade, as they imagined, started, and built their firms—and ultimately as they decided whether or not to sell what they'd created—we can absorb their stories, learn from their mistakes, and internalize their actions. Ultimately, my goal is to help you understand how they practice what I call "high-percentage entrepreneurship"—and to show you how you can, too.

WHO THE HECK IS BILL MURPHY JR. AND WHAT DOES HE KNOW ABOUT ENTREPRENEURSHIP?

Fair question. They say all writing is autobiographical, and this book is no different. It grew out of a number of my personal experiences.

First, I'm a journalist, not an academic. I've been a business owner and an entrepreneur. (I was a cofounder of a publishing company, and later one of the first employees at a dot-com.) I've always been interested in entrepreneurship and leadership. Not long ago, I wrote a book about a different kind of leadership—West Point's class of 2002 and those young military officers' experiences in the wars in Iraq and Afghanistan. When I finished, I realized that I'd learned far more about the military and warfare than I'd actually used in the book. I learned how the gun sights work on an M1A1 Abrams tank. I learned what the computerized voice of the pilot warning system sounds like on an Apache Longbow attack helicopter. I learned, at least in theory, a good deal about infantry tactics and what it takes to lead men in war. I interviewed hundreds of America's best-educated soldiers. They'd thought a lot about what they had experienced, and they spent many hours with me, sharing what they'd learned.

But with no plans ever to operate a tank or a military helicopter, much of what I learned was of limited practical use. As I considered what I wanted to do next, my thoughts kept circling back to my experiences as an entrepreneur. Ultimately, the businesses I launched and joined never got past the startup stage. Frankly, they failed.

I'd always wondered whether I might have succeeded if I'd had better mentors, or if somebody, somewhere, had discovered and boiled down what it took to become a successful entrepreneur—someone who could have told me in advance what to expect so I'd have been better able to deal with each challenge as it came along. West Point teaches young men and women to become first-rate soldiers; was there an equivalent institution that teaches people how to succeed at entrepreneurship? Looking for the answer, I cast a wide net. Before long I found it at the so-called West Point of capitalism: Harvard Business School.

Beginning in early 2008, I sought out and interviewed more than one hundred entrepreneurs from the Harvard Business School classes of 1997, 1998, and 1999, years in which many alumni launched companies either right after graduation or in the first few years afterward. My overriding goal during these interviews was to learn everything I could about entrepreneurial best practices. But I also knew that I wanted to tell an engaging and instructive story.

Instinctively, I knew it would be a mistake to write about entrepreneurs who were blessed at the start with advantages far beyond the normal founder, or who achieved success too easily. Honestly, what lessons can we learn from a hypothetical founder who might say, "Well, the first thing I did was to convert part of my trust fund into five million in cash" or "Since my father was the managing director of a venture capital firm, I asked some of his tennis friends for advice."

Meanwhile, a handful of HBS graduates in the late 1990s were blessed with incredible timing, and they built and sold businesses for extraordinary amounts of money in ridiculously short periods of time. I got to know some of them, and although they are interesting people with good stories, they are clearly anomalies. Besides, challenge and hardship can be the best teachers. Certain that their long, hard journeys would provide some very useful lessons, I wanted to find and write about entrepreneurs who had launched, stumbled, fallen, recovered—and learned.

That meant focusing on a small number of entrepreneurs who would be willing to tell me everything—the good, the bad, the downright ugly—about their efforts to start and build new companies. Over time, I came up with three criteria that helped me to identify the entrepreneurs who would ultimately play the starring roles in this story.

- **They had to be successful.** Nothing builds credibility like success, so I wanted to tell the stories of a few entrepreneurs who came up with a great idea and over time made it a reality. When considering which enterprises to write about, I looked at several standard measures of success, such as annual revenue, market share, and in some cases the founders' ultimate financial windfall. Each of the three entrepreneurs who became the main characters in this story started more or less from zero and then built firms that generated at least $50 million a year in revenue and/or netted their founders more than $20 million in personal profit.

- **They had to have endured.** The most useful experiments are those that observe their subjects over time, and I wanted my accounts of these entrepreneurial ventures to be what a social scientist might call longitudinal case studies. Rather than track a startup for a year or two, I wanted to tell the story of what happens to entrepreneurs and their enterprises during a five- or ten-year period. As you read this book, you will get to know:

  - the founder of a national retail company who grew her venture over eleven years (and counting);

  - an entrepreneur who started and sold one Internet-based business, and then started and sold another, both of which are still thriving; and

  - an entrepreneur who spent the first five years after graduation from HBS figuring out which venture to start, and the next seven or so building it into a very profitable and successful firm (it, too, is still going strong).

- **They had to be candid.** My entrepreneurs had to talk honestly about their ups and their downs, their inevitable failures as well as their exhilarating triumphs. They had to have thought long and hard about what led to their success, and be willing to explore their experiences further with me. They also had to be willing to open their books, open their lives, and make introductions to people who had known and worked with them. In fact, one of the first things I asked my top candidates to do, once I was satisfied that they met the other criteria, was to ask them to introduce me to five people they'd known at various points in their lives and encourage those people to speak freely with me. College roommates, old romances, ex-employees, the whole bit. I asked them—and they agreed—to provide thousands of pages of documentation so that I could explore and back up their stories of what happened. They forwarded me hundreds of e-mails and lent me journals and photo albums. I even had to buy an old 1.44 MB disk drive so that I could go through some of their original (and now technologically outdated) computer files. I wanted to be as confident as possible that the stories I'd be telling were true.

HOW TO READ THIS BOOK

Virtually every class at HBS is taught using the case method. Students read and prepare case studies recounting real-life stories about all sorts of businesses. The idea is to put the student in the decision makers' shoes and, over time, to instill confidence and familiarity—if not with the outcomes of any particular dilemma, at least with the decision-making process. Think of this book as an extended case study, one that weaves together the stories of three successful entrepreneurs. Collectively, these three stories—and the lessons we will draw from them—will help you develop confidence and familiarity with high-percentage entrepreneurship.

In a way, though, this is really two books in one. There are twenty-two chapters here; in the odd-numbered chapters, we'll follow the stories of our three intrepid entrepreneurs—Marla Malcolm Beck, Chris Michel, and Marc Cenedella—just as they unfolded in real life, highlighting their challenges and their triumphs. In the even-numbered chapters, we'll step back and explore the key rules of entrepreneurial success that Marla, Chris, and Marc learned along the way. (In case you're the impatient sort, the ten rules are summarized on pages 36–37.)

Over the course of a decade, these three entrepreneurs built successful businesses, made millions of dollars, and created hundreds and hundreds of jobs. As you read their stories, I hope you'll keep in mind that they are living, breathing human beings who started out just like most of us—with a hunger to succeed, but also with the usual array of fears and insecurities. Each of them sat alone in a room with a blank sheet of paper (or, more likely, a blank screen) and developed an idea. They wrote business plans. They attracted teammates and partners. They raised money. They built prototypes. They launched; they built brands; they scaled up their businesses. They also made big mistakes, faced serious hardships, and in a few cases nearly lost everything. Along the way, they learned to overcome the obstacles—real and imagined—that held them back. And ultimately, they persevered and prevailed.

Over the course of a decade, after much trial and error, Marla, Chris, and Marc became intelligent entrepreneurs. More important—at least for our purposes—they learned the ten rules of successful entrepreneurship. My fervent hope is that, by following their examples and understanding the rules they learned, you will be able to achieve your entrepreneurial goals as well.

CHAPTER 1

> To be nobody but yourself in a world which is doing its best, night and day, to make you everybody else means to fight the hardest battle which any human being can fight; and never stop fighting.
>
> —E. E. CUMMINGS

MEET MARC

Marc Cenedella was pumped. He had blazed his own path after graduating from college in 1992, moved clear across the country, and struck out on his own. Just two years later, his audacity was about to pay off. He was on his second sales job now, and when he'd landed this position with an import-export firm in San Diego, he'd negotiated an incentive-laden employment deal. Entitled to a third of everything he brought in, Marc had enjoyed a heck of a run over the past twelve months. He'd made the company $420,000. His share of the profits would be well over six figures.

He walked into the office on the morning of his annual review, understandably excited about the money that would go into his pocket. But he was prouder still of having charted his own course. He'd made good deals by developing good relationships. He'd gotten to know the U.S. manufacturers whose products he represented. He'd flown to Japan to learn about his customers. He'd kept his eyes open and used his brain. As just one example, when he'd learned that two of Japan's most powerful status symbols were pet ownership and American clothing, he'd come up with the unorthodox but lucrative idea of exporting

American-made pet food to Tokyo. He'd thought of some great ideas, and he'd seen them through.

Marc had grown up in a big family outside Buffalo, New York, with three brothers and thirty first cousins. He'd done well in high school—class president, editor of the student newspaper, captain of the swim team—and he'd graduated near the top of his class. With dark, thick hair, a round face, and a perpetual smile, Marc was both restless and methodical. He'd won a partial scholarship to Yale and worked hard for the rest of his college money—waiting tables at Favorite's Pizza in New Haven, Connecticut, tending bar at official university events. He'd poured drinks at homecoming and reunions, listening as the alumni talked about their success at the firms his classmates aspired to join: Morgan Stanley, Goldman Sachs, Fortune 500 firms like General Motors and IBM. He heard talk of law schools and MBA programs. To Marc, Yale in the late 1980s and early 1990s seemed like it could be a stairway to untold riches. Everyone was eager to climb to the top.

Early on, though, Marc realized he wasn't built for stairways. He wanted something different. He wanted something more.

He read constantly, and as Marc perused business magazines and newspapers, he read again and again that "international business" would be the high-growth area of the 1990s. He liked the sound of that—Marc loved the idea of traveling, and he was eager to add stamps to his passport and see the world. Meanwhile, after reading a book called *Places Rated Almanac*, he decided to move to either Seattle or San Diego after graduation. The weather in San Diego made the difference; after growing up in Buffalo, he wanted to live somewhere sunny and warm.

Marc followed through on his plan, but if California promised plenty of sunshine, the American economy did not. When Marc graduated from college, in 1992, the United States was mired in the longest recession since the 1930s. *Time* magazine predicted that the eventual recovery would be "one of the slowest in history," and that the 1990s would be "a decade of lowered expectations."

At the outset, Marc knew virtually no one in California and had no network. Jobs were scarce. He eagerly took an unpaid internship at the World Trade Association, a San Diego–based organization comprised of 850 local businesses that were all engaged in "international business" of one sort or another. The job offered one invaluable perk: access to the association's membership list, with the name, address, and employee roster of all the import-export businesses in the San Diego area. Marc sent résumés to every company that looked interesting; before long, he had an offer to work on "special projects" at a tiny local firm. Within weeks, he persuaded the company to allow him to pick up extra duties, such as managing a few small international sales accounts.

"You've got South America" was his boss's direction. "Call and see if they want to buy anything."

Marc soon proved that he had a knack for sales. But he also discovered that his boss had the habit of cracking open a new bottle of Chivas Regal every morning. Things went sour fast. Within a few short months, Marc and half the other employees were laid off.

Marc's parents wanted him to return home, but he persevered. Eventually, he received an offer from a much larger import-export company, and the incentives were extremely attractive—he would get to keep one-third of the profits he brought in. It was a handshake deal, and although Marc made several attempts to get the agreement in writing, it never quite happened.

Written contract or not, Marc was excited about his new job. He dove in headfirst, reasoning that the best thing he could do was become indispensable. Each week, he compiled a list of overseas business contacts, then set up the company fax machine to blast faxes all weekend long. On Mondays, he always had at least a few inquries from overseas merchants who wanted to buy and sell all kinds of products. Today, batteries; tomorrow, software. Next week it might be dog food or Levi's jeans. One month in early 1994, Marc realized that at age twenty-three he'd become the single largest U.S. importer of prune juice.

Marc loved the travel, loved the work. He quickly built a reputation as an outstanding performer. And he looked forward with great anticipation to the day when he'd sit down with his boss for his annual review.

But when the boss reviewed his sales figures and saw his calculation of his share of the profits, he seemed genuinely shocked.

"We really can't do that," he told Marc. "This is more than the president of the company makes, more than anyone makes. You're a rookie here. We can't do that."

Marc protested vehemently, but his boss now claimed to have no recollection of offering a one-third commission. Marc felt incredibly naive for having believed in the handshake deal. It was a very painful and expensive lesson.

Ready to quit, Marc marched out of the office and headed toward the beach. Staring out at the Pacific Ocean, he tried to decide whether his boss sincerely didn't recall the agreement or whether he was simply getting screwed.

How could I have been so careless? Marc asked himself. *How could I have failed to get the agreement in writing?*

And then, watching the waves break on the sand, he asked himself the harder question.

What the hell am I going to do now?

After getting burned by his boss, Marc didn't quit immediately, as he couldn't afford to be without a job. But he started thinking a lot harder about his future, and he took two important steps.

First, he applied to business school. Maybe all those Yale alumni had the right idea. Marc ordered applications for Harvard, Stanford, and the Wharton School at the University of Pennsylvania. He took the GMAT, called his old professors for recommendations, and started crafting essays.

Second, he started to think about launching an import-export business of his own. He'd spent a full year making deals, he reasoned. If he'd brought in more than $400,000 working for someone else, why couldn't he do at least that well working for himself?

Starting a new company would be a huge step, not just practically but emotionally. Marc thought of himself as an introverted person. For all his audacity in moving out west, he still felt like the nine-year-old kid he'd once been, riding the swim team bus and reading *Time* magazine cover to cover while the other kids screamed and played. But he also recalled a couple of times when he'd shown flashes of an entrepreneurial mind-set. As a college freshman, for instance, he and some friends had written the dean of students, griping that their dorm's snack shop was run-down, losing money, and open only a few nights a week. Let us take it over, he and his friends had written, and we'll do better. The hostile takeover worked; they ran the shop five nights a week and made it much more successful.

But that was a tiny operation. In contrast, Marc remembered another friend in college who seemed to be a natural entrepreneur. The guy had started a laundry service, charging other students to take their clothes to a coin-operated Laundromat in town. Marc remembered thinking he couldn't ever be the type of person to come up with creative ideas like that and make them work.

Even so, Marc was a bit more experienced now, and he was still young and single. He had very little to lose. He knew the industry, he reasoned. He'd already discovered that exporting pet food to Japan could be very lucrative; maybe that should be his specialty. If he could keep a high percentage of the clients he'd brought into his old firm, and scale up his business quickly, he figured he could gross a million dollars before costs. He needed about $250,000 to launch, but he thought his pet food industry suppliers might be interested in funding him, especially since he'd be using a lot of the money to buy their products.

By early 1995, Marc had decided to take the leap. His mother's maiden name was Forbes, so he named his company after her: Forbes Pacifica Trading Company, LLC.

Launching the company proved much tougher than Marc expected. Few customers followed from his old firm. He was barely making ends meet. But then, just a couple of months into the new venture, Marc came home one evening to find a fat envelope from Harvard Business School in his mailbox. He'd been offered a spot in the HBS class of 1997.

This seemed like deliverance—a chance to far exceed his expectations and hopes for his little import-export company. HBS was the alma mater of wildly successful entrepreneurs and businesspeople, men and women who had made fortunes in industries that Marc didn't even pretend to understand. No, he reflected, he hadn't succeeded in business—but what did that really matter now? Who could possibly fault him for giving up his struggling little company to attend perhaps the most prestigious business school on the planet?

But he kept hearing a little voice in the back of his head: *You're a product of all the decisions you make.* This one didn't feel right.

He couldn't do it. He couldn't leave his three investors—who had only just put up the money he needed to start the company—and he couldn't let Forbes Pacifica die an early death. Besides, he'd been taken to the cleaners by his former company; more than anything, he wanted to get his revenge by taking away their business.

Marc turned down Harvard. He gave his full attention to Forbes Pacifica.

Over the next year, Marc made six long trips to Asia, pushing his clients' products and working to open new markets. Soon his pet food business took off, and Marc began looking around for other unusual products to sell. At one point, he heard from his customers that a drought in Thailand had led to a shortage of brine shrimp—better known in the United States as "sea monkeys," thanks to the old comic book advertisements that promoted them as pets. In Asia, they were used primarily as feed in commercial shrimp farms. Marc went to Salt Lake City, tracked down about ten tons of the stuff from a supplier, and made a deal. The tip proved extremely valuable. His trip brought about $50,000 in profit.

By mid-1995, Forbes Pacifica was on track to do $3 million in revenue for the year, of which Marc would bank about $195,000. His investors were happy; he was happy. But before long he began thinking about Harvard Business School again. As someone who had declined an offer of admission, he figured he had a good shot at getting in if he were to apply again, especially since he could talk about how he'd built a successful business in the intervening year. And, he thought, if he were doing this well with no formal business education whatsoever, what might he accomplish if he had the education and the network of a place like HBS behind him?

One morning, Marc lay awake in a hotel room in Tokyo, mulling things over.

He asked himself: *If I could be the king of the Japanese pet food market by the time I turn thirty, would that be enough?*

When he put it that way, the answer came easily: *No. It's not enough.*

MEET MARLA

Marla Malcolm's blue Honda Prelude had been a gift. But as she pulled onto the freeway heading south toward Silicon Valley one morning in

October 1993, she reminded herself that the car was also the result of a deeply disappointing outcome.

Her California-girl good looks—blond hair, blue eyes—were what people saw first. But underneath, Marla was introspective, quiet, and driven. Her parents had given her the car a few years before to commemorate her graduation from high school, but also because she'd chosen to attend the University of California at Berkeley—a much less expensive option than the Ivy League colleges she'd long aspired to. Marla had thrived at Berkeley, but she was well aware that she would have had more opportunities if she'd gone to a more prestigious college.

Her peers at Stanford and Harvard seemed privy to a secret. In Marla's mind, they all knew how to find the well-traveled highway to professional success, a route on which the best and the brightest young people were identified, recruited, groomed, and rewarded. But the on-ramps to this highway were hidden to people like her, and Marla had spent years trying to find them.

Her immediate destination this morning was Palo Alto. Her boyfriend, a recent Stanford graduate, had suggested that she think about working in the management consulting industry. Marla was an economics major, and her boyfriend had told her that some consulting firms paid as much as $40,000 a year to the smartest young liberal arts graduates—a very healthy starting salary at the time. But their definition of "the smartest" was narrow, and it generally excluded Marla and her classmates. The biggest firms didn't recruit at Berkeley, but they had well-established interviewing programs at Stanford and around the Ivy League. If that was where the management consulting firms looked for talent, Marla decided, that was where she'd go.

Growing up in nearby Oakland, Marla was the daughter of a stay-at-home mom and a hardscrabble entrepreneur dad who had built an insurance agency and a real estate business out of virtually nothing. Her father had put her to work in his office at a young age. By seven she was organizing his files; by twelve she was doing simple bookkeeping and accounting. Marla grew up thinking about business, but also knowing she aspired to a bigger, better future—even before she had any idea what that might mean.

The important moments in her life passed almost unnoticed by those closest to her. Her mother was attentive and involved, but there were times when financial constraints meant they couldn't have everything they wanted. Back in grade school, all of the other kids started wearing Izod brand shirts, the ones with a little alligator label on the chest. Marla badly wanted an Izod shirt of her own, but her mother said no. They were too expensive.

"When I grow up," she decided quietly at the age of nine or ten, "I want to make sure I can afford the things I want."

Another moment came a few years later, at her sister's soccer game. Her sister was younger, but taller and more naturally athletic, and in Marla's mind her parents had categorized each girl. Marla had been encouraged to play piano; her sister played sports. Sitting next to her mother at the game, Marla decided she didn't want to be shoehorned anymore, and she announced that she wanted to play soccer. At first her mother reacted with surprise, but she quickly agreed. No problem; if Marla wanted to be an athlete, she could be an athlete.

Earn enough money. Become what you want to be. They were simple tenets, but they had driven her ever since.

Marla was focused and high achieving throughout middle and high school. She worked hard to become a successful athlete; she made the varsity volleyball and softball teams as a sophomore, and by her senior year she was captain of the volleyball team. Her grades were good enough that she could sit in the back of Mrs. Kubicek's math class and read romance novels without suffering any consequences. Marla liked the idea that the heroes in these books were all proud, powerful women— one of her favorite books focused on a young woman who took over her family's perfume empire. The books were fantasy, but to Marla the stories carried a very real message: she could achieve anything she wanted to achieve.

While in high school, she also began reading books and articles about business and the people who ran America's biggest companies. Often enough, the leaders had attended Harvard Business School. As time went on, the place became almost mythical to her. One day she had another one of her moments.

Harvard Business School, she thought. *Someday, somehow, I'm going to go there.* She could see her future, almost as if it had already happened.

Marla mapped out her course. To get to HBS, she focused first on getting into a top college—Stanford, one of the Ivies, or another name-brand university. But then Marla did not do as well as she should have on the SATs, and suddenly those schools were out of reach. She reflected afterward that nobody had ever explained just how important the test was, or that many of the students with whom she was competing had spent hundreds of dollars on test-prep courses. Marla was deeply disappointed in herself, but she also felt naive and let down. Soon, she took the obvious lesson to heart. She would have to figure these things out for herself.

Marla kept studying, kept working for her father. She settled on going to Berkeley and got her new Honda. Early in her freshman year, she sought out mentors and joined clubs. She rushed for a sorority and played intramural volleyball. But she found her passion with a student organization called AIESEC (Association Internationale des Étudiants en Sciences Économiques et Commerciales).

Rooted in post–World War II Europe, AIESEC's mission was to set up internships in the United States for foreign college students, while placing Americans in similar positions abroad. For Marla, AIESEC provided the perfect mix of collegiate life and the corporate world she longed to be part of. Her work for the organization forced her to overcome her natural shyness. It was her job to call executives at The Gap and other Fortune 500 companies in the Bay Area and ask them to take on foreign students. She felt grown up, a true businesswoman, and with each incremental success she grew more and more confident. By midway through her sophomore year, she was elected the chapter's president.

Marla did very well during her four years at Berkeley. She spent her summers working for a law firm, traveled for AIESEC, and met with fellow students and top executives from all over the world. She grew friendly with her fellow AIESEC president at Stanford—over time, they started dating. And when her boyfriend graduated and went to work for a consulting firm in the Silicon Valley, Marla learned from his experiences. Soon she was convinced that consulting would be her ticket. Serious money right out of college. A pipeline into Harvard Business School. Who could ask for anything better?

But landing a job after graduation at a firm like McKinsey, Bain, Andersen or Boston Consulting Group wouldn't be easy. Marla knew she had to start early, and her first objective was to land a summer internship with one of the top-tier firms. Since they didn't recruit at Berkeley, Marla put her AIESEC cold-calling skills to work, and during her junior year she landed a summer job at Monitor Consulting in Los Angeles. With Monitor on her résumé, the other big firms would be willing to talk with her—but on their terms, at their offices. Now, in the fall of her senior year, it even meant driving to Stanford to talk with recruiters who wouldn't come to Berkeley.

Marla spent the day in a Palo Alto hotel where the interviews were conducted, the only Berkeley interloper in a room full of Stanford students. She'd managed to get interviews with McKinsey & Co. and several other consulting firms, but to talk with a recruiter from Boston Consulting Group she practically had to crash their interview session. Maybe it was her nervousness, she later reflected, but that firm turned her down. No matter; she had proven that she had the necessary self-confidence and record of accomplishment, and she was now collecting other offer letters.

Finally, the one she really wanted arrived: "On behalf of the entire Firm," the letter began, "I am delighted to invite you to join McKinsey & Company as a Business Analyst in the San Francisco Office."

McKinsey. It was the most prestigious firm, the most competitive, the highest-paying—and the one with the best-traveled path to HBS. The list of her salary and benefits took up an entire single-spaced page, including pay ($38,000, to start; $55,000 within two years), a signing bonus, and perhaps the biggest benefit of all: if she could get into HBS or another top business school, McKinsey would pay for it.

Marla started at McKinsey in late summer 1994, the only Berkeley graduate in an office full of Stanford and Ivy League alumni. After a short orientation, she was assigned to her first big client projects. She quickly developed a reputation for being confident, smart, and ambitious. One of her first team leaders was a recent Harvard Business

School graduate, and she impressed him with her resilience. He couldn't help but laugh one morning when they were running to a client meeting and the heel snapped off of Marla's shoe. Hardly breaking stride, she discarded it and ran the last five blocks hobbling on one foot.

Marla enjoyed the work and found her projects challenging, whether she was analyzing market opportunities for utility companies or trying to help clients find innovative ways to cut costs. She was learning the language of business and developing analytical skills that would serve her all her working life. If her early performance reviews were any indication, she was well on her way.

"In my four plus years at McKinsey," one manager wrote about a year after her arrival, "Marla has been the most outstanding Business Analyst I have worked with."

By the time of her second anniversary at McKinsey, Marla decided that it was time to start assembling her application to HBS. Her team leader gave her a copy of his successful HBS application from a few years before, and Marla methodically put together long outlines for her recommenders. She wrote draft after draft of her essays, emphasizing the many leadership roles she'd held over the years. Even her essay describing a "typical day" required multiple rough copies. Marla settled on a hypothetical Friday that began with "read[ing] the editorials in the *Wall Street Journal*," arriving at McKinsey by 7:30 a.m., collaborating with clients, taking meetings with colleagues, working for a local nonprofit organization, and finishing with "a night at the symphony or the opera."

In her response to a question asking her to describe an ethical dilemma, Marla wrote about a McKinsey project involving a company's organizational structure. The McKinsey client wanted to slash costs by 15 to 30 percent, and the only way to do that was to cut jobs.

"I wondered how I could be responsible for eliminating people's livelihoods," Marla wrote. Someday, she promised, "when I am a senior manager of a company," she would hire responsibly and not make promises to her employees that she couldn't keep. "It does not seem fair that the lower levels of organizations need to pay for poor management."

Marla submitted her HBS application in early 1995, confident that she had done everything possible to maximize her chances. But a few weeks later, she received bitterly disappointing news: she had been wait-listed, and the spot she'd coveted in the HBS class of 1997 went to someone else. Perhaps she would be admitted the following year—but by then she'd be competing with the McKinsey class behind her as well. Marla worried that she might have missed her chance.

She put on a full-court press, asking her former professors and coworkers to write more recommendations, to persuade HBS that it would be an absolute tragedy if she were not admitted. She wrote her own updates as well, reiterating her interest, describing the kind of work she'd been doing for McKinsey in the interim, and explaining why she thought she was now an even more compelling candidate.

By August the admissions office gave in. The class of 1997 was full, but Marla was offered one of the first places in the class of 1998.

Things never seemed to come easily for her, Marla reflected, but over-coming these kinds of challenges had taught her something about herself. When she figured out what she wanted to accomplish, she would work as hard as needed to make it a reality.

MEET CHRIS

Lieutenant Chris Michel sat perched on a radar console between the pilot and copilot of the navy P-3 Orion patrol plane on a late March morning in 1994. They climbed out over the Atlantic Ocean and headed south toward Cape Cod as the raw chill and rocky coast of Maine vanished behind them.

With red hair and an outsized personality, Chris was one of the most visible young officers in the squadron. He had been commissioned as a navy officer in 1990, during the era of *Top Gun* and the high-tech, tele-vised battles of the Persian Gulf War. He and his fellow officers were proud of their jobs, and they knew they looked good in their uni-forms, peering at the world from behind dark sunglasses and confi-dent smiles.

Their patrol plane was the size of a civilian Boeing 737, and although it lacked the flash of the navy's fighter planes, it was a legendary work-horse with a long history. Teams like Chris's spent their time chasing drug smugglers, patrolling vast stretches of ocean, and practicing for a war they hoped would never come.

The Orion was packed that day: three pilots, two navigators, a host of flight engineers and sonar operators. They quickly gained altitude, the plane's dials spinning steadily past ten thousand, fifteen thousand, twenty thousand feet. Visibility outside fell to nothing as they climbed, but when they leveled off the crew relaxed. The pilot leaned back in his seat. Chris looked out the cockpit window at the thick, gray clouds.

And then—

Whooosh!

With no warning, the plane's nose jerked violently toward the sky, like a racehorse stopping short. Chris was thrown from his makeshift seat, crashing into the ceiling of the plane. Then, just as quickly, the plane veered into a deep dive, plummeting toward the ocean. As the G-forces multiplied, Chris was slammed downward and glued to the floor. The pilot and copilot gripped their yokes with both hands, their feet planted on the plane's dashboard, trying to get leverage.

They fell and fell and fell.

Chris's military file listed Illinois as his home of record, but in truth he had grown up all over. An only child, he'd been born in Florida to an American mother and a Greek father, but his parents had separated when he was young. His mother remarried, and the Michels—Chris, his mother, and his stepfather—shuttled back and forth between the United States and France, and then bounced from one small town to another in Illinois and Connecticut. Chris had even taken a year off from school after third grade, traveling throughout Europe with his mom. Later, he attended three high schools before graduating. Chris was a happy kid, but he was always the new guy, never putting down roots anywhere.

He didn't begin to feel settled until he reached college, at the University of Illinois at Urbana-Champlain. Chris majored in political science and began thinking about a career in the military; he remembered with particular clarity and admiration the sailors he'd seen at a submarine base near where they'd lived in Connecticut. He joined the navy's ROTC program, which was dominated at Illinois by a group of former enlisted marines who were unimpressed with their civilian counterparts. Chris won them over with his determination and charm. At graduation, he was named the Distinguished Naval Graduate.

All that moving as a child had made Chris extremely adaptable as an adult. As one example, Chris had always pronounced his last name the way the French did, so that it sounded like *Michelle*. But when he joined the navy, his fellow officers Americanized it, pronouncing it like *Michael*, with a long "I" and a hard "ch." Instead of constantly correcting them, Chris simply changed the way he pronounced his name.

Chris imagined going to flight school after college and then working his way up in the navy, and he could easily see himself doing twenty years or more in uniform. Lousy depth perception meant he couldn't qualify as a pilot, so he became a navigator instead. At his new squadron, VP-11 in Maine, his primary focus was learning how to be a competent flight officer, but his commander quickly named him the squadron's "bull ensign" as well.

It was an unofficial navy tradition to put a junior officer in charge of the unit's morale, and the job gave Chris latitude to be brazen, even outlandish, sort of like a medieval court jester. Not long after he was appointed, Chris and some of his squadron mates were at the officers' club, and Chris noticed that the commander of a rival squadron had left his hat hanging on a rack near the door. Chris swiped the hat, took a photo, and ran an ad in the base newspaper.

Found. One skipper's cover. If lost please report to Ensign Chris Michel, VP-11.

Another time, the squadron's brand-new executive officer, a commander named Anthony Winns, gave an introductory presentation entitled "Rules for Getting Along with the XO." It was filled with advice like "Check small things" and "Share the credit when things go well."

Chris recognized some of the language in the speech, and at the next squadron meeting he made a presentation of his own. He had some shocking news, he said. General Colin Powell, then the chairman of the Joint Chiefs of Staff, had copied their new XO's rules without permission.

Using two overhead projectors, he compared General Powell's similarly entitled "Rules for Getting Along with the Chairman" with Winns's speech the week before. By the time he finished, the crowd of officers was roaring. Commander Winns hadn't meant to deceive, but he acknowledged he had cobbled together his rules from presentations he'd heard over the years without knowing where they'd all come from.

Though based in Maine, Chris's squadron had done rotations in Saudi Arabia and Puerto Rico. They patrolled the Adriatic Sea and the Caribbean and lived the adventures they'd later tell in sea stories. He and his crew helped capture millions of dollars' worth of cocaine and called in helicopters to pick up Cuban refugees and the crews of disabled fishing vessels. Chris traveled the world, had girlfriends around the country, and took leave to fly to Greece and London to visit his father. ("Lots of good food and drinking," he wrote in his diary after one such trip.)

He felt he had found his calling. He loved flying and loved just about everything about the navy. And on that March morning in 1994 when he got the word that another navigator in his unit had to spend the day getting his annual physical, Chris was happy to volunteer to take his place on the flight.

The Orion fell for forty-five seconds, plummeting more than ten thousand feet. For much of that time, Chris remained pressed to the floor. But gradually he came to his senses, surprised at how steady he was. Up front, the pilot and the copilot were losing the battle with their airplane.

This is it, Chris considered calmly. He'd had a good life. Now he was going to die.

The dive eased slightly, and Chris pulled himself off the floor. He worked his way down the fuselage and strapped himself into a compartment between two large computer consoles. He and the other crewmembers were like hockey goalies, batting away debris hurtling from the back of the plane to the nose. Folders, binders, papers, even the coffee pot went flying. Sonar buoys and a fifty-pound camera had been ripped away from their straps. Chris realized that if any of the heavier debris fell forward to the cockpit, one of the pilots trying to control the plane could be hit on the back of the head and knocked unconscious.

Finally the plane stopped falling and leveled off. A minute passed.

Chris and the other officers checked one another out, making sure that bumps and bruises were the limits of their physical injuries. The pilots tried to figure out what had gone wrong.

And then—

Whoosh!

Once again they were tumbling, falling hundreds and then thousands of feet, almost completely out of control. Both pilots struggled with their yokes and regained control of the plane—only to lose it again. They limped back toward Maine, but the pattern held: every time they gained some altitude, they would lose it again in an abrupt dive. As the base finally came came into view, they all realized that another uncontrollable dive as they tried to land would be fatal.

Somehow the pilots managed to put the plane on the runway and then bring it to a stop. The mud of an early Maine spring had never looked so beautiful.

Chris and the crew emerged from the plane, badly shaken. Some cried. Most were nauseous. Many swore they'd never fly again. A team of investigators appeared on the scene, interviewing everyone separately while the episode was still fresh in their minds. Commander Winns raced out to meet them and decided he wanted them all back in the air soon—the next day if possible. Like riders getting right back on a horse after a bad fall, they needed to fly again immediately or risk never flying again.

"Almost died today," Chris wrote that night in the journal he kept, filling the pages with a spare, acronym-peppered account of the incident. "Never came that close before."

The cause of the plane's near disaster was a mystery; it was officially considered a freak accident. In hundreds of thousands of hours of flying, no Orion had ever malfunctioned that way. Chris carried on, undeterred. He'd learned firsthand just how fleeting life could be. He swore he wouldn't waste his.

His time as a junior flight officer would soon come to an end—Chris would have to move on to make room for the others coming up behind him. This meant he would be reassigned to some sort of "shore billet," as the various positions for staff officers, instructors, and students were called. Many young officers called it quits at that point, heading off to graduate school or to the business world.

With his near-miss still fresh in his mind, Chris explored his options. Somebody told him a bit about the profession of business consulting; intrigued, he sent résumés to companies whose names he hardly knew and whose businesses he only halfway understood. When he was advised to look at McKinsey & Co., for instance, his first reaction was to wonder why a Scottish firm would want to hire an American naval officer.

But then another option emerged. Chris learned that he was one of the finalists to be the aide-de-camp to the top admiral in charge of the Naval Reserve at the Pentagon, who also happened to be the senior P-3 admiral in the navy. The position seemed to offer the perfect bridge between the military and civilian worlds. Chris flew to Virginia for the interview, and he sold himself as aggressively as he ever had in his life. It paid off. He got the job.

This was a different kind of navy. Chris's new Pentagon position required all of his organizational skills and charisma. Early on, he set out to learn the names and backgrounds of everyone the admiral dealt with—not just their jobs but their families and interests outside the military. Aides like Chris were known in the navy as "loops," a reference to the cordlike epaulettes they wore over the left shoulder of their uniforms. Soon, Chris emerged as one of the leaders of the thirty-five or so young loops in the Pentagon, organizing happy hours and other events. He kept a running tab in his diary of the famous and quasi-famous people he met. The work was fun, and he loved the travel. In one especially busy week, he noted in his journal, he accompanied his boss on trips to both Hawaii and Chile. And the more he got to know the admiral he worked for, the more impressed he was.

But seeing the military's power center in Washington, D.C., up close was also disillusioning. Chris was struck by the simple realization that the people at the top who made the big decisions were human, no different than he was. It might be another ten or fifteen years, he realized, before he had a shot at making those kinds of decisions himself. He wondered whether he could be happy waiting that long.

Meanwhile, Chris learned about a navy program that sent promising young officers to places like Harvard's Kennedy School of Government and other top graduate schools. He could hardly fathom the idea of getting a degree from an Ivy League university, but he put in for the scholarship anyway and applied to KSG.

In late 1995, the far-flung community of navy P-3 Orion pilots and flight officers held a two-day conference in Washington. Thousands of naval aviators descended on the Washington Navy Yard to attend a few classes, play a little golf, and knock back a few drinks together. The highlight was an evening reception at the Navy Yard, and Chris donned his dress uniform and walked into the dark, heavy room, thick with navy memorabilia and models of ships and aircraft.

He mingled with other officers roughly his rank and age. Looking at the uniform name tag of a lieutenant commander he hadn't met, Chris thought the name seemed familiar. Then he remembered: the officer, Scott Leftwich, had received the same fellowship Chris had just applied for. Leftwich was now returning to the navy after a two-year assignment at Harvard.

Chris introduced himself, explained that he'd recently applied for the navy's fellowship, and started to ask what life had been like at KSG.

Leftwich cut him off.

"No, not the Kennedy School," he said. "Harvard Business School."

Chris was surprised; he hadn't realized that the navy's program also sent officers to business school.

"They love navy guys," Leftwich told him.

Chris had lots of questions, but nowhere near enough time to ask them all. After chatting for ten or fifteen minutes, Chris offered Leftwich his business card and thanked him for the advice.

"I hope you'll give me a call sometime," Chris said.

"No," Leftwich replied. "But if you get serious, you give *me* a call."

Chris did get serious. He used the essays he'd written for the Kennedy School and the London School of Economics as jumping off points and worked through the application for HBS as quickly as he could. Then he got some bad news: the navy turned down his application for the scholar-ship. It was too early in his career, the rejection letter said. Maybe he'd have a good shot next year.

But not getting the scholarship galvanized Chris. He took the Metro downtown and interviewed with Andersen Consulting. By early spring, Chris had a job offer in hand. He would start as an entry-level consul-tant in Andersen's Washington, D.C., office in August. His salary would be $43,000 a year ("including compensation for overtime worked")— roughly comparable to what he was taking home as a seventh-year navy officer.

Chris still hoped he'd be accepted at HBS. But even if that didn't hap-pen, he planned to resign his commission in the navy and get started on a career in business, one way or another.

It turned out that Chris was right on the borderline for acceptance to HBS. One day, the admissions office got in touch with him, asking if he'd be willing to do a phone interview. Rumor had it that only a small percentage of those being considered got interviews, and those who did had about a 50 percent chance of being admitted.

Chris agreed, of course, but this seemed absurdly high-pressure. So much of his future rode on the outcome of a single phone call.

At lunch the day before the interview, he shared his anxiety with a more senior navy officer who had become a mentor.

Why don't you drive up there and do it in person? the officer suggested.

Chris drove through the night to Massachusetts, stopping to buy a shaving kit and to change into his dress blue navy uniform. But when he got to campus, things went poorly. Showing up unannounced—with his polished shoes, colorful ribbons, and aviator's wings—was clearly a bad idea, and Chris could see that he had thrown the interviewer off guard. Moreover, he was exhausted after the drive. He handled the interview questions as best he could, but he was sure he'd blown his chance.

As he walked off the HBS campus, Chris threw his application mate-rials in the trash. He drove back to Washington in disgust.

A few days later, though, his mail included a thick packet with a return address from the HBS admissions office. Chris tore it open and read with amazement: "I am pleased to inform you . . ."

He was in! The letter suggested, on a more cautionary note, that he take some more math and accounting classes over the summer. And instead of beginning in September, Chris had been assigned to a compressed program that would begin in January 1997 and go straight through without a summer off until graduation in May 1998. But Chris didn't care. He was as exhilarated as he'd ever been in his life.

"I am afraid of the competition," Chris wrote in his navy journal. "Perhaps for the first time in my life, I might be out of my league. I am committed, however, to do everything in my power to succeed. VERITAS!"

CHAPTER 2

ENTREPRENEURSHIP CAN BE LEARNED

There are skills, attitudes, and a fundamental base of knowledge that education and experience can provide. You won't turn me into a world-class athlete by sending me out to practice with a coach, but I will certainly play a better game. Entrepreneurship is no different.

—PROFESSOR HOWARD STEVENSON,
HARVARD BUSINESS SCHOOL

THEY WEREN'T BORN WITH IT

I first got to know Chris, Marla, and Marc well after everything you've just read. In fact, we met years later, after they had graduated from Harvard Business School, tried different career paths, launched their companies, and achieved success. And because I didn't meet them until later, it took some time before I realized something so obvious that I had missed it at first.

They weren't born entrepreneurs—never mind successful entrepreneurs.

They're different from most of us now, but they weren't always. In the years after college, something happened—and a big part of what happened is that they *learned* how to become successful entrepreneurs. And that leads to another obvious but crucially important truth: if they can do it, so can you.

Surprisingly, this maxim flies in the face of what we are often told. We hear stories about people who were natural-born entrepreneurs—as children, they sold lemonade, hawked T-shirts, and squirreled away their allowances and birthday money to fund toddler-sized ventures. Or we hear about the famous experiment where psychologists give little kids a marshmallow and tell them that if they can stare at it for twenty minutes before eating it, they'll get a second marshmallow. (Besides giving the researchers the chance to tease little children in the name of science, the study supposedly proves that kids with the patience to sit and stare wind up more successful later in life.)

Seriously, are our fates really predetermined by our genes, not to mention our childhood hobbies and obsessions? Are some people destined to become successful entrepreneurs, while the rest of us are doomed to spend our lives splashing around in the shallow end of the startup pool?

After hundreds of hours of talking with my trio of protagonists and many other HBS graduates and intelligent entrepreneurs, I can provide an unequivocal answer: no. Marc, Marla, and Chris were not predestined to become high-percentage entrepreneurs. Yes, they were impressive people before they started their companies. They all had ambition, and they were all admirably accomplished. Right out of college, Marc learned enough about the import-export business to start his own small company. Marla fought her way into McKinsey and HBS. Chris was rated highly in the navy. But they weren't born entrepreneurs. Step by step—some forward, some back—they had to learn.

WHAT THEY TEACH YOU AT HARVARD BUSINESS SCHOOL

At Harvard Business School, the core belief about entrepreneurship is quite simply this: *it can be taught, and it can be learned.* Entrepreneurship is, to use HBS's quasi-official definition, "the pursuit of opportunity without regard to resources currently controlled." It is not so much a set of skills as it is a process, a belief, and a commitment. It is a mode of thinking and acting—a way of observing the world, of figuring out how to change it (hopefully for the better), and, perhaps most important, of becoming the person who is capable of implementing that change. Skills are important—the HBS catalog is filled with courses on funding and managing entrepreneurial ventures—but skills are commodities. Besides, the non-MBAs among us can hire MBAs to perform or advise us about such business functions as finance, marketing, and human resources.

Entrepreneurship itself, however, is more valuable, more challenging—and sometimes more difficult to explain, even for those who practice it and teach it. And as you will see, becoming a successful entrepreneur requires courage, character, and faith.

"One of the reasons people get very excited about entrepreneurship is that nobody really knows what it is," says Stig Leschly, an HBS 1998 graduate turned entrepreneur turned HBS lecturer. "There is no stable definition for this thing, and so the focus is on technical components—mostly entrepreneurial finance, the specialized vocabulary of term sheets and valuations and so on. We strive to put as high a conceptual bow on it as we can."

While working on this book, I was sometimes asked: Why are you writing about Harvard Business School alumni? Why not Stanford, for example, in the heart of Silicon Valley? Or why not write about MBA programs at places like Babson College or the University of Southern California, which pride themselves on their entrepreneurship curricula?

In truth, I don't think places like HBS have a monopoly on teaching intelligent entrepreneurship. But even during the early days of my research, I kept hearing stories about several hugely successful entrepreneurs from the HBS classes of the late 1990s. Moreover, it became clear as I dug deeper that HBS itself had gone through an impressive process of reinvention, after its academic leaders realized how important serious research about entrepreneurship was—and the extent to which it was lacking. HBS launched its inaugural business-plan competition in those years, and several of the winning student teams attracted millions of dollars in investment before their members even graduated. A decade later, entrepreneurship is a big part of the school's curriculum, as will be apparent to anyone who walks around the campus, talks with the professors, or visits the entrepreneurship page on the HBS Web site (http://www.hbs.edu/entrepreneurship). There is now a $25 million Arthur Rock Center for Entrepreneurship on campus. And in the course catalog, prospective students will find twenty-five MBA Entrepreneurial

Management electives, ranging from "Venture Capital and Private Equity" to "Building a Business in the Context of a Life," a course dedicated, in part, to helping students "understand and apply a process and frameworks for developing an integrated life plan."

Clearly, Harvard Business School is deeply committed to teaching its MBA candidates how to become successful, intelligent entrepreneurs. But that hasn't always been the case.

A NEW DISCIPLINE

Let's go back to the mid-1940s. It was just after World War II, and soldiers streamed into colleges and graduate schools on the GI Bill. HBS had to shift quickly to a three-times-a-year entry program just to keep up with demand. Professors added more courses. New faces joined the faculty. Among them was a member of the HBS class of 1938 named Myles Mace, just back from service with the army air forces in the Pacific. He was in a special position to understand what the military veterans who were attending the school aspired to. They'd faced death and the horrors of war. They'd seen how fleeting life could be, and they wanted to make their mark, control their destinies. But they were fed up with bureaucracy and big organizations. They were saying (as one veteran put it), "When I get out of this damn uniform, I can tell you that I'm never, ever going to work for a large corporation and just be another number!"

Mace listened. He developed a course designed to help HBS students start their own businesses. When "Management of New Enterprises" appeared in the 1947 course catalog, it was the first time any course at HBS had used the word *entrepreneur* in its description or focused on problems faced by people in new businesses. The course proved wildly popular, and HBS had a great opportunity to be at the forefront of entrepreneurial research and teaching.

But the school allowed that opportunity to fall by the wayside.

Why? Well, because it was the 1950s, and Harvard Business School was practically a flagship for the era of corporate America and the man in the gray flannel suit. As a later HBS account of its own history put it, an inclination toward entrepreneurship was seen as a "personality defect," and the prototypical entrepreneur was presumed to be "a chronic malcontent." The HBS placement office loved big companies; after all, their recruiters showed up, made offers, and kept the school's employment stats high. Professors who wanted to win tenure focused on subjects that the employers of HBS graduates wanted them to master—corporate finance, for example, and general management of large organizations.

Now scroll forward to the 1960s and 1970s. HBS students pushed back, at least a little. A group of them raised $5,000 to run a full-page ad in the *Wall Street Journal* asking small, entrepreneurial businesses to come interview on campus. But while students oversubscribed just about every entrepreneurship class the business school offered, the subject had "almost no stature among academics," as one history put it. By 1980, very few entrepreneurship courses were offered at HBS at all. Those that did exist were often listed in the course catalog with the initials "TBA"—"to be announced"—where the professor's name would normally go.

Finally, in the early 1980s, the school started to change. Howard Stevenson, a veteran HBS professor who had left for a career in private business, returned at the invitation of the school's new dean and began to develop a real entrepreneurship curriculum. Around the same time, the school surveyed its alumni and the results were a shock. Half of its graduates claimed to be entrepreneurs fifteen years after graduation. Entrepreneurs, the school learned, tended to be happier, healthier, and less likely to be divorced than their classmates who worked for large firms. For the most part, they loved what they did. As Stevenson put it, "They never wanted to retire."

The curriculum he and his colleagues designed, Entrepreneurial Management, was broken into five sections, each representing a stage in the process of entrepreneurship.

Evaluate the opportunity.

Assess required resources.

Acquire the resources.

Manage the venture.

Harvest the value.

Most important, Stevenson and his colleagues become evangelists for their cause. Their core conviction, reflected in every aspect of the new curriculum, was that entrepreneurship could be learned.

"It was no longer a case of 'if you're not a born entrepreneur, you're out of luck,'" as the official HBS history later put it. "Instead, it was, 'these are skills and attributes that you can learn, and upon which you can draw when circumstances require you to do so.'"

Howard Stevenson has been back at HBS for more than a quarter of a century, and the school now has three dozen faculty members specializing in entrepreneurship, making it the second-largest department on campus.

There were false starts. "One guy made a big deal about the fact that roughly 44 percent of entrepreneurs were firstborn," Stevenson recalled. "It turns out that the same fraction of the population is firstborn. So that wasn't a very remarkable finding."

But professors like Stevenson, William Sahlman, and Joseph Lassiter developed innovative courses and performed valuable research. By the mid-1990s, the entrepreneurship department at HBS had become a powerhouse. Students had always wanted the school to get serious about entrepreneurship, but now the HBS alumni—many of whom were successful entrepreneurs—wanted it, too.

Granted, HBS has many other strengths and disciplines. Want to make a mark in venture capital? Roughly one in seven American venture capitalists is an HBS grad. Want to run a huge corporation? About a fifth of Fortune 500 CEOs have an HBS degree on the wall. Even during the entrepreneurial heyday of the late 1990s, a large majority of HBS graduates took positions with big institutional employers—investment banks, consulting firms, and large companies—all of which offered the big salaries and signing bonuses that almost anyone would be reluctant to pass up. Furthermore, many of the HBS graduates who thought of themselves as entrepreneurial often took a job with someone else's startup as a relatively early employee, instead of starting a venture of their own.

Even so, entrepreneurship at HBS has grown from its origins as little more than an afterthought to one of the school's most important disciplines. When you walk into the lobby of the Rock Center today, you'll find a prominently displayed glass case filled with baseball caps—memorabilia from companies launched by HBS alumni.

THE TEN KEY RULES

Those baseball caps were created for companies started by people like Thomas Stemberg (class of 1973 and the founder of Staples), Scott Cook (class of 1976 and the founder of Intuit), and David Thompson, Bruce Ferguson, and Scott Webster (all class of 1981 and the founders of Orbital Sciences Corp.). But the caps and the names associated with them don't begin to explain what drove would-be entrepreneurs to attend HBS. As I began interviewing alumni, I asked them about their childhoods, their college years, and their hobbies, all versions of two very basic questions: who are you and how did you get here?

One HBS alumnus told me that he'd figured out how the school decides who to admit: find people who will clearly achieve great things no matter what, accept them, and take credit for their inevitable success. Then there's the 3M theory: some are convinced that HBS is especially inclined to admit those who have worked at McKinsey, served in the military, or are members of the Mormon Church. Other observers express a mixture of admiration and disdain for the degree to which the school seems to fill each section with precisely calculated percentages of former consultants, investment bankers, armed forces veterans, men, women, ethnic minorities, international students, and a small handful of people with quirky, unusual backgrounds. They call it the Noah's ark theory of admissions.

But the more HBS alumni I talked to, the more I became convinced that, for the most part, the people who attend the school are pretty normal. Sure, they are high achievers. They had good grades as undergraduates and they crushed the GMAT. Moreover, only about one in ten applicants is admitted, and that's from among a self-selecting group. But, even so, they're really not all that different from anyone else who is serious about succeeding in business. And if those HBS students who are determined to make it as entrepreneurs do indeed have something of an advantage because Harvard Business School is on their résumés, plenty of people start wildly profitable companies without ever having graduated from HBS or any other business school.

"Do you need to go to HBS?" asks Stig Leschly, the 1998 HBS graduate who went on to found a $200 million company that he sold to Amazon, before returning to HBS to teach for several years. "Of course not. Warren

Buffett didn't go to HBS. Bill Gates didn't go to HBS. The answer is no. But that is not to say HBS doesn't add any value. Thank God we do it the way we do it. We teach by the case method, grounded in good examples, and force students in class to interact the way that they will in the real world. You don't *need* HBS, but we do what we do very well."

It's worth pointing out, by the way, that starting down the path toward becoming a successful entrepreneur is about more than simply making money. Beyond your personal ambitions or mine, our society needs entrepreneurs. We need tinkerers, risk takers, creators, and builders. We need ambitious people who will put themselves on the line to build real firms that add value and create jobs. Planet Earth is, as always, a bit of a mess, and we're not going to improve our lot much by continuing to produce the same products and provide the same services. Incremental changes in the status quo will not change the world; entrepreneurs who solve difficult problems and invent entirely new industries will.

In the case of the HBS class of 1998, a few of its members—Marla Malcolm, Chris Michel, Marc Cenedella, and a minority of their peers—had the audacity to take up the challenge of entrepreneurship and launch their own ventures. Any one of them could have pursued many other attractive opportunities, which leads to a few deceptively simple questions. What made Marla, Chris, and Marc decide to become entrepreneurs? What lessons did they learn as they launched and built their companies? And most important: how can we make best use of those lessons ourselves?

Answering these three questions is what I set out to achieve. And as my research proceeded, I became increasingly convinced that the lessons learned by my trio of entrepreneurs—and the many others I interviewed—could be distilled into what I now think of as the ten rules of successful entrepreneurship. As you'll see, I discuss each of these rules as the story goes along. But it wouldn't be fair to keep you in suspense, so here without further ado are the ten rules.

1. Make the commitment.
2. Find a problem, then solve it.

3. Think big, think new, think again.

4. You can't do it alone.

5. You must do it alone.

6. Manage risk.

7. Learn to lead.

8. Learn to sell.

9. Persist, persevere, prevail.

10. Play the game for life.

More—much more—on these ten rules as we go along. For now, though, it's worth saying that during my early conversations with Marla, Chris, and Marc I was struck over and over by a simple truth: these three very different people had all made an unequivocal, pedal-to-the-metal choice to throw everything they had into realizing their dreams of building successful companies. As I began thinking about what else they had in common—and then began to suspect that it might be possible to distill some rules for winning the startup game—I had no trouble identifying the first step that any intelligent entrepreneur must take: you've got to make the commitment. With a clear head and your whole heart, you've got to decide that you absolutely, positively will become a successful entrepreneur.

CHAPTER 3

Chance favors the prepared mind.

—LOUIS PASTEUR

WORM DECK, POWER DECK, AND WARNING TRACK

Marla Malcolm began her Harvard Business School career smack in the middle of the middle. Assigned seats were a big deal, and she was given the center place in the center row of tables in one of the classrooms in Aldrich Hall. She and the rest of Section A in the class of 1998 would meet there every day, every class, for a full semester.

The rooms in Aldrich were virtually identical: five concentric U-shaped rows of tables, each elevated slightly above the next, with the doors to the room at the top and a section called "the pit" at the bottom from which the professor taught. The rows themselves had taken on nicknames, and even the relative merits of each seat were passed along from one incoming class to the next. Sit in the uppermost row, dubbed the Sky Deck, and you had the psychological advantage of being above the action. Sit in the lowest row, the Worm Deck, and you were right in front of the professor—good if you were prepared and wanted to participate on a particular day, horrible if you weren't and didn't. Between the three were the Warning Track, the Power Deck, and the Garden Deck, so called because it was just above the worms.

In past years, students had shown up absurdly early for their first class in an effort to grab the best seats—before dawn for classes that started at eight or nine in the morning. But eventually HBS decided to end the mad scramble. In September 1996, Marla and her seventy-nine section mates entered their room in Aldrich Hall for the first time and found a seating chart waiting for them.

As Marla sat in Power Deck, she was surrounded by an assortment of former military officers, investment bankers, and consultants. (Up in the Warning Track, all the way to the right, sat a Yale graduate from Buffalo, New York, by way of San Diego, who had nearly become the American Pet Food King of Japan.) Ever the underdog, Marla was concerned that many of of her fellow students might be better qualified and better connected than she. But now that she had finally made her dream of attending Harvard Business School a reality, she felt confident that no one would outwork her or be more committed to succeeding.

Early in the first semester, as a part of a class called Organizational Behavior, the incoming students were required to take the Myers-Briggs Type Indicator, a test that divided people into sixteen categories based on personality. Marla and her classmates spent several hours taking the test and got the results a week later. They speculated endlessly about what the results meant for their future success. Historically, a plurality of HBS students came up as ENTJs—which stood for extroverted (as opposed to introverted), intuitive (as opposed to sensing), thinking (as opposed to feeling), and judging (as opposed to perceiving).

"Frank, decisive, assumes leadership readily," read one official description of the ENTJ type, sounding as if it had been written by the HBS admissions office itself. Being pegged as an ENTJ was seen by many HBS students as an accomplishment, a badge of honor.

But Marla was labeled an ISTP, almost the exact opposite of an ENTJ. The "I-for-introverted" part was hardly news to her. She had always thought of herself as quiet, driven, and thoughtful, and it was sometimes difficult for her to interact with people she didn't know. She had spent years forcing herself to overcome her shyness, but during those first few weeks of school, her voice would sometimes shake with nervousness when she was called on or when she offered a comment in class.

"Logical, analytical, and objectively critical," the Myers-Briggs report on Marla began. "Unlikely to be convinced by anything but reasoning based on solid facts." ISTPs could be "intensely but quietly curious. Socially they may be rather shy except with their best friends. Quiet and reserved ... [they] often use their talents to <u>bring order out of unorganized facts.</u>"

Marla read the report with fascination. It struck such a powerful chord that she underlined the last six words. She hated to admit it, but the test had described her exactly.

Up in the Warning Track, Marc Cenedella's Myers-Briggs results pegged him as an ENTP. The description sounded familiar: "Bored by routine, will seldom do the same thing the same way, apt to turn to one new interest after another." Perhaps this explained his drive to do things like pack up after college and move to a city where he knew no one and had no job. Marc had always felt guilty that he couldn't organize his life a little better; even when he tried to use one of those day planners that supposedly turns you into a blindingly well-organized person, he had real trouble sticking to any sort of plan or schedule. But now it all made sense—this was just the way he was wired.

Marc stood out from the very first day of school. He sat next to a former Monitor Company consultant named Aaron Pempel, who initiated a little ice-breaking scheme by betting people twenty dollars that they couldn't name all fifty U.S. states from memory. Marc took his new classmate up on the challenge during one of those first days in class and rattled off all fifty states in less than two minutes.

Double or nothing, Marc proposed, offering this time to include the state capitals. Pempel declined.

Later, Marc learned that a classmate named Steve Perricone was in danger of having his twenty-eighth birthday pass unnoticed. Marc's response was to organize an outing to a Boston sushi restaurant involving about twenty students, none of whom really knew one another. Before long, Marc developed a reputation as a hard-partying student who was nevertheless "scary smart," in the words of one classmate.

Marc found the work at HBS interesting, but he recognized early on that business school did not require that its students study, memorize, and master a rigorous corpus of knowledge, the way law schools and medical schools did. There were a few exceptions to this rule—classes like accounting and finance included problem sets that had to be completed before each session. But more important than teaching any particular skill or set of facts, HBS taught its students how to approach and break down problems. The case studies invariably included too much information, and few students retained much of a case's detail after they were finished with it. Instead, Marc and his classmates developed the ability to analyze complex business problems and judge which information was important and which was not. Perhaps better than many of his classmates, Marc understood that HBS wasn't all about "credits on the right, debits on the left." It was about refining your instincts.

A week's worth of reading at HBS might amount to ten or so twelve-page case studies. Many of Marc's peers put in endless hours of study, but to Marc's way of thinking, it was like being asked to read a dozen magazine articles a week. He set aside Sunday afternoons to do his reading; as he reviewed the cases, he underlined the important parts and wrote comments in the margins.

By Sunday evening, his preparation for the week was done. His perceptive comments in class made it clear to both his professors and his classmates that this was more than sufficient. He still had Forbes Pacifica to run from afar, and he'd hired two employees to manage it day-to-day while he was gone. Most of his classmates made do without any income during the nine-month school year, but Marc took in roughly $30,000 from his pet food exporting business.

Otherwise, though, his undemanding schedule left virtually every weeknight free. Marc filled his time with socializing. On Thursdays, he would arrange margarita parties; on Friday afternoons, he'd get together to jam with a group of friends who had at least a passing musical interest. They'd print out the lyrics to Bob Dylan and Grateful Dead tunes, beat up on a guitar or two, and take turns singing lead vocals. And, that first fall, Marc's cousin Loraine was a junior at nearby Boston College. Marc started spending time there as well, expanding his playing field and getting to know the BC undergraduate girls.

As the semester went on, Section A developed a close camaraderie. HBS purposefully structured the "Section experience," so that it became a 24/7 commitment. You attended class with the same people, studied with them, went to the gym with them. You ate dinner and went to parties with them, and you traveled to warmer climes together on spring break. The section even had a budget for social activities, which meant that HBS practically forced you to develop friendships. This was a mixed blessing for an introvert like Marla Malcolm, but for Marc Cenedella it was like winning the networking lottery. He realized that the most important thing about the HBS program was that it provided an opportunity to meet a big group of interesting high achievers. Just about everything he did while pursuing his MBA was designed to allow him to get to know as many of his classmates as possible. And as Marc understood very well, when one person's network expanded— both at and after Harvard Business School—everyone else's network expanded, too.

HBS students were advised to come to campus with their résumés prepared. Just weeks into the first semester, the investment banks, consulting firms, Fortune 500 companies, and other employers came calling. The suitors held elaborate cocktail receptions at area hotels and bars, plying students with drinks and hors d'ouvres, making informal notes about who was who. A satirical article in the weekly *Harbus* newspaper described a fistfight between recruiters for two top-tier consulting firms when they both approached the same student.

"A six-person brawl erupted during which representatives from the Boston Consulting Group managed to sign up the student in question." It was a joke, of course, but it didn't seem all that far off. The *Harbus* brimmed with full-page ads from top employers, blue-chip firms that seemed to promise both opportunity and stability—companies with names like Andersen Consulting, Bear Stearns, and Lehman Brothers.

One full-page ad read:

The journey begins…

ENRON

wishes you well

as you travel through the new school year.

(For the record, *Harbus* also carried ads for firms that still existed a decade or so later.)

Stability wasn't necessarily something Marc Cenedella was looking for. He planned on doing something much bigger after graduation than he'd done before. What, precisely, he wasn't sure—that was the whole point of spending two years at HBS.

Over time, he started focusing on private equity investing. Those firms generally wanted people with investment banking experience, so Marc planned to use his HBS summer to get it. He interviewed with every investment bank that came to campus and accepted an offer for a summer internship at Donaldson, Lufkin & Jenrette. He even arranged to go to the Los Angeles office—once again, he'd be back in southern California.

CREATING OPPORTUNITY

Marla Malcolm enjoyed HBS, although she wasn't crazy about Boston. She'd never lived in a place that was so cold in the late fall and winter. New England seemed a little strange culturally, too—when she went to dinner with people outside of school, they often talked about religion or the merits of everyone's hometowns. Laid-back Californians just didn't do that kind of thing.

Guaranteed a position with McKinsey & Co. after graduation, Marla faced little of the intense career pressure that her peers did. But McKinsey encouraged its employees who were on MBA sabbaticals to work elsewhere during the summer, and Marla wanted to make the most of the opportunity. She took up residence in Baker Library, searching through newspaper archives for intriguing people and firms operating under the radar. One name came up over and over: a 1983 HBS graduate and former investment banker named Jonathan Ledecky.

Ledecky, who lived in Washington, D.C., was clearly an outsized personality; his exploits had often been written up in the *Washington Post*, and the stories were laced with equal parts consternation and admiration. In 1994, Marla read, he had gone to extraordinary lengths to put together his first real deal on his own: the acquisition of a Minnesota office supply company. He'd sunk his entire net worth into the contract, and he'd lined up a friend and mentor who was also eager to invest. But he was still short, and he'd made up the gap by taking out $250,000 in cash advances on his personal credit cards. The up-front cash came easy, but on the back end he'd be paying interest rates of 17, 19, even 23 percent.

This was a go-for-broke risk, but Ledecky had made it pay off. He quickly acquired five more companies, funding each deal with stock in a new holding company he formed called U.S. Office Products, or USOP. He'd immediately taken USOP public and used the additional money to buy even more companies. The technique was usually called a roll-up, though some wags called it "poof! financing" because it enabled big companies to appear out of nowhere.

Increasingly intrigued by Ledecky, Marla browsed through more stories about him. "Ledecky's Billion-Dollar Run: 52 Weeks + 52 Acquisitions = 1 Empire for U.S. Office Products Chairman," was the headline on one *Washington Post* article from the year before. It was accompanied by a photo of Ledecky in a T-shirt and shorts as he ran through the streets of Georgetown. An avid marathoner, he averaged between six and ten miles every day.

USOP was focused on the business-to-business market, selling to law firms, corporations, and anyone else who used huge amounts of office products. Because the company let the affiliates it acquired keep their names and management teams, many customers never even noticed the switch. USOP's stock price rose, based on incredible earnings, which were in turn pumped up still higher by adding the performance of newly acquired companies. In just three years, USOP had gone from Ledecky's cash-advance checks to revenues so high that the company was knocking on the door of the Fortune 500 club.

Theoretically, bringing all those companies together meant operating more efficiently—pooling buying power, centralizing and sharing distribution systems. But in practice, Marla read, that wasn't happening much. Ledecky had built something truly impressive, but he clearly needed help from people who knew how to cut costs in large companies. Since this was precisely the kind of strategic project Marla had been involved with as a McKinsey consultant, she reached an obvious conclusion.

Jonathan Ledecky and USOP needed her. They just didn't know it yet.

THE ADMIRAL'S NIECE

As Marc and Marla finished their first term at HBS, Chris Michel was still in Washington. His accelerated program would begin in January 1997; until then, he was still an admiral's aide, now running out his last few weeks in the military.

Every year, the navy held a ten-day orientation session in Washington for its newly promoted admirals. As the aide-de-camp to the top admiral in the Naval Reserve, Chris was very busy during the orientation period. One evening in late 1996, the group of new admirals split in two, with the full-time active duty officers going to one event and the nine new reserve admirals and their wives heading to a dinner at the home of Chris's boss, Admiral Tom Hall. They chartered a bus, and Chris sat across the aisle from a newly promoted admiral named Hank White and his wife. Their conversation turned to Chris's imminent departure from the navy.

"You're going to Harvard Business School?" Mrs. White asked when she heard Chris describe his plans. "Our niece is going there." Her husband jabbed her in the side—*leave the poor guy alone*—but she got Chris to give her his business card.

Later, Chris looked up the admiral's niece in the directory of admitted HBS students. Anne Dwane, twenty-six, was a graduate of Georgetown University. She had worked in market research for a small consulting firm in North Carolina, where her clients included Nabisco. She also happened to be quite attractive, so Chris was pleasantly surprised a few days later when she called him.

Attending HBS had been a goal of Anne's since high school, although she had gone through a tough decision process once she'd been admitted. Lately she'd spent quite a bit of time in Silicon Valley, where everyone understood that an exciting new frontier was opening up. She'd been very tempted to try her luck in California, and she found it difficult to accept that attending HBS would mean paying not just an expensive tuition but a significant opportunity cost as well. But in the end she'd decided it would be worth it.

Chris and Anne talked on the phone for a while, the conversation polite but guarded—probably inevitable under the circumstances. (Anne had looked up Chris in the directory as well; with his short navy haircut and his expression, she thought he looked very young.)

Anne seemed nice enough, but Chris didn't think she seemed interested in getting to know him better. *So much for that,* he thought as he hung up.

Chris was assigned to Section H, and as he walked into his first class on the first day—Leadership and Organized Behavior—he was chagrined to find he was assigned to the center seat in Worm Deck. Class had hardly begun before the professor cold-called him to discuss the twelve-page case study they were due to analyze that day, about a telecommunications company. Chris had been up half the night reading the case, highlighting it in purple and doing calculations in the margins. Truth be told, the case thoroughly confused him, but when called upon he managed to muddle through and offer at least a few cogent thoughts. Later the professor confided to him that he liked to call on a military veteran first, on the theory that no matter what else happened, a former soldier or sailor would be very unlikely to cry under the pressure.

Chris was pleased to come up as a classic ENTJ when he got the results of his Myers-Briggs test, but he was still worried that he was out of his league, that he'd one day be remembered as the first former military officer to flunk out of HBS. Marc Cenedella may have found the course materials easy to master, but Chris was intimidated and felt out of control. What did he know about accounting or business? How could he possibly compete with all these consultants and investment bankers? Much of what they talked about in class might as well have been in Swahili.

Flanking Chris on the Worm Deck were Amar Singh—an outspoken Sikh who took pride in describing himself as "the only guy at HBS in a turban"—and Sergio Monsalve, a former Morgan Stanley investment banker. When they learned about Chris's military background, Singh and Monsalve began a daily ritual at his expense. After everyone filed into the room and settled down, and just before the professor began the first class, they would make a big show of leaping to their feet, standing at attention, and saluting Chris.

"Good morning sir!" they would call out—every single morning.

Chris tried to laugh it off, but the teasing made him very uncomfortable. He was certain that he was the admission committee's big mistake for the class of 1998—and that everyone knew it.

On Chris's first day at HBS, as he was moving into his new graduate dorm room in Morris Hall, he noticed an attractive, red-haired woman struggling with boxes. He introduced himself and offered to help—and lo and behold, this was Anne Dwane. He graciously took charge, and this time she found him a lot more impressive. When he stopped to ask one of the maintenance workers for directions, for instance, it became apparent that the man spoke no English. Anne was charmed when Chris immediately switched into the basic Spanish he'd picked up during deployments to Puerto Rico.

Anne was assigned to a different section, but they'd bumped into each other a few times during the first few days of class. Then, a week or so into the semester, as the men and women of the January cohort began forming study groups, Anne was asked to join a group started by a classmate she'd known at Georgetown named Tom Goundrey. A two-time academic all-American in swimming, Tom had worked for Morgan Stanley Capital Partners after graduating from college, helping to manage a $2 billion investment fund. Still a few months shy of his twenty-third birthday, he was one of the youngest students in the business school. (Later, when they discussed a case about a baby food company, Tom was inevitably called on to discuss it.) But he was also extremely confident. He'd applied to HBS—and only HBS—sure that he'd get in.

Tom had already recruited two other students to the study group, and he thought that Anne's background in marketing would be a good complement to their finance and accounting experience. Anne signed on—and then persuaded Tom that it would make sense to include Chris Michel as well.

Chris was eager and grateful, but he remained extremely anxious about his ability to catch up to his peers. One early case in Financial Reporting and Control focused on a ski company; to prepare for the discussion, the students were advised to do a pro forma projection of the company's financial outlook. Chris didn't know what the words *pro forma* and *projection* actually meant in that context, never mind how to prepare such a statement. He bought a college-level accounting textbook and spent many late nights teaching himself accounting. Chris decided that although he was never going to be as proficient as someone like Tom Goundrey, he was determined to learn enough to get by.

MARLA'S FULL-COURT PRESS

Much as she had once done while trying to set up internships through AIESEC at Berkeley, Marla Malcolm continued to mine news articles for mentions of Jonathan Ledecky's key leadership and executive team. In time, she wrote letters to him, to his chief financial officer, and to his general counsel. When she didn't hear back, she wrote again. She followed up with phone calls, leaving voice mail after voice mail for Ledecky and his executive staff, refusing to get discouraged when her calls went unreturned.

Logistics made her pursuit difficult. This was still an era before everyone had a cell phone and used e-mail constantly; besides, Marla was in class half the day. Then, one day, she came home to find that Ledecky had returned her call and left a message on her voice mail. But he was frustratingly noncommittal.

Great to hear from you, he said. *When you're down here in D.C. sometime we should go and get a beer together.* He didn't even leave his phone number.

Marla kept making calls. Finally, she got through to Ledecky's general counsel.

"I think I understand the challenges you're facing," she began, at last making the pitch she'd rehearsed many times. "A roll-up like USOP is all about integration and cost-reduction. That's precisely what I did at McKinsey." She described her experience in a bit more detail.

The general counsel had no involvement in any of these areas at USOP, but he told Marla that Ledecky had just brought aboard a new chief operating officer. He promised to pass her résumé along.

Marla kept pursuing Ledecky and his people, and before long she landed an interview with the new COO. By the time she flew to Washington and visited the USOP headquarters in Georgetown, just a few blocks from the Potomac River, the company had clearly decided that hiring her was almost a no-brainer. Marla was a once-and-future McKinsey analyst, so bringing her aboard for a summer would be a bit like getting a McKinsey & Co. study done for a fraction of the usual cost. Besides, if things didn't work out, she'd be gone in a few months anyway.

Marla was happy to get the offer, but her one disappointment was that she still had never met Ledecky. A few weeks later, he happened to come to HBS to give a speech, and she decided that this was her chance. Still only thirty-nine, he was a dynamic speaker—funny and energetic; he had an "aw-shucks" demeanor that belied his smarts and acumen. He built his talk around a series of lessons he'd learned in business. The most important of these, he said, was "DROOM," which was short for "Don't Run Out of Money." Money bought resources and credibility, but it could also buy time. Most entrepreneurs didn't succeed with their first idea, but if you had the resources to fuel your tenacity, your chances of success improved. That was what had led him to hoard credit card offers all those years.

Afterward, the students crowded around Ledecky as if he were a rock star.

Marla patiently waited for a chance to speak with him. Finally she shook his hand and said, "I just wanted to introduce myself. I'm working for you this summer."

"You want to work for me?" Ledecky replied. "Great,"

"No," Marla replied. "I *am* working for you. I already have the job."

He invited her to have a cup of coffee with him, and then Marla drove her future boss to Logan Airport for his flight back to D.C. Ledecky had made quite an impression on her over these past few months. But Marla liked to think she had made a good impression on him as well.

THE ROARING '90s

In the mid- to late 1990s, the world was changing at lightning speed. It was the era of "irrational exuberance," and as one Internet company after another went public their stocks soared. Netscape held its initial public offering in 1995, and in a single day its share price rocketed from $28 to $75. In 1996, Yahoo!'s IPO opened at $24.50 a share and on its first day jumped to $43. Amazon's market capitalization reached an astounding $560 million before its first day of trading in 1997 was done.

Some of life's outcomes can seem inevitable in retrospect, and the emergence of the Internet as an enormously lucrative marketplace may be a good case in point. At the time, however, it required true vision to see where the Internet mania would lead; no one knew which companies would succeed and which would fail. By and large, the HBS classes of 1997 and 1998 weren't sure what to make of it all. They were excited about the possibilities, and many of them at least considered pursuing opportunities with these young companies. But few actually took the leap; mostly they applied for jobs with I-banks, consulting firms, and companies in the Fortune 1000. True, a few HBS students like Marc Cenedella had slightly different aspirations—private equity, for example— but most of them sought to join stable companies, or at least established and growing enterprises. Internet companies were simply too risky. When Amazon's founder, Jeff Bezos, came to speak at HBS in 1997, Chris Michel asked a question that in effect suggested that Amazon should aim to be acquired, since Barnes & Noble was about to launch its own competing Web site. Chris was quite confident that the well-known bricks-and-mortar retailer would ultimately destroy the upstart Internet site.

Despite all the skepticism, HBS found this new frontier impossible to ignore. In 1996, a pair of MBA candidates had obtained permission to do a field study for credit, during which they analyzed the business plan competitions sponsored by MIT and other top schools. They and some of their classmates hoped that HBS would start a similar competition, even though some of the faculty objected. But by spring 1997, the first HBS Business Plan contest was under way. Competitors ranged from a pair of students with plans to start a dessert-only restaurant in Boston, to another group that wanted to start an Internet chemical marketplace. The following year, a student with an idea for a site that would help people find collectibles like old records, stamps, and rare books entered the contest; his competition was a plan to build the first Internet-specific consulting firm. The restaurateurs raised enough money to open a restaurant, the chemical company signed a multimillion-dollar investment deal, and the consulting startup raised $2 million in venture capital right out of the gate. The entrepreneurial collector revamped his company's Web site, relaunched, and eventually sold the whole thing to Amazon for $200 million.

Heady stuff, yes. But even then, most of the proposals submitted to the contest involved old media—a plan to produce and sell a golf bag on wheels, a "personal emergency signaling device," and two separate entries to start chains of car and truck washes. And although the contest did inspire many interesting ideas for new businesses, the professors consistently told their students that coming up with good ideas was the easiest part.

In one speech given to a huge crowd of HBS students around this time, Professor Bill Sahlman warned them that starting a successful new company would be very difficult. It will take a lot of research, Sahlman said. You'll have to want it. You'll have to follow through, even while your friends and classmates are enjoying themselves. But most important, he added, get over the greatest myth about entrepreneurship— the false notion that all you really need is the one truly great idea.

"Ideas are a dime a dozen," Sahlman said. "Execution is what is important."

U.S. OFFICE PRODUCTS

Marla Malcolm had sought out U.S. Office Products primarily because of Jon Ledecky, but when she reached Washington, D.C., that summer she found that she had little contact with him. She worked instead for the senior vice president for operations, David Copenhaver, who had joined the company—how else?—when Ledecky bought his business.

We have a great financial model, Copenhaver confirmed in an early conversation with Marla, but the operating plan was a shambles. Cutting costs and building synergy across so many firms was daunting, largely because they kept adding firms so quickly. With hundreds of acquired subsidiaries around the world buying tens of thousands of different products, it was next to impossible to keep track of everything. A subsidiary in Florida might buy a certain product at $3 a unit, while another subsidiary in Texas bought the same item at $2.20, and a third subsidiary in California paid $4. Some of their newly acquired companies were buying office furniture at full price from outside competitors, even though USOP now had affiliates that specialized in office furniture. Ledecky had been buying companies at such a fast clip that headquarters had trouble keeping up with the list of everything its subsidiaries sold. Marla's most important project was to design a computerized inventory management system—later dubbed "PowerSku"—that could account for each of the company's many thousands of products. Marla worked with computer programmers to develop different algorithms, oversaw the people who entered all the product information into the giant database, and then had to persuade the individual subsidiary presidents to insist that their people actually use the system.

Marla enjoyed her work, but since she was working on day-to-day operations, and Ledecky was focused almost exclusively on the big picture, she wondered if the entire summer might go by before she ever got the chance to sit down and talk with him. Then, one hot summer Sunday, she was out for a morning walk in Georgetown when Ledecky happened to jog by. He stopped to say hello.

"So," he asked her, "what do you think about U.S. Office Products?"

Marla thought for a second, and gave a much more complex answer than he was expecting from a sidewalk encounter. She'd spent a lot of time talking with the presidents of the USOP subsidiaries, Marla told him, and there were a number of things they needed to address. She ticked them off, starting with PowerSku and moving through a long list of ideas about cost containment and inventory control.

"What we need is a centralized distribution warehouse," she said. USOP had eight subsidiaries in Florida alone—each with its own facility, its own inventory, its own staff. The entrepreneurs who had started these firms each thought their systems were best, and they weren't working together. You've got a great business model, Marla told Ledecky, but eliminating all the inherent efficiencies would be difficult to achieve.

Before Marla realized it, she had gone on for a good five minutes. Ledecky was both charmed and impressed: from the minute she got up in the morning, Marla Malcolm had obviously been thinking about U.S. Office Products and how to make it better.

The following week, Marla noticed that Ledecky began reaching out to her. He called her into meetings that had little or nothing to do with her official job. It struck Marla that at least from one point of view, all those hours of researching USOP and fighting to get a summer job at the company had prepared her to take advantage of a chance encounter on a street in Georgetown.

BIRTH OF A SALESMAN

Chris Michel, Anne Dwane, and the rest of the January cohort went to school straight through the summer of 1997 so they would catch up with Marla, Marc, and the rest of the HBS class of 1998. Among the classes they began in June was General Management, perhaps the quintessential HBS course, in which students studied business policy and corporate leadership. Even at a school where the faculty included men and women who were famous in the business world, their professor for this course, Ed Zschau, stood out.

With his bachelor's degree, MBA, and PhD from Stanford, Zschau had represented Silicon Valley in Congress in the 1980s. More recently, he had been a candidate for vice president of the United States, running for the nomination of the Reform Party in an ill-fated effort to wrest control of the party from its billionaire founder, Ross Perot. But for all of that, Zschau had first made his mark as a technology and business entrepreneur. He'd founded a company called System Industries in the 1960s that manufactured computer products, and had gone on to be both a partner in a venture capital firm and the CEO of another tech firm. He'd even run a division of IBM.

With the beginning of the summer semester, Chris had finally been able to escape his front-and-center seat in Worm Deck. But Zschau greatly impressed him and from their first meeting the charismatic professor had his full attention. The feeling was mutual. Chris's humility and maturity, and the fact that he'd served in the military, all appealed to Zschau. Moreover, through his stepfather, Chris had a very distant relative named Robert Michel, a prominent congressman who had served with Zschau and become close friends with him.

This was Zschau's second stint at HBS—he'd taught management at the school in the 1960s—and he could look back on a number of the students who had been in his classes then with pride, thinking of the many companies they had started. Not surprisingly, he was an evangelist for entrepreneurship, not just as a business strategy but as a way of life. Toward the end of the semester, Zschau burst into song one morning, belting out a version of Frank Sinatra's "My Way," with the altered lyrics espousing the merits of starting a company and going your own way.

But he also knew how to ask the hard questions. "Just out of curiosity," he asked the class one day, "how many of you can imagine yourself being an entrepreneur, either right after school or soon after?"

Many of the students raised their hands.

"How many plan to be in sales?" Zschau asked.

Most of the hands fell.

"Well," Zschau told them. "If you are planning to be an entrepreneur, you should be planning to be a salesman. You're constantly selling. You're selling yourself when your company doesn't even exist yet; you're selling the concept to potential employees; you're selling to customers. And you're trying to convince suppliers that this teeny company of yours, that isn't well financed—you're selling them the belief that you're going to succeed."

As his education at HBS continued and Chris gained in confidence, he developed the zeal of a convert. He and Anne spent more and more time together—the secret was out; they were dating—and from the very beginning she had been all about entrepreneurship. Between her enthusiasm and Ed Zschau's example, Chris was beginning to see his future in a new way: someday, he wanted to start a company of his own.

BREVITY

One summer of working for an investment bank was enough for Marc Cenedella to realize that he did not want to be an investment banker. He was still primarily interested in private finance, so in the fall of his second year at HBS he applied to every bank and financial firm that came to campus. But he was also enjoying running Forbes Pacifica on the side, and for a time he wondered whether there might be a way to scale the business beyond what he'd done before. Overall, he enjoyed the process of trying to figure out what sort of job would suit him, and he liked helping his friends and classmates think through their options— identifying their strengths, finding careers they might be good at and enjoy. For a day or two he wondered whether he might go into the career advice business, so he launched an intensive study of the headhunting industry. But the more he looked into the field, the less appealing he found it. Headhunting meant developing a professional practice over a long period of time, like a lawyer or a doctor or a dentist. You might succeed in building a Rolodex of three or four thousand people, but then you'd have to stay put. Marc loved to travel—he had a goal of visiting thirty countries by the time he turned thirty—and so the idea of staying in one city was a nonstarter.

Marc also came to understand that he wouldn't be a very good fit with many of the large, traditional employers who came to campus, even in the financial field. One afternoon, he went for an interview with GE Capital, and the first person he met gave him a form to fill out that was about ten pages long. It was the most bureaucratic thing Marc had ever seen.

"Why would GE Capital be interested in a guy whose background includes being an entrepreneur and exporting dog food?" Marc asked the woman.

"At GE, we're looking for all kinds of different people, especially those who think outside the box."

"I'm sorry," he said. "Entrepreneurs who think outside the box don't fill out ten-page forms." He handed the blank forms back to her.

He also interviewed with an old-line famous private equity firm, but after his less-than-inspiring experience with a bank over the summer he knew his heart wasn't in it. Besides, he didn't click with the senior partner. When the man asked Marc to name his greatest weakness, Marc couldn't help himself.

"Brevity," he replied.

Then he sat, stone-faced and silent, in a staring contest with the interviewer.

He didn't get an offer. It was probably just as well.

———

As the fall semester continued, however, Marc developed a plan. He didn't want to follow his classmates—whether that meant taking a job with an American investment bank or joining the growing number of students considering, but most often ultimately rejecting, dot-coms and other startups. Just as "international business" had been hot when he graduated from college, now some of the excitement in business was in "emerging markets." These were the overseas investment opportunities that carried with them both the biggest risk and the biggest possible upside. Among the regions near the top of the list at the time was Eastern Europe. The Iron Curtain had fallen only a decade before, and hundreds of millions of Eastern Europeans were clamoring for Western goods and services.

Trying to make money in emerging markets would probably be an all-or-nothing bet. But Marc had always been attracted to the idea of taking well-thought-out risks, and the volatile economies that often caused wild swings in emerging markets represented big opportunities for foreign firms. With a little luck, you could make a fortune.

Marc interviewed with several companies involved with emerging markets. Of all of them, Marc was most intrigued by Creditanstalt, an Austrian investment bank. When the bank made him an offer, Marc gave up on Southern California for good and agreed to work for the firm in New York City. If you were young, smart, and willing to work hard, emerging markets seemed the place to be.

WHY CHRIS MICHEL IS NOT A
PHARMACEUTICAL MAGNATE

For the January cohort, the accelerated course schedule meant an abbreviated summer break. HBS students with lots of experience and a clear idea of what they wanted to do after graduation could simply relax, but for career switchers like Chris Michel, taking even a two-week summer internship was considered vital.

Chris envisioned returning to Washington, D.C., after graduation, so he was happy to accept a brief internship with Mercer Consulting in the nation's capital in August. He lived in a hotel for two weeks and worked on a project involving what was known as multimodal trans-portation, which basically involved moving cargo by air, land, and sea. Chris went to a lot of Mercer-sponsored happy hours, and he was wined and dined by the firm. They clearly wanted him to come back full-time after graduation. But enjoyable as his internship was—Chris liked a lot of the people he worked with in Mercer's D.C. office—he simply wasn't excited about joining the company.

HBS had transformed him, and when Chris returned in the fall he was thrilled to be back. When the class of 1999 arrived, Chris was one of the members of "Old H" who came to meet the new members of Section H and help them get oriented. Meanwhile, he and Anne Dwane were committed to either joining a new company or starting one of their own. They brainstormed constantly, hoping to write a business plan and enter it in the HBS contest in the spring. But then another opportunity emerged: along with Tom Goundrey, they registered to do a field study with Harvard's office of trademark and technology licensing. It quickly struck Chris that if he and other HBS students could work with profes-sors in Harvard's other colleges, they could help turn their research and inventions into businesses. They formalized the program, calling it "Har-vard Entrepreneurial Action Teams," or HEAT, and teamed up with a chemistry professor who had developed a computer-modeling program that could lead to major advances in pharmaceuticals.

Thus began many hours with the professor and his colleagues, trying to come up with a business plan. They discussed many options. Should they license the program to a drug company? Should they create a brand-new company? Chris helped to draw up the papers to incorpo-rate the firm—which they called Initio Pharmaceuticals—and after meeting with the professor and his colleagues a dozen or more times, he started to believe that this would turn into a job offer after graduation. Maybe he'd be the chief operating officer or take on some other senior operational role. They got some good press for their effort, including a front-page article in the *Harbus*, and they were featured in various offi-cial university PR announcements. They wrote a business plan and the chemistry professor pitched it to local venture capital firms. For a few weeks, they were brimming with confidence about their prospects.

But by the early months of 1998, they had nothing concrete to show for all their efforts, and suddenly it seemed highly unlikely that this venture would result in a full-time job for Chris. He'd been so excited about the idea that he hadn't even interviewed anywhere else. He still had the offer to join Mercer, of course, but taking it would feel like moving backward.

Meanwhile, he and Anne were getting along better than ever, and as time went on she became completely focused on finding a job with a startup in San Francisco or the Bay Area. Chris flew out to the coast with her a couple of times when she interviewed, since the companies always paid travel expenses for an interviewee's "significant other." At first he didn't much care for San Francisco. He still shared some of the military's conservative tendencies, and San Francisco was perhaps the most liberal city in America. But over time the city grew on him. He decided to find a way to follow Anne out west.

SO MUCH FOR MCKINSEY

Jonathan Ledecky had made a decision, too: after graduating from Harvard, Marla Malcolm should come to work for him full-time. But Marla had a hard time envisioning working for him long-term. To begin with, she was focused on getting as much as possible out of her second year at HBS. She founded a student organization called the Women's Entrepreneurship Seminar and worked to bring female executives to campus for talks. Recruiting the speakers and coordinating the events became nearly a full-time job in itself. But she also invited Ledecky back to campus to give another talk, and he simply wouldn't let up with his recruitment pitch.

Though she was intrigued, and now sensed he was serious, she hesitated. For one thing, she felt she had little choice but to go back to McKinsey after graduation; otherwise, she would owe the firm more than $50,000, since they had covered her Harvard tuition. Moreover, as excited as she'd been to spend a summer working for U.S. Office Products, now that she was back at HBS her experiences at the company seemed oddly ephemeral. And despite Ledecky's entreaties, Marla wasn't even sure what business she'd be working for. That fall, he had stepped down as the CEO of U.S. Office Products. Then, just before Thanksgiving, he did something truly remarkable: he formed a new company called Consolidation Capital Corporation and then took it public without clients, revenue, or even an industry. On the strength of his reputation alone, he raised half a billion dollars of seed money on Wall Street.

Ledecky's new venture was groundbreaking, like poof! financing squared. But from Marla's perspective, his sudden departure from USOP was also quite disconcerting. She kept in touch with him, and he kept telling her he wanted to hire her away from McKinsey. But he was slow to make a firm offer, which made Marla all the more reluctant to sign on. Finally, in January, Ledecky sent her an e-mail and committed himself.

"You know you have an offer to join (for lack of a better description) 'Ledecky Enterprises,'" he wrote in his e-mail. He then spelled out the terms—$100,000 a year, a signing bonus equal to what she owed McKinsey for leaving, and stock options. Ledecky was not one to get bogged down in details, so he simply asked her to tell him what else she needed to make her comfortable.

"Protocol these days is a detailed offer letter," Marla replied, and she drafted one herself, including a full page of terms designed to ensure she'd work on only the most important and interesting projects, and also learn how to build and run businesses.

"You have to learn when to stop negotiating a deal," Ledecky replied. He moved fast, and he wanted Marla to move quickly, too. Even now he was filing plans with the SEC to poof-finance yet another new IPO—this time a company called Unicapital that would roll up lease-financing companies.

"Every day now a new deal comes in," he wrote. "Stripping it all away, it really doesn't matter what you get paid, what your title is, what the stock options are, etc. You either understand the unique opportunity you are being given"—and, he added, he knew she *did* understand—"or you don't. Since you do, sign up and let's go!"

Marla realized that it was time to make the call. She explained the situation to her father, who told her she was crazy to consider giving up her prestigious, high-paying, secure job at McKinsey.

Next she sought out Ed Mathias, one of Ledecky's mentors, who had been his first investor in the deal that eventually became U.S. Office Products. Ledecky had introduced them during the previous summer. Mathias was very enthusiastic.

Finally, Marla asked one of her favorite mentors, Dick Darman, a former White House official and investor who now taught at Harvard's Kennedy School of Government. He'd even worked at McKinsey, so he understood her situation precisely.

"What's the risk?" Darman replied when she laid out her dilemma. Even if you try working for Ledecky and things don't work out, he added, "You could still go to McKinsey, no problem."

That made sense. But just to be sure, Marla interviewed with the managing directors of McKinsey's offices in both Washington, D.C., and San Francisco, getting their firm commitment that if she wanted to rejoin the consulting firm a year after graduation, she would be able to. With those assurances in hand, she knew Darman was right. There was no risk.

Marla accepted the offer. She would take the plunge with Jon Ledecky.

GRADUATION AND "THE NEW 'BROADBAND' INTERNET"

The day before graduation, the HBS class of 1998 was addressed by Treasury Secretary Robert Rubin, who advised them to remember the role that pure luck and happenstance had played and would continue to play in their success. Rubin's point was well taken: it was hard to imagine how the class could have chosen a better moment to attend the business school. On average, the men and women of the HBS class of 1998 fielded three and a half job offers each. Their average starting pay packages, including salary and signing bonuses, exceeded $160,000 a year. Most had asked for—and received—stock options, and more than half picked up guarantees of additional bonuses at the end of the year. Three in ten went into consulting; 11 percent joined tech companies; another 11 percent went to work for investment banks.

Flipping the pages of the *Harbus* in those last few weeks of the spring semester, readers were provided with a telling glimpse of how the HBS community saw the world—and how the world saw HBS. Big firms ran full-page advertisements congratulating the members of the class who had accepted offers to join them—Andersen Consulting, Bain & Co., Bear Stearns, PricewaterhouseCoopers, and many others. Chris Michel was among the ten graduates listed in the Mercer Consulting ad; he'd accepted the firm's offer on the conditions that he could work out of the

San Francisco office and that he could take most of the summer off first to travel.

One feature article was headlined "A Conversation with a McKinsey Partner." Other articles included a review of "the new 'broadband' cable modem Internet service . . . which promises access to the Internet with none of the delays associated with our telephone modems." There were also features on "publishing your own personal Web page" and "how to publish your resume on the Web in five minutes."

On graduation day itself, a cloudy, windswept spring day, sixty-six flags flew near the stage, each representing the home country of at least one person in the class. The members of the class of 1998 walked across the stage quietly; a few who had become parents during their two years in school carried their young children. The new graduates shook hands with the dean, got their diplomas, and then began the next chapter of the lives.

The days around graduation were some of the best of Marc Cenedella's life. He had received excellent grades during his two years at HBS, and on June 2, the day before graduation, he was celebrated as one of forty-two Baker Scholars in the class of 1998, an honor bestowed on the top 5 percent of the class. His parents and three brothers watched him receive the honor; he also made sure to provide tickets to the occasion for his cousin Loraine from Boston College, and then went out of his way to introduce Loraine to a friend and classmate of his named Tom Morgan. (He'd been trying to set them up for quite some time.)

Marc and his classmates graduated on June 3; on June 4, Marc sold his interest in Forbes Pacifica Trading Company, the import-export firm he'd started before attending HBS. He told friends that he cleared only enough to put aside some "travel and furniture money," but selling the firm, as much as graduating, marked a major milestone in his life.

For many of Marc's colleagues, two years at HBS had opened their eyes to myriad opportunities. Their ambitions had expanded exponentially; not only did most of the graduates believe they could make a lot of money, they also now had the confidence to try. Marc, as always, was a little different. He had never lacked either courage or confidence. He was certain that whatever he did, it would be rewarding and lucrative.

Walking across campus one day, Marc turned to a close friend, Steve Perricone, and said: "Can you believe we're going to be millionaires?"

Steve looked at him incredulously for a second. "Maybe you are."

"No, Steve," Marc said matter-of-factly, without breaking his stride. "You do know it's inevitable now. Don't you?"

GOING WEST

Anne Dwane had found her startup: a Silicon Valley Internet company that designed Web-based content management systems. Chris Michel, meanwhile, had worked out his deal with Mercer, trading the excitement of finding a similar job with some other Internet startup for the opportunity to spend most of the summer visiting his father in Greece. He wasn't an entrepreneur yet, but he was increasingly certain he would become one. And at least he would be moving to the city where entrepreneurs seemed to be starting companies on every street corner.

He and Anne packed everything they owned into her maroon Ford Explorer and began following a meandering route west—first down to Tennessee, where Chris's mother and stepfather now lived, then north to the Canadian border and Glacier National Park in Montana. Finally, they reached San Francisco. A day later, Chris took off for Greece—Anne would find him an apartment while she also looked for one for herself.

While he was gone, Anne had a bad career scare. The day before she was due to start work, the company's cofounder called to tell her that the firm was folding. Anne experienced a day or two of panic, but she was amazed at how quickly the HBS network kicked in. The startup's main investor, a technology incubator called Interval Research that had been founded by Microsoft cofounder Paul Allen, soon offered her a job in business development. She jumped at it.

Anne took to her job at Interval Research immediately; she found it hard to imagine that working for the small startup she'd originally come west to join could have been more exciting. By the time Chris returned from Greece, she was commuting to Interval's office on Page Mill Road in Palo Alto, Silicon Valley's investment and capital heart. "Business development" was a nebulous term, but Anne's position meant that no one in any startup business in California would ever turn her down if she called and asked them to present to her. Just weeks after graduating from HBS, she had somehow landed in the catbird seat.

Anne had found Chris a studio in the same apartment complex where she now lived, in the northeast corner of San Francisco near the financial district. Chris's apartment was a studio with a view of the Bay and the Coit Tower. Though she didn't have a great view, Anne's place was larger.

"Same college, different dorms," was how Anne described it when Chris returned.

Chris started at Mercer in early September 1998. He tried hard to stoke his enthusiasm for the job but, even in his first few days, he knew it wasn't for him. The energy just a few miles south in Silicon Valley was awesome, Anne told him each day when she came home. Change was afoot. It was a time to be bold.

Anne was right, Chris knew. It was the time to start something of their own.

MARLA AND BARRY

Right after graduating, Marla went to work for Jonathan Ledecky in an office east of Georgetown, overlooking the White House. He'd finally chosen an industry for his new company: commercial building maintenance services. But Consolidated Capital seemed too generic a name for the company, and he soon came up with something more descriptive: Building One Service Solutions. On the NASDAQ exchange, the company's stock ticker was "BOSS." (Leaving no doubt about his overall business strategy, Ledecky had chosen "BUYR" as the stock symbol when the company had been called Consolidated Capital.)

Marla quickly became Ledecky's right-hand woman. In the six months before her arrival, he had acquired twenty-seven maintenance and janitorial companies; now, week in and week out, they brought in more founders and chief executives so Ledecky could pitch his vision. Watching Ledecky fold in so many companies so fast, Marla soon came up with a medium-term goal for herself: persuade Ledecky to make her the CEO of one of the BOSS subsidiaries.

Marla thought that Building One had a couple of real drawbacks, however. First, she didn't think building maintenance was an especially interesting industry from a business-strategy standpoint. At least with office products, you could lay out a plan to consolidate operations and cut purchasing costs. But janitorial services didn't sell products, so there was no opportunity to save money by consolidating everyone's inventory, as she had done at USOP.

And second, Marla couldn't help but acknowledge that she and Ledecky were missing an enormous opportunity. The excitement, the Wall Street money—everything was moving to the Internet. Marla knew that Ledecky was an incredibly effective salesman; he had boundless energy, and already his mind was racing toward other ventures, other ideas. Throughout the final months of 1998, Marla rarely missed a chance to tell Ledecky that he had picked the wrong industry. His talents were being wasted. They should try something different, something to do with the Internet.

During her first months with Ledecky, Marla developed a friendship with an executive at one of the companies they tried to acquire. Barry Beck, dark-haired and driven, was a natural salesman and a forceful negotiator. His older brother and a friend had started a maintenance company called Tower Systems in the late 1980s, and after Barry had graduated from Cornell University in 1990 he'd joined them as a sort of third founder. Now thirty, he was running a company that was generating something like $50 million a year. But Barry was restless.

One of his competitors had sold his business to Building One, and when the competitor offered to make an introduction, Barry came to his first meeting with Ledecky eager to hear the offer. He shook Marla's hand, Barry later confided to her, and had presumed at first that she was Ledecky's assistant or secretary.

But when Ledecky turned the meeting over to Marla, Barry was blown away. Sitting at the conference room table, surrounded by the founders and general managers of other companies not all that different from his, he suddenly realized that as successful as he, his brother, and his brother's friend had been, Ledecky and Marla were playing the entrepreneurial game at a much higher level.

Although Barry and his partners didn't sell their business to Building

One in the end, he and Marla kept in touch. In Barry, she found a kindred spirit—he was smart, ambitious, and stuck in an industry he no longer found exciting. He was looking at opportunities elsewhere, and soon Marla realized that she was, too. Eventually, she confided in Barry and told him about her hope that Ledecky would someday soon make her the CEO of one of his companies.

Barry was incredulous. "You're crazy if you think that," he told her bluntly.

Pointing out that she'd made herself into Ledecky's indispensable deputy, Barry insisted that Ledecky wouldn't dream of letting her go. Besides, Marla wasn't even a year out of business school. Nobody was ever going to make her a CEO at this early stage in her career. And then he added two of the most prophetic, resonant sentences she would ever hear.

"There's only one way that's ever going to happen," Barry told Marla. "You'll have to start a company of your own."

CHAPTER 4

MAKE THE COMMITMENT

You can't wait for inspiration. You have to go after it with a club.

—JACK LONDON

DECIDE, LEARN, BECOME

So, how badly do you want this?

That may sound like some sort of challenge, and in a way it is. But my question also provides an opportunity for self-reflection. Thinking hard at the outset about what's really motivating you to launch a company can make all the difference down the road.

Becoming a successful entrepreneur is hard. As our story develops, you'll see that Marla, Chris, and Marc faced serious, high-stakes threats to their businesses. They were often under intense pressure, and they continuously dealt with enormous amounts of stress. Along the way, they had several opportunities to throw in the towel and still come away more or less whole.

But they didn't. And one of the most important reasons they persevered is that they had begun their careers as entrepreneurs by making a crucial decision. Before they developed their business plans, recruited teams, raised money, learned to lead, and built their ventures, Marla, Chris, and Marc each made a conscious and very personal commitment to become successful entrepreneurs.

That choice made them, too. Even at this early stage of the story, we can see that their decision to start companies was greatly influenced by people they trusted. Anne Dwane, for example, knew from her first days at HBS that she wanted to join or launch a startup, and her passion for entrepreneurship had a profound effect on Chris Michel. And although the idea of launching a company didn't take hold of Marla Malcolm while she was at HBS, her outlook changed dramatically once she worked with people like Jonathan Ledecky and Barry Beck. Their social environments encouraged Chris and Marla to believe that becoming an entrepreneur was not only possible but something they fervently wanted to do.

Wait, you might say—what about Marc Cenedella? Perhaps most interestingly, Marc recognized that even though he'd achieved some pre-HBS success as an entrepreneur, he wasn't eager to start another company immediately after graduating. He remained interested in entrepreneurial enterprises—and investing in emerging markets certainly qualifies—yet he wasn't quite ready to become a full-fledged entrepreneur again. But think back—remember that voice that spoke to him when Forbes Pacifica was failing and he'd been offered a slot at HBS? He'd made a serious commitment to the company and its investors, and he knew he absolutely had to stick it out and make the venture successful.

Remember my earlier point that most would-be entrepreneurs launch their businesses without thinking hard enough about innovation, without plans for growth, and without large amounts of capital? Here's an even more surprising fact: many companies are founded by people who never truly set out to become entrepreneurs. Instead, new ventures are often launched because their founders have lost jobs—the unemployed are twice as likely to launch companies—or because they don't want to work for others. As I got to know high-percentage entrepreneurs like Marla, Chris, Marc, and their colleagues, I concluded that these kinds of "accidental entrepreneurs" skew the statistics. They may as well plan to fail, because they fail to plan.

As with any field requiring exceptional talent and creativity—the arts, athletics, and many of the so-called white-collar professions—making it as an entrepreneur involves much more than simply deciding that you're going to start up a company that will ultimately make millions of dollars. But the depth of your commitment matters greatly. In the long run you are much more likely to succeed if you can draw on a deep reservoir of resolve. And if you make that commitment first—even before finding an opportunity, building a team, and launching a venture—your odds of success will be that much higher. So think hard about the question I asked at the beginning of this chapter. Making a conscious choice to become a real entrepreneur—rather than simply finding a way to make a living or starting a business—is essential.

HARD TO DO, EVEN WHERE IT SHOULD BE EASY

Even at a place like HBS, where students seem to graduate armed with every advantage—excellent business training, an unparalleled network, access to plenty of capital—relatively few make the decision to become entrepreneurs, especially early in their careers. Maybe even those of us who clearly have an interest in entrepreneurship are still at risk of falling into the trap of seeing the entrepreneurial mind-set as some sort of "personality defect," as Professor Howard Stevenson once put it to me. But the truth is, the high-percentage entrepreneur is by definition an unusual person, if not an outright iconoclast.

Most of this book takes place far from Harvard Business School itself—in New York City, San Francisco, and Washington, D.C., the cities where our three founders started and grew their businesses. But while researching and writing this book, I kept returning to HBS, both to understand better what Marla, Chris, and Marc had experienced there and to interview professors and learn more about their entrepreneurship curriculum.

Early on, I was encouraged to talk with Professor Joseph Lassiter, who is a bit of an iconoclast himself. He arrived at HBS in the fall of 1996—the same time, as it happens, as most of the members of the class of 1998—after teaching ocean engineering (of all things) at MIT and serving for twenty years as a vice president of one company and president of another. Sitting in his office in the Rock Center, Lassiter rattled off some useful statistics about HBS alumni and entrepreneurship:

- On average, about 5 percent of any graduating HBS class starts a business within one to three years.
- By five years out, 25 percent of HBS alumni say they work in a company

in which they have a material interest and that employs ten or more people.

- By fifteen years out, another 25 percent say they work for a company in which they have a material interest and that employs at least ten employees.

But, I asked him, is having stock options or working for a relatively small company the same as being an entrepreneur? Maybe these graduates are being more *entrepreneurial* than those who took a seemingly safer route and went to work for big corporations. Still, it sounded kind of junior varsity to me, like riding the coattails of a true entrepreneur rather than becoming one yourself. And besides, I wondered, how many of these entrepreneurs—even those who fit the HBS alumni office definition—dedicated themselves to the task beforehand? How many became entrepreneurs only after they were boxed into doing so because other options—such as getting a promotion or a big raise—disappeared?

We both recalled an old *Dilbert* comic in which a beleaguered employee is squeezed out of his company. In the punch-line panel, he walks away saying, "I think I just became an entrepreneur."

"Organizations are a pyramid," Lassiter continued. "As you approach the top, there are fewer chairs, so people leave larger companies and start smaller ones. Some of these entrepreneurs end up running small organizations; some run big ones. Are the small companies somehow inferior? That depends on how you think of a four-person firm running a $2 billion hedge fund. It depends on what you think about someone who has a consulting business. And there, I have no opinion. I just want my students to have a lot of choices and be free to make the choice that matters to them."

You can't talk with many of the faculty in the entrepreneurship department at HBS without a sense that they view their role as more than simply teaching courses and offering occasional career advice.

"What we do is we plant these time bombs," Professor Stevenson told me during another conversation. "We say go to Goldman. Go to McKinsey. But when you find that's not what you really want, think about launching a new company as a legitimate use of your talents."

As I continued my interviews with the professors at HBS, I came to understand that they see the entire discipline of entrepreneurship as necessary, life fulfilling, and at times almost spiritual. They're not just teaching business strategies and processes; they're inspiring students to embrace a way of life.

"My hope," Lassiter said, "is that we help our students find the courage to actually take the leap. It's extremely easy to follow an established, well-traveled path, and their lives can matter and they can find fulfillment and all of those other things. But some people want to take a different path, and yet they hesitate because they're fearful about the consequences—because they can't explain it to their mom and dad, because it's riskier than another path, because it's lonelier than another path. But I would much rather that they die regretting what they *have* done than what they have *not* done."

Lassiter and I talked more generally about some of the success stories I'd heard—the HBS grads about whom you'll read more in this book, and others I'd come to know during my research. He knew many of them personally, and almost all of them by reputation. Not surprisingly, he seemed to take pride in the idea that he'd contributed to a body of knowledge that might have helped them to succeed.

"The sad conversations I have," Lassiter told me, "are the ones with the students who come back to see me and say, 'I always wanted to be able to do this, but I just haven't been able to get it done.' And you know what? I have that same dadgum conversation with them every time they come back. And that breaks my heart."

CAN YOU (OR SHOULD YOU) MAKE THE COMMITMENT?

As I got to know Marla, Chris, and Marc, it struck me that they were in their late twenties and early thirties before they truly considered themselves to be entrepreneurs. (Marc, of course, started Forbes Pacifica Trading Company in his early twenties, but by his own account he didn't consider himself to be a committed entrepreneur until . . . well, until things that happen later in this book.) But whether they made a commitment to becoming entrepreneurs during their two years at HBS or during the months and years that followed graduation, all three ultimately decided to take the leap that Lassiter spoke about. And as I came to understand how they arrived at this momentous decision, I realized that each of them had answered several important questions that you or any aspiring entrepreneur should consider before deciding whether to make a similar commitment.

What other obligations will compete for time and resources? Launching a business, even a highly promising one, entails risk. While we can manage and even minimize those hazards (a very important point, and one we'll examine in detail in chapters 13 and 14), the risk-free venture is rare. As they began their careers as entrepreneurs, Marla, Chris, and Marc had few competing commitments. They didn't have children to raise, extra mouths to feed, or other significant demands on their time and their finances.

But if you do have a lot of obligations, it may not be wise to give up a steady paycheck to start your own company. "I just talked to a friend of mine from our class at HBS," Marla told me during one of our interviews at the headquarters of the company she went on to found. "He's been in private equity forever and now he's thinking about starting his own company and he's hemming and hawing. He's like, 'I don't know what it would be like to go without a salary.' You know what I mean?"

So ask yourself: If I make the commitment to become an entrepreneur, who else will be coming along for the ride? Who will it affect? And if the answer leads you to conclude that the risk is too big, figure out how to reduce that risk before proceeding. On the other hand, if you realize the risk isn't really all that large, maybe what has been holding you back is more about irrational fears and a lack of commitment.

What kind of support systems do you have? HBS gave Marla, Chris, and Marc confidence. It surrounded them with people who were willing to provide emotional support, encouragement, and good advice as they embarked on their entrepreneurial careers. As we've seen, Ed Zschau inspired Chris, and Chris and Anne Dwane spent a great deal of time talking about business ideas. Marla worked with Jonathan Ledecky, a famously aggressive entrepreneur, and Barry Beck pushed her to realize that she could achieve her goals only if she became an entrepreneur.

Just as important, Marla spent many hours talking with established entrepreneurs who ran companies that Ledecky wanted to buy. "That showed me a completely different world than I had ever seen before," Marla told me. "I would be sitting across the table from them—a table just like this one—and I'd find myself thinking, 'I can do that.' So it's conceptualization. I think some people have trouble seeing themselves as entrepreneurs—they don't feel like they can start companies because they don't know or work with other people who have started companies. So if you're at McKinsey your whole life . . ."

Marla trailed off, perhaps imagining how her life might have been different if she had made the seemingly safer choice.

Entrepreneurship can be a hard and lonely life. Without the support and encouragement of others, success will be more elusive. Having mentors and role models matters. So before you launch headlong into the process of starting your own company, ask yourself: "Who's really got my back?"

Who can you count on to take a genuine interest in your efforts? Who will offer good advice but also enthusiastic encouragement? If people who are important to you won't provide that sort of support, can you at least inoculate yourself from their negative influence? And if you don't have mentors and role models who can help you achieve your dream of becoming an entrepreneur, you'd better make a serious effort to seek them out.

What is the opportunity cost? In the next several chapters, we'll learn how Marla, Chris, and eventually Marc found the best entrepreneurial opportunities for their particular experience and talents. But as you'll also see, all three thought hard about the true cost of pursuing those opportunities before they ever took them on.

Marla, for instance, hedged her bet by getting assurances from McKinsey that the firm would welcome her back if her stint with Ledecky didn't go as well as she hoped. Chris, as will become evident, recognized that his opportunity cost was fairly low—becoming an entrepreneur would require that he give up a job at Mercer, but he didn't imagine staying at Mercer long-term in any case. As for Marc, he once again provides an indirect but instructive illustration of this point.

"Coming into HBS, " Marc explained to me much later, "I was thinking that I'd been the founder of a rinky-dink little company and had experienced what it's like to not have any capital. And that's very difficult. So why don't I find a way to become an entrepreneur who isn't capital-constrained? Maybe I shouldn't be stuck in pet food but should instead have a hand in a lot of other industries. I can be in merchant banking, for instance—which we now call private equity—and be a meta-entrepreneur."

Marc, in other words, had experienced firsthand how risky it is to be underfunded when starting up a business. By going to HBS and then working in private equity, he was going to shore up that risk. Besides, he instinctively knew that he wanted to do other things before he launched another company. He was making the choice—the intelligent choice—not to do this quite yet.

All these examples illustrate the point that you need to carefully consider the opportunity costs of making a commitment to become a high-percentage entrepreneur. You may also find it useful to list the worst-case outcomes in the event that you choose to launch your own company. Sometimes, after all, naming your fears can make them much less scary. For instance, giving up a salary isn't necessarily as risky as it might have been some years ago. As the recent recession has proven, the supposed security and stability of working for someone else's firm sometimes turns out to be a cruel myth.

What is your record of achievement, creation, and reinvention? All three of the entrepreneurs featured in this book have a gift for what I think of as self-creation. Marla Malcolm reinvented herself time and again, and her creativity and persistence landed her jobs at two elite consulting firms, a coveted slot in the class of 1998 at HBS, and a position in the previously nonexistent MBA internship program at U.S. Office Products. Marc Cenedella went from waiting tables at Favorite's Pizza to selling tons of sea monkeys in Asia in just three years. Chris Michel had launched a successful service project at an elementary school, when he was in the navy, and he'd tried to launch a pharmaceutical startup even before he'd left HBS.

Similarly, you need to take inventory of your own accomplishments, and ask yourself whether your record of achievement and creativity suggests that you'll be likely to succeed as an entrepreneur. And don't limit yourself to the business world. Consider your academic career, your hobbies, your involvement in sports and the arts, even your experiences with your family.

If you find you're coming up short, it may be a good idea to consider setting more limited goals before undertaking the challenges of high-percentage entrepreneurship. Modest accomplishments may not be a predictor of ultimate success as an entrepreneur, but they can provide a storehouse of readily available memories and confidence if you do decide to launch your own business.

What is your tolerance for risk? While researching this book, I interviewed HBS alumnus Stig Leschly, who started a company called Exchange.com, sold it to Amazon for many millions of dollars, and came back to the business school to teach. Leschly made an essential point about risk more effectively than I ever could.

Leschly was simultaneously enrolled in both Harvard Business School and Harvard Law School, but he began skipping a lot of classes to work on what became Exchange.com. This, he explained to me, was a "career decision." Acknowledging that it was an unusual strategy, he went on to insist that "it was not risky—I hate when people say it was risky. I don't think that's true. If you factor in every aspect of a decision, we are all optimizing uncertainty." But, he added, "HBS students are usually not willing to go off into the wilderness, work in solitary confinement, and tolerate the fact that if they fail, they will make no money and everyone will think that they're a leper."

For Leschly, the biggest risk was the danger of becoming mediocre. When I asked why he practically abandoned his post-graduate education to start Exchange.com, he replied, "The honest answer is the following: I was scared to death of going back to McKinsey, or Skadden Arps, or a buyout shop, or a venture firm—or, God forbid, Procter & Gamble or any of those places."

Marla, Chris, and (later) Marc clearly made this calculation as well. Marla's tolerance for risk may seem lower than Chris's or Marc's, but she carefully gauged the level of risk she was willing to accept before going to work for Ledecky by getting a guarantee from McKinsey that she could return.

Chris, meanwhile, remembered how dissatisfied he was when he worked for Mercer in San Francisco. He recalled feeling as if "the world was passing me by. I felt I could have been doing so much more. I remember walking down the street with Anne and passing all these offices of startup companies." It was somehow humiliating, he told me, almost as if these successful startups were taunting him.

By then, Chris knew he *had* to become an entrepreneur. Even though he had never run a business before, hadn't found the right opportunity yet, and hadn't even begun thinking about assembling a team of people, he had made his choice. As he put it to me: "By then I was thinking constantly about starting my own company. I was always asking myself, Where will I come up with the idea?"

SPEAKING OF WHICH, WHERE WILL YOU FIND *YOUR* BEST IDEA?

Maybe you started reading this book thinking that you already have the core concept behind a company you want to start. Or maybe you find yourself asking yourself the same question Chris Michel asked constantly back in late 1998: "Where will I come up with the idea?"

Would it surprise you to learn that making a firm commitment to entrepreneurship as your first step will almost certainly help you come up with your best ideas? Or that even if you've come to this story with an idea in mind, focusing on succeeding as an entrepreneur will likely guide you to reevaluate and improve the idea you started with? They say that comedians live in the same world as the rest of us; they just see everything differently. It's the same with entrepreneurs. Once you've truly made that commitment, you'll be amazed at how quickly you begin to see the world in a different light.

Problems give way to opportunities.

"Why?" becomes "Why not?"

"It's always been done this way" turns into "What if we tried something different?"

So much of what is written about business opportunity focuses on so-called growth industries or game-changing technologies. But Marla, Chris, and Marc learned that approaching entrepreneurship that way can be terribly counterproductive. For the intelligent entrepreneur—and especially for the first-time entrepreneur—opportunity is personal, not universal. It grows out of your talents, experiences, interests—and the problems that you're uniquely positioned to perceive in the world.

Our three intrepid entrepreneurs ultimately succeeded, in part because once they had made the commitment to start their own companies, they thought constantly how the world around them could be improved. Think about this as you read the next chapter: Marla, Chris, and Marc began by focusing on a problem they wanted to solve. And only then did they start looking for the solution.

CHAPTER 5

Every problem has in it the seeds of its own solution. If you don't have any problems, you don't get any seeds.

—NORMAN VINCENT PEALE

MARC: STARTING OVER (AND OVER)

Marc Cenedella was on top of the world in June 1998. He had finished in the top 5 percent of his HBS class, and he was eager to seize the platinum opportunity he was sure he'd found in the world of emerging markets.

Four months later, he was out of a job and starting over yet again.

After graduating from Harvard, Marc hoped for a summer that was both busy and fun. He and a group of friends planned to spend more than a month vacationing in Europe before they started work. They rented a house in Tarifa, Spain, a beautiful town on the Mediterranean coast. But before leaving the country, Marc and Steve Perricone—who had decided to share an apartment together in New York—gave themselves three days to find a place to live. Marc had big plans for their new home; he wanted something centrally located in a nice, hip neighborhood, and it had to be big enough to accommodate the three giant parties that Marc had been throwing almost every year since high school—one for Halloween, another sometime in January or February, and a third celebrating Cinco de Mayo.

Their first day in the city mysteriously disappeared, perhaps because they stopped at a bar for a celebratory beer—and then had a second and a third. When Marc and Steve finally started looking for an apartment on the morning of Day Two, they were shocked and discouraged to discover that rentals in New York were unbelievably expensive. Landlords and brokers wanted $200 just to take their applications, and most of the apartments in their price range were ridiculously small. As the hours passed, the only apartment they found worth considering was a dark, tiny two-bedroom in the West Village—so small that they would practically be on top of each other.

Maybe this is just what life is like in New York, they thought, taking solace in the fact that Marc's job would likely require that he spend half his time in Eastern Europe. Reluctantly, they decided to rent the apartment in the West Village, but as they headed back to their hotel they saw a "For Rent" sign in the window of a building on East Twelfth Street between Second and Third avenues. On impulse, they knocked on the door.

Bigger and brighter than anything else they'd seen, this apartment covered the third floor of an 1850s brownstone, with bedrooms at either end and the kitchen and bathrooms in the middle. Marc quickly hit on the idea of converting the closets into tiny bedrooms, which would allow them to open the two large rooms and the kitchen into a giant space where a hundred people could gather.

The landlady offered each of them a glass of wine, and within minutes they could easily see themselves making the apartment their home. Next morning, just hours before their flight, they signed the lease.

"You don't need a cashier's check?" Marc asked the landlady, surprised that she was so trusting.

"Of course not," she replied. "If the check bounces, you just won't have a place to live when you get back."

Tarifa was a blast. While Steve took language classes, Marc wiled away the afternoons devouring books (Robert Penn Warren's *All the King's Men* was a favorite) and *bocadillos*, the delicious Spanish sandwiches. At night, they and their HBS friends hit the bars and clubs. Eager to see more of the region, they visited Portugal and Morocco. Every couple of days, Marc wrote long e-mails to friends and family back home and described his exploits. Later he was gratified to learn that his missives were forwarded far and wide.

They returned to New York in August, and Marc quickly fell in love with the city. It was wonderfully vibrant and exciting: Marc was astounded that so many people from so many diverse backgrounds and cultures lived together more or less peacefully in such a small space. He'd enjoyed living in San Diego after college, but now he couldn't believe that he hadn't lived in New York all his life.

On the first Monday in August, proud and excited, Marc started his new job at Creditanstalt. To his way of thinking, he was one of the few HBS students who had displayed true fortitude and foresight by choosing to work in emerging markets investing. He was absolutely certain that he'd made a shrewd move.

But after only fourteen days, his glamorous new career came to a screeching halt.

In retrospect, Marc saw that his bet had in fact been extremely risky. His focus as an investor was on Russia and Eastern Europe, which only a decade earlier had been part of the Soviet Union. But the Soviets' industrial and manufacturing capability had been nowhere near the equal of that in the West, and in the late 1990s nearly half of the Russian economy was tied to exporting raw materials—everything from oil and gas to timber and steel. The country was thus especially susceptible to global demand for these raw materials, and when the world market for them declined and then collapsed in 1997 and 1998, Russia was hit hard. Soon the country was blindsided by a full-blown financial crisis; in the first two weeks of August, just as Marc was beginning his new job, Russia devalued its currency. Overnight, the ruble lost two-thirds of its value.

Investing in Russia or the other countries in the former Soviet bloc suddenly made no sense at all, for Creditanstalt or anyone else. Marc had no illusions about what this would mean for his career; sure enough, in mid-September his boss called him into his office.

"The bad news is," his boss began, "I'm afraid we're all out of a job."

Marc replied that he understood, and that he realized that he was being terminated due to events beyond anyone's control. If he wanted to blame someone, he reflected, he might as well blame Boris Yeltsin.

Then he brightened. "So," he asked, "what's the good news?"

"I have Blue Man Group tickets for tonight if you want them," his boss said. Marc smiled. This wasn't exactly a golden parachute, but then again he'd been at the company for only about a month. Besides, he'd wanted to see the show.

He took his girlfriend that night and they had a great time. The fact that it happened to be his twenty-eighth birthday made the evening all the better.

Steve Perricone was impressed by Marc's equanimity. Marc would have to start all over again, but there was no panic and no visible anxiety. He also didn't seem to be in any special hurry to find a new job. Steve would sometimes come home from work (he was an associate in the equity derivatives division at Deutsche Bank) and find Marc looking exhausted, only to discover that his friend had stayed up all night playing the computer game Civilization or teaching himself how to program HTML.

That fall, Marc interviewed with a dozen or more investment firms around New York, but he was careful not to jump at the first job offer he received. The economy was booming—well, the U.S. economy was, anyway—and if you had to be on the street looking for work, being a recently minted Harvard MBA who had graduated in the top 5 percent of your class helped stave off any feeling of urgency. He could afford to be picky.

Marc was now very clear about the kind of place he wanted to work, and about what he wanted his role to be. If it wasn't the right moment to be investing overseas, it was a great time to invest in the United States, and Marc was confident he could find a role at a merchant bank focused on the domestic market. The trick was to find a firm with both the ambition and the capital to make interesting and potentially lucrative investments. Meanwhile, the investments had to be small enough that a twenty-eight-year-old MBA just a few months out of Harvard Business School could have an impact.

While looking for the right job, Marc took the opportunity to explore his new city—but he also spent a lot of time in the apartment on East Twelfth Street.

"Thank God we didn't take that other place," Steve said to him one day, thinking of the tiny, dark apartment they'd almost rented—and their mistaken belief that Marc would be out of the country much of the time.

MARLA: CALM, STRONG, AND SWIFT

One weekend afternoon in February 1999, Marla Malcolm sat in the Georgetown town house she'd bought after she'd decided to move to Washington. Her desk was cluttered with paper; her computer was running Microsoft PowerPoint. Barry Beck was just down the street; browsing the reference section in Barnes & Noble, he was thumbing through a thesaurus and talking to Marla with his cell phone pressed to his ear. Over the past few weeks, Marla had come up with what she and Barry both thought was the perfect idea for an Internet business. Now, they were looking for the perfect name.

Marla had been inspired by Jon Ledecky. She'd gone to work for him in large part because he had a proven track record. It made sense to attach herself to a winner who was likely to win again. But she also knew she could learn a lot from him. Ledecky had drive, smarts, incredible financial acumen, and an uncanny ability to predict how people would behave in a wide variety of circumstances. What he didn't have, though, was a long attention span. And Marla found his impatience contagious.

The current object of Ledecky's waning interest was Building One Services Solutions. Ledecky had come to agree with Marla: the commercial maintenance industry was staid and "old economy," and there wasn't much upside to consolidating operations. He had loved the company when it was still Consolidation Capital—he was enchanted by the idea of starting up a company and taking it public based solely on his reputation. But he was a bit like a kid who desperately wants a toy, gets it, and then sees another toy he wants even more. By the end of 1998, he was making plans to hand over the reins of Building One to a new CEO. Ledecky planned to stay on as chairman of the board, but running the day-to-day operations would become somebody else's challenge.

Like many others, Jon Ledecky and Marla Malcolm were riveted by the sudden growth of the Internet. In the first weeks of 1999, the share prices of Internet stocks grew at an absurd rate. In early January, the price of Yahoo! nearly doubled in the space of eight days, rising to $402 a share. Broadcast.com traded at $223 by the middle of the month—almost three times its share price on New Year's Day. A Massachusetts-based Internet company called CMGI had seen its stock price rise sevenfold during 1998, and now its upward momentum seemed unstoppable. On January 7, CMGI traded at $57.25 a share. By January 12, it traded at $130.75; a few days later, it rose to $151.

In the face of both Ledecky's decision to step away from Building One and the deliriously exciting opportunities offered by the Internet, Marla's already marginal interest in the janitorial and maintenance industries withered away to nothing. Technically, she was still employed by BOSS, but in reality the company was her third priority at best.

Priority number one was helping Ledecky come up with his next venture. She and Ledecky kept looking at that Massachusetts-based Internet company: CMGI. Most people had never heard of it, because CMGI was a behind-the-scenes player. An incubator for Internet companies, CMGI seemed to have taken some of the guesswork and gambling out of the new economy by putting together a wide portfolio of Internet firms. They didn't have to win every bet—they just needed a few of their investments to pay off in a big way.

How different was this from rolling up companies and using poof! financing to create giant conglomerates? To Marla, it seemed exactly the sort of thing that had made Ledecky's reputation. Intrigued, she researched the history of CMGI, investigated its investment strategy, and tried to convince Ledecky that his best next move would be to start a sort of USOP or BOSS of the Internet. Acquire several startup Internet companies, she told him, and then figure out how to coordinate their development and marketing. In a year or less, he could take the entire thing public and make tons of money. He'd done it before. It was simply a matter of employing the same strategy in a new marketplace.

But Marla's second priority—which often seemed to be tied for first—was to get into the Internet startup game herself. She had already taken several huge imaginative leaps, first by walking away from McKinsey & Co., and now by following Ledecky into one frenetic entrepreneurial business after another. As her determination to go out on her own grew, she hoped Ledecky would take her ambition to start a company as a compliment; maybe he'd even see it as part of his legacy as an entrepreneur.

And although she wasn't telling him her plans, exactly, she had dropped some heavy hints.

"Key learning from this year, which you clearly learned a long time ago," she wrote him in an e-mail around this time, is that "the best situation is to reap your own rewards from leveraging your own talent, not relying on someone else to 'reward' you for it. I see all of these entrepreneurs here, and those in the Internet space, and know that I have the potential to really 'knock it down.'"

Barry Beck was also encouraging her to take the plunge. He was still running the Washington, Maryland, and Virginia regions for the maintenance company he and his brother had started, and he had an office in the D.C. suburbs. But he and Marla were spending more and more time together; they talked constantly about launching an Internet startup, maybe even as partners. They spent hours researching different products and markets. Barry—who tended to dominate just about every conversation he engaged in—admitted that Marla was one of the few people he'd met who could go toe-to-toe with him when talking about business or any other subject. They'd walk together from Georgetown along the Potomac River to the Lincoln Memorial, the two miles going by quickly as they traded ideas for new companies. For a while they explored the idea of a company that would offer "certified e-mail," enabling a sender to get proof that the recipient of an e-mail had received and read the message.

But neither of them knew much about the demand for this product. It was a classic case of finding a clever idea and then looking for the problem it would solve. Were people really dying for a way to send certified e-mail? Marla wasn't sure.

She also thought that she and Barry might be missing another opportunity—one that she personally found much more appealing. A few Internet ventures targeting women had attracted huge amounts of investment capital, and Marla hit on the idea of doing something in the beauty industry. Ever since she was a teenager in California, she'd been what she called a "skincare junkie," the kind of girl who went to a spa for facials before most of her peers even knew what facials were. She was devoted to certain high-end brands of cosmetics, and she remembered that when she was going to business school in Boston she could never find them. She particularly favored a lipstick made by a company called

MAC, she explained to Barry, but only one store in the Boston area had carried it. She hadn't thought twice about driving forty-five minutes just to buy a half-ounce tube of the stuff. Happily, she didn't have to travel nearly as far to find good beauty products now that she lived in D.C. Just a few blocks from her house in Georgetown, a small retailer called EFX carried many of her favorite brands.

Of course, she could always shop for cosmetics at high-end department stores, Marla explained to Barry. But the merchandise in those stores was displayed in glass cases; sometimes it was even hidden from the customer. You had to deal with salespeople who worked mostly on commission, and usually for a single brand. The salespeople would always steer you to the brands they got paid to sell, rather than guide you to what might actually be the best product for you. The irony was that cosmetics were among the most profitable items sold in department stores. That's why they were always on the first floor right when you walked in.

Wouldn't it be easier, Marla asked herself, if you could just go online and purchase these beauty products? But as of January 1999, no one had launched a Web site dedicated to cosmetics. Marla knew, because she was constantly in the market for them.

"Forget certified e-mail," Marla told Barry. "Cosmetics are the perfect commodity for the Internet."

Barry was eager to jump into this new marketplace, but he was also leery of some of the crazy ideas that investors were pursuing. He hadn't gone to business school, but he was smart and experienced, and frankly, he believed that an MBA degree got in an entrepreneur's way as often as it helped. He'd get agitated when he read about some of the crazy Web businesses that people were starting—not to mention all the baloney about vertical portals and measuring Web ventures based on how many people visited the sites rather than on how much money they made. He was a hardheaded businessman—"a brass tacks kind of guy," as he put it. That sort of talk made no sense to him.

But makeup and cosmetics? That was a real business. "Women have been buying lipstick for hundreds of years, at least," he told Marla. "Marie Antoinette—heck, even the Egyptians."

He loved the idea. If Marla wanted to give it a shot, Barry told her, he was in.

———

Thanks to her work for McKinsey and Jon Ledecky, Marla had read hundreds of business plans, and now she started working on a plan for an Internet cosmetics supplier. The business model was straightforward and simple. She understood what investors would be looking for, and she saw that the key to success was to get high-end makeup manufacturers to offer their products on her site. Marla reasoned that if they were already distributing their cosmetics to a little outfit like EFX, which had only two retail stores, they would probably be willing to sell their products through a well-designed Internet portal. She had to admit, however, that she'd have to solve a chicken-and-egg problem. The cosmetics companies created a sense of cachet by making their products available only in exclusive stores. Likewise, she would have to persuade the companies to deal with her by developing an Internet company and Web site that communicated that same sense of exclusivity and class.

Marla also had another problem: "Untitled Cosmetics Internet Company" would hardly make for a compelling first slide on a PowerPoint presentation when it came time to raise money. Marla wanted to come up with a name that implied strength, simplicity, and speed, but deciding what to call her company proved extremely difficult. Finally, she concluded that she wanted the name to incorporate the color blue, since it symbolized calmness and possibility, like the ocean or the sky. Barry liked the idea, but they both knew that "blue" was at best only half the name.

That was why, one afternoon in early February, after yet another discussion about what to call the company, Barry had walked down to the Barnes & Noble store on M Street in northwest Washington. Thesaurus in hand, he called Marla on his cell phone They tried several different combinations of words, and suddenly Barry hit on it: *Mercury.* Strength, speed, swiftness.

Bluemercury. The perfect name. Then Marla had another thought: even better, she would call the company *bluemercury* with a lowercase "b."

For the immediate future, however, bluemercury would have to wait, because Jonathan Ledecky was now serious about his own Internet play. Once again, his plan was deceptively simple—and the concept owed a lot to Marla's ideas about how to adapt his earlier business strategies to the Internet. He proposed to pick five or six promising Internet ventures in their earliest stages of development, and his new company would invest a small but healthy amount of seed money in them. As quickly as possible, he'd take the new company public, just as he'd done with U.S. Office Products and Consolidated Capital. Step one, of course, was to find the Internet companies to pull into his new umbrella company, and Marla suggested that they begin with visits to Stanford and HBS. Venture capital firms had invested tens of millions of dollars in companies started up by recent graduates of both business schools, including the winners of the 1997 and 1998 Harvard Business School business plan contests. Marla was particularly interested in one of the winning HBS companies, an online chemical marketplace called Chemdex.

"We need to go up to these schools, announce that we have money, and find out which promising graduates have the next Chemdex," she told Ledecky. She also forwarded Ledecky a news story about Stig Leschly. "Classmate of mine just sold his business, exchange.com, to Amazon for $200MM. Founded fall, 1998."

"This could be you one day," Ledecky replied. "Keep those dreams coming!"

Soon he and Marla settled on a name for the company: E2Enet. As Marla had already discovered with bluemercury, just having a moniker for the project made it seem so much more real. Marla was now working practically around the clock, drafting the E2Enet business plan and the S-1 filing for the Securities and Exchange Commission. By February, she and Ledecky had finished a draft of the plan, and their presentation promised that E2Enet would become a publicly traded Kleiner, Perkins (the country's best-known venture capital company). For good measure, the plan also suggested that E2Enet would become a Berkshire Hathaway (Warren Buffett's company) of the Internet.

On the page labeled "Management Team," the plan promised that the president and chief executive officer and chief operating officer positions would be filled by executives with significant experience in Internet industries, individuals who would be esteemed by their peers for being strong leaders and forward thinkers. But no names were mentioned—the two titles were followed by "TBA"—and the implication was that finding and recruiting these people were comparatively minor challenges that would be addressed later. The most important and compelling part of the presentation was the slide titled "growth strategy." Using only lowercase letters, the plan promised that E2Enet would:

- raise $250 million investment pool
- invest in compelling private Internet companies
- foster portfolio community
- realize options for portfolio companies.

If it had been anyone else's plan, this to-do list might have read something like the old Steve Martin bit on how to be a millionaire and pay no taxes. (It began, "First, get a million dollars.") But with Ledecky's track record, achieving the promised goals seemed more than possible, perhaps even inevitable.

Ledecky put the word out that he was looking to invest in young Internet companies, and within days Marla was meeting with bright-eyed entrepreneurs and reviewing dozens of business plans. Her schedule was crazy, especially since she had to be careful to work on Ledecky's new projects either after she left Building One for the day or on the weekends. After all, even though Ledecky had negotiated her employment deal, he had now left Building One and she had a new boss.

"You're worse than I am in the sleep department," Ledecky wrote to her one morning, after reading a series of e-mails from her and realizing she'd written the last one just before two a.m. On another occasion, she e-mailed him after midnight on a Saturday to provide an analysis of one of the companies she'd been looking at.

"Marla," he replied. "I am disappointed that you are on the Internet at midnight on a Saturday. It's one thing for a clown like me to be [reading] e-mail, another for you to be."

Meanwhile, Marla was waiting for the right moment to mention bluemercury to Ledecky, but she wanted to cover every base before doing so. She asked her old professor Dick Darman to look over her business plan; she even reached out to Ledecky's brother and asked his opinion. Not surprisingly, she also began to hope that Ledecky might want to add bluemercury to E2Enet's portfolio. Knowing his penchant for investing in companies with broad reach, Marla realized that if she rethought the concept of bluemercury as not simply a cosmetics site, but a high-end, luxury destination for women, she might be able to get him to invest in it.

"bluemercury is building a new 'Nieman Marcus of the Internet,'" she wrote in the business plan now—"the Internet's foremost, upscale specialty retailer focused on busy, professional, and affluent women." If there was one demographic Marla knew forward and backward, that was it: busy, professional, affluent women.

Marla e-mailed Ledecky on March 31 to report she'd registered the domain name e2enet.com along with many variations of the name. But if she was going to try to bring bluemercury into the deal, she knew she was running out of time. Early the next morning, at 12:39 a.m., she tucked her first mention of bluemercury into an e-mail to Ledecky—a status report on all of the issues she was working on for him and the Internet entrepreneurs she was meeting with.

"I should head to NYC on Monday," Marla wrote in the sixth paragraph of her seven-paragraph status report. "Darman and a couple of others have taken a look at a concept I came up with and they think there's something there . . . not sure if it makes sense here."

That was it—an opaque, guarded reference to her ambitious plan to start a company of her own. But Ledecky saw immediately what she was up to. He replied within an hour, writing quickly in all lowercase letters. "you're either in on this or you're out doing your own thing. can't have it both ways, my friend!"

Ledecky's e-mail made Marla extremely anxious—she was worried that she might have seriously damaged her relationship with him. But a few hours later, his sense of humor had returned. He forwarded Marla a marketing solicitation he'd received by e-mail.

To: Ledecky, Jonathan
From: Patty0824@aol.com
Subj: FW: Profit from the Internet growth explosion

"Okay, let's drop everything else we are doing and join Patty," Ledecky wrote to Marla. "How do WE get this spam?"

Whatever qualms Ledecky might have had about losing his right-hand woman to her own business quickly evaporated as other people he trusted reviewed her plan. Moreover, her approach seemed to match perfectly with his own thinking about which Internet ventures had the most potential for success. Established brick-and-mortar businesses would have a hard time launching effective Internet complements, he had suggested during one of his many conversations with Marla about the future of this new marketplace. If these old-line businesses were big enough to matter, Ledecky pointed out, they were usually public companies, and the managers and directors of public companies were inevitably more concerned with meeting their quarterly earnings targets than with launching new business models. Only entrepreneurs could embrace the kind of creative destruction necessary to build the bridge to the Internet.

Marla had listened as Ledecky concluded that the most interesting e-commerce proposals were those that proposed to build their businesses online and then link up with traditional retailers. And as she had drafted and redrafted her plan for bluemercury, she emphasized that model. Her new company was much bigger than an idea to sell cosmetics over the Internet, she emphasized. "We are focused on a demographic, not a product category."

As she pointed out in the plan, her recent research had revealed that there were twenty-one million affluent women in America, "65% of whom are in the work force, who crave time, and whose needs are underserved." This wasn't just a makeup and cosmetics Web site she was pitching; it was a "foundation for a multiple category upscale retailer."

By now, Ledecky was convinced: he was eager to include bluemercury among the initial four or five companies that E2Enet would fund. But it had also become clear that since Marla was working so much on the overall plan for E2Enet, they had to make sure she was no longer on the payroll at Building One by the time E2Enet was announced. The timing had to be very precise, which made Marla nervous. But by mid-April, she and Building One had agreed on an exit date of May 1, 1999. And only then did Ledecky offer her his terms for bluemercury. His new fund would invest $1 million with her, in exchange for 49 percent of the company.

Marla was less than thrilled with this proposal. In late March, another women-focused Internet site called ivillage.com had gone public. With no revenue whatsoever, its stock price had quadrupled from $23 a share to nearly $100 on the first day of trading alone. Even though she only had a plan, not an actual business, Marla thought such a large stake in bluemercury was worth an investment much greater than a million dollars given the stock market frenzy around Internet companies. She told Ledecky as much.

Fine, he replied. As an alternative, he would invest $500,000 in exchange for 24.5 percent of the company. If Marla could do better with other investors, great; if not, he'd come in later with the extra half a million dollars. Marla was happier with this proposal, and she immediately began looking for other investors. One of the first people she pitched to was Ed Mathias, who had been Ledecky's first investor in the U.S. Office Products deal. Mathias bit; he came in as in investor for Marla and immediately wrote her a check for $100,000. Just as important, he introduced her to other likely investors, and before long she had all the funding she'd need.

Ledecky understood that Marla would soon have to spend all of her time on bluemercury, so she would no longer be able to assist him with the launch of E2Enet. But even as their working relationship came to an end, he wanted to look out for her. He knew that Marla planned to launch bluemercury with Barry Beck as her cofounder, and he wanted to be certain that he was the best partner for her. Since he didn't know Barry that well, he offered to "fly speck the Beck," meaning have other people he trusted interview Barry and get their take on him.

Marla would always welcome Ledecky's perspective, but she was confident that Barry would be a strong partner. With a great concept, a persuasive business plan, and now funding and investors, Marla believed she had all the necessary pieces in place. She was ready to launch.

CHRIS: THE OBVIOUS OPPORTUNITY

As he began working for Mercer Consulting in the late summer of 1998, Chris Michel felt as if the world was passing him by. HBS had been well worth the $50,000 or so he was now paying off in student loans. He was convinced that he'd gotten more out of the experience than a lot of his friends who had been accountants, bankers, or consultants. People like his friend Tom Goundrey, for example, had already spoken the language of business and finance, so HBS merely refined and expanded Tom's base of knowledge. But for Chris, HBS had opened up an entirely new world.

Still, it bothered Chris that he was essentially right back where he was before going to HBS: taking a job at a consulting firm, pulling down a salary, chained with golden handcuffs to someone else's plan for his life.

Virtually every Sunday night or Monday morning, Chris boarded planes for Texas or Southern California, where the Mercer clients whose projects he worked on were located. On the bright side, he had been able to work into his deal with Mercer the right to focus mainly on tech-related projects. One of his big efforts was helping a major airline build its first Web interface and transition its frequent flier program to the Internet. Later, he worked with a Web development firm that built a Web site to complement a book written by a Mercer partner. But all that amounted to nibbling, and Chris wanted to take as big a bite of the new economy as he could. Every time he walked back to the coach section on an airplane and stuffed his carry-on bag in the overhead compartment, he felt as if he were falling farther behind.

He had the Ed Zschau disease. He desperately wanted to be an entrepreneur. But thus far he hadn't been able to think of an idea for an entrepreneurial venture that would be exactly right for him.

Even as Chris spent a lot of time trying to come up with a concept for a new company, he still missed the military. The civilian world could be a little impersonal, and Chris wanted to find a way to regain that wonderful feeling of camaraderie that came from flying for the navy. When he'd decided to leave active duty and go to HBS, he had consoled himself with the idea that he could one day join the Naval Reserve; now, he did just that. He was assigned to a reserve squadron about eighty miles from Los Angeles, where the pilots and flight officers flew P-3 Orions, the planes he knew so well. He would spend one weekend a month with the squadron, and he was also committed to undertake two weeks of training a year.

Chris traveled light—since enrolling in HBS, he hadn't even owned a car. Many drill weekends, Anne would drive him to Moffett Airfield in Silicon Valley. He would hop out of her Ford Explorer, change into his flight suit in a secluded area right near the runway, and then catch a military flight to the base in Southern California. Once, Air Force One landed at Moffett only a few hundred feet away from Chris just as he was about to change out of his civilian clothes. Without thinking, he walked around to the back of the Explorer and reached deep into his duffel bag. Then he froze, realizing how suspicious he looked digging through his bag while standing just a few hundred feet from Air Force One. He imagined a Secret Service sharpshooter watching him through the scope of a sniper rifle.

The reserve unit provided just the balance Chris needed. He loved being back in uniform, and he was proud that his continuing service in the military set him apart from the other consultants and MBAs he worked with. He couldn't requalify as a navigator and flight officer immediately, so for a while his weekends in the reserves were taken up with meetings and administrative matters. Still, Chris felt a sense of purpose and direction that he hadn't experienced since arriving in San Francisco.

As the months went by, Chris's life settled into a reasonably satisfying routine. Then, one weekend in early spring 1999, he was attending a squadron-wide officers' meeting during his once-a-month navy drill. He and his fellow officers had gathered in what looked like a high school classroom crammed with small desks. The meeting was much like the ones he used to go to in Maine, during which he had always entertained everyone as the bull ensign.

Chris was still the new guy in this unit, and he hadn't met everybody yet. Before the commander called the meeting to order, the pilots and flight officers milled around, making conversation and in many cases trying to establish their earlier connections to one another. The P-3 Orion community was a fairly tight one, and almost any reserve officer could walk up to just about any other officer in the room and make a connection—through assignments and experiences, or at the very least through their passion for the navy and their country. This was as true for Chris as for anyone else. One pilot might have rotated to his old squadron in Maine just as he had left; another flight officer might have known his old commander years earlier, when they'd flown together at another base. Inevitably, Chris and his fellow reservists had traveled to many of the same places and undertaken the same kinds of missions—flight school in Florida, service in the Persian Gulf, drug-interdiction patrols in the Caribbean.

One of the officers Chris met that morning had heard that Chris had graduated from Harvard Business School, and he wanted to know all about it. Another recent addition to the unit chimed in, saying that he hoped to go to graduate school, too, but he was having a heck of a time navigating the web of educational benefits that military officers were entitled to. Chris and a couple of other officers started giving him advice on how to best use the GI Bill and other benefits. In fact, Chris explained, he had had to tackle some of these issues himself, when he'd started at HBS—

Just like that, in midsentence, Chris's world changed. Instantly, the nondescript room in which he stood seemed to morph into something much more exciting. He looked around and saw clusters of officers—standing, talking, making connections.

"Why isn't this group on the Internet?" he asked himself. "If there's a women.com, there has to be room for a military.com."

The formal meeting began, but Chris was barely able to contain his excitement or pay attention to the commander and the other presenters. He'd been feeling so restless, so disappointed that he hadn't gotten into the Internet game. And now here it was, he realized—the Big Idea had been hiding right in front of him all the time: the United States armed forces. He could be the one to connect and empower all those who served, and the Internet offered the perfect way to do it.

This group was unique, he told himself, but it was also huge. Add up everyone serving in the military, those who *had* served, those who aspired to serve, their loved ones—the total was in the tens of millions at least, with trillions of dollars in buying power. Usually, Chris knew, the larger a group was, the less affinity its members had to one another. But the military was different.

He thought about women.com again. "When two women see each other across the street," he thought to himself, "they're not going to drop what they're doing and walk over to say hello. But introduce two navy guys, and they'll start a ten-minute conversation."

Was there already an Internet site targeting military members and veterans? If so, Chris decided, either he'd been living in a cave or the site had done a pretty horrible job of marketing itself.

Imagine all the things you could offer, he thought. People in the military were transferred from base to base all the time—so a new site could offer practical information about each base and possibly even military discounts on moving services. Soldiers and sailors were entitled to take advantage of various educational benefit programs, but Chris knew many veterans who—just like the aspiring graduate student he'd spoken to a few minutes ago—had trouble figuring out how to use the GI Bill. Veterans also felt great connections to their units and services. Just think of all the cars on the highway with marine corps bumper stickers, Chris thought, as well as all the veterans wearing baseball hats with the names and logos of their navy ships and army divisions. A new site could give every one of them a virtual place to reconnect with their old shipmates and army buddies.

And why limit this to current soldiers, sailors, and veterans? What about the spouses and children of people who served? What about the young people who were thinking of joining?

Chris's mind raced. The squadron meeting was easily the longest thing he had ever sat through. After it finally ended, he ran from the room, trying to be discreet and polite but also seized with a desire to know whether any other Web companies were already trying to target this demographic. He knew of only one computer in the building that had an Internet connection; he made a beeline for it. He pulled up Yahoo! and Altavista and ran search after search trying to find organizations and ventures that were helping members of the military establish connections with one another.

The American Legion. *Check.*

The Navy League. *Check.*

Veterans of Foreign Wars. *Check.*

Chris found nothing other than nonprofit organizations. Moreover, they all seemed to cater to older veterans, those who'd served in World War II and Vietnam. Then Chris keyed in the domain name www.military.com. Up came a Web page with two simple lines of text: "This domain does not have a web site. The domain name is not for sale. For further search assistance, click here."

The link led to a page called locate.com, which carried links to all the big search engines of the era: HotBot, Altavista, Yahoo!, and the like.

Odd, Chris thought—the domain name is taken but it doesn't seem to be active. No matter, he started looking for other domains. The name MilitaryAdvantage popped into his head; when he checked, MilitaryAdvantage.com was available. He immediately registered it.

He had never been so excited about an idea in his life. He ran to the phone and called Anne.

"This is it!" he told her. "This is the idea we've been looking for!"

CHAPTER 6

_____

FIND A PROBLEM, THEN SOLVE IT

I'll bet the military.com guy was in the military. I'll bet the woman who started the makeup company really likes lipstick.

—STIG LESCHLY, FOUNDER OF EXCHANGE.COM AND
FORMER LECTURER AT HBS

WHAT'S YOUR PROBLEM?

Let's say that you've made the commitment and are determined to become a successful entrepreneur. Maybe you're looking for the right idea for a business, or maybe you want to be sure that the idea you've seized upon is indeed both ripe and exactly right for you. In either case, this will help: Start with a problem you really want to solve. Do *not* start with a solution and then go looking for a problem.

So many entrepreneurs make the wrong call here. But if we take the cases of Chris and Marla (and later, as we will see, of Marc), it's clear that they found the opportunities that afforded them success because they began by identifying problems they knew something about. Not only that, they chose problems that they personally wanted to solve.

Here's a hard question worth asking yourself, over and over again. You're certain you want to become an entrepreneur, and now you're waking up in the middle of the night thinking about how to start whatever it is you think you want to start. You've thought about whether the timing is right for you, and whether you're truly up for this. And you've started considering and rejecting a range of ideas. You think you want your new venture to be in . . . green technology . . . or kids' games . . . or medical devices—whatever it is.

As you consider idea after idea, here's the question you want to ask yourself: who cares?

It's a tough, almost rude question, isn't it? In truth, it's shorthand for a few questions that you ought to be asking over and over. If you can't think of good answers, consider that a warning sign that you probably haven't come up with the right idea yet. If you go ahead and start anyway, you're likely in for a world of heartache.

"In business school," Chris Michel recalled in one of our interviews, "I had a lot of conversations with my friends driven by questions like, 'How do we triangulate on a market?' Or, 'How do we find an idea that looks like it would be at the center of a good business?'"

That's precisely the sort of analytical, dispassionate analysis that led Chris to try to start up a pharmaceutical company during business school. It's also the sort of analysis that prompted Marla to think about starting a company dedicated to certified e-mail.

It's not as if these were foolish ideas, or even that they didn't identify problems worth solving. But it's important to understand that every good entrepreneurial opportunity is personal, and these two ideas simply weren't the *right* opportunities for Chris and Marla, given their experience, strengths, and personalities.

Even at this early stage of our story, doesn't it make perfect sense that Chris would incorporate his love for the armed forces in the concept for his company? Or that Marla would build her venture around not only her interest in beauty products, but also her understanding of what an ambitious, intelligent, professional woman would want out of life?

Chris and Marc couldn't have started bluemercury. Marla couldn't have started military.com. They got their ideas—the ideas that worked—because they began by identifying problems and then focused intensely on problems they were personally eager to solve.

"It's funny because today I sort of feel like I could do that," Chris told me recently—meaning that after starting two successful companies, he feels he knows enough about entrepreneurship that he could launch a company in a field that he didn't have a personal background or interest in. "But that is a confounding position to be in, and frankly I haven't seen it work very well for people."

"It's easier when you really care about solving a problem," Marla agreed. We talked about how many entrepreneurial ventures that target women as customers are in fact led by women; bluemercury, of course, is a good example. "It's definitely easier to stick with it if you like the business," Marla told me.

True, she loved business strategy. But she was also her own ideal customer.

THE LURE OF THE BETTER MOUSETRAP

Professor Howard Stevenson has a similar point of view. "Part of what we try to teach the students is the importance of knowing the economic model of the business, and understanding whether there is a compelling need," Stevenson told me in an interview. "Most of our graduates become entrepreneurs—it used to be fifteen years out, now it's probably seven to ten years out. That's probably appropriate, because they've had the time to get to know something about their customer, and know something about their industry. We try to point out—gently—that actually knowing something really helps."

Notice that Stevenson didn't say a word about innovation or technology in that comment. While successful entrepreneurship does indeed require innovation, focusing first on the solution rather than the problem that needs to be solved can be a recipe for failure.

"Part of the reason that you have a lot of failures in technology startups is that the founders don't know the marketplace," Stevenson continued. "They may know the technology, but often there is no compelling need for the customer to buy."

In fact, Stevenson says, this was his objection to the Harvard Business Plan contest to begin with. "I felt the contest would encourage students to undertake things they didn't know anything about. And it was particularly true in the context of having a business plan contest, where your objective was to hide the fatal flaw."

The same pitfalls apply in less innovative industries as well. Author Michael Gerber has performed a lot of research testing the observation that many companies are started by technicians who either come up with a new way of doing something or decide they want to do for themselves what they've been doing for others.

Stevenson pointed to aspiring restaurateurs as a good example of this shortcoming. "They'll say to themselves, 'People need to eat; I like to cook.' But they don't do the calculations. How many people do you have to serve to make even a crappy living? If you're selling meals at $20 a ticket, and you can only make a 25 percent margin, you've got to sell food to a lot of people just to make the minimum wage. And then you have a stacking problem. If the seat is full, you cannot serve another customer. So you're also limited by the number of seats."

Ironically, MBAs from a place like HBS may be especially likely to make this mistake. Armed with a sophisticated understanding of the latest research in business strategy and finance, entrepreneurially minded graduates of top MBA programs can mistakenly conclude that their knowledge is applicable to almost any industry. A typical HBS student in his or her midtwenties probably worked for three or four years in a field like consulting or banking before coming to the school. They're very smart, but in the view of many of the professors I talked with, they haven't lived and learned long enough. As a result, HBS often advises its students to work in two or three different fields after graduation. The hope is that after some experimentation you'll find an industry that really interests you and then get a job that allows you to learn a lot about it.

When Stig Leschly taught at HBS, he made exactly this point, but he put it more bluntly: "You have to go and become interesting and interested in something," he implored his classes on the last day of each semester. "It's been bred out of you, because you've been kissing people's asses since you were sixteen."

The data about entrepreneurship back up the wisdom of this advice. Want to increase your odds of being a successful entrepreneur? Finish school, because startups founded by college grads have 25 percent higher sales than those with only high school diplomas. And startups founded by those with graduate degrees do 40 percent better than startups founded by college graduates. Work for someone else first. Learn as much as you can about an industry that interests you. And if you're serious about starting your own company, you'd be wise to learn to supervise, manage, and lead on someone else's dime.

In short, experience matters. "On average, businesses founded by people between the ages of 45 and 54 tend to perform better than those founded by people less than 35 years old," writes Scott Shane in his book *The Illusions of Entrepreneurship*.

But what if you haven't been able to identify a problem that's crying out for a solution? And what if you haven't even found an industry that particularly interests you? If you're certain you want to become an entrepreneur, follow the good advice offered by Professor Bill Sahlman to the men and women of Marla, Chris, and Marc's HBS class. Decide where you want to live, pick an industry with good prospects and ample opportunity, find the best job you can, and then look for good mentors. If things go well, you will soon have firsthand knowledge of the industry—and as time goes on there's a good chance you'll be able to identify the problems that people truly want someone to solve.

"Sahlman's advice had a really profound effect on me," Marc Cenedella told me. "And I didn't even take his class. I heard about it secondhand."

PLEASURE VS. PAIN

"Making sure you are solving a real customer problem is something that differentiates entrepreneurs," Noam Wasserman explained to me. Equally important, you've got to understand that there are different kinds of problems. The real dividing line is simple: does the problem you've identified relate to the promotion of pleasure, or to the prevention or termination of pain? And intensity matters, too. As Wasserman put it, you've got to distinguish between "ideas that only rise to the level of 'nice to have,' versus things that people really need or greatly want."

Wasserman then explained that although HBS spends a lot of time trying to teach its students how to distinguish good ideas from bad ones, it's surprisingly difficult to develop a data-driven, objective study of what makes a good entrepreneurial opportunity. "It's definitely done at the case level, but developing anything more systematic is much tougher," he told me.

In an effort to explore this issue further, I decided to talk with several people whose job it is to identify promising startups and invest in them. Since they put their money on the line, I thought they would have a well-honed sense for what makes a good opportunity versus a not-so-good one. Although no one claimed to be able to make broad, quantitative judgments about one entrepreneurial idea as opposed to another, the distinction that came up over and over was, again, the difference between a pleasure business and a pain business.

"That's a theme we talk about frequently," said one partner at a top-tier venture capital firm. He suggested that it would be worth trying to locate the chosen problem on Maslow's hierarchy of needs, which takes the form of a pyramid and ranks needs from the most basic (breathing, food, water, etc.) to the most sophisticated (morality, creativity, spontaneity, etc.). "Pain businesses are those that solve a significant problem, and people will rarely hesitate to pay money to solve that problem," he pointed out. "Pleasure businesses solve less urgent problems. They can sometimes be great, but the success rate is much lower."

WHAT DOES THIS MEAN FOR YOU?

I never liked those self-help books that ask you to list your strengths so that you can begin to focus on them. To me, that approach doesn't work very well.

Instead, I'm going to ask you what I think is a better question. Let's say you're struggling to come up with an entrepreneurial idea; for now, forget what you're good at. Instead, ask yourself: what am I interested in?

If that question proves hard to answer, try this one: what do I do with my time?

The more honest your answer, the better. Seriously, this is a judgment-free zone. If you like to watch TV and take naps, don't feel that you've got to make up some phony, college application–style malarkey about how you're deeply interested in helping underprivileged kids or working on complex math problems.

Once you've focused on what you're interested in or how you spend your time, think about the problems you encounter in your everyday life. You're much more likely to find a problem you care about—and one that other people will care about as well—if you focus on something that's personally interesting. So, if you're a musician, or a fan of music, think about what annoys you about the way you play or listen to music. If you have kids, identify a problem that makes your life miserable whenever you spend time with your children.

This approach even works with less, um, high and mighty interests. Suppose you picked up this book in the hope that you could glean what they teach at Harvard Business School, launch a company, sell it two years later for a zillion dollars, and spend the rest of your life hanging out with your friends and drinking beer. If so, then maybe the best idea for you is to start by thinking hard about the problems—the little annoyances and major pitfalls—that come with hanging out and drinking beer.

I can't necessarily promise you that you'll come up with a money-making idea. (What about developing a better portable Breathalyzer, or designing an exercise machine that magically eliminates beer guts?) But at least you'll be working on something you care about.

Most of the successful HBS entrepreneurs I interviewed founded companies by following the guidelines I've been describing. They either identified problems they wanted to solve and built businesses around the solutions or they launched firms in industries they knew extremely well and about which they felt a genuine passion. For instance, I interviewed a member of the HBS class of 1999 who had been a medical researcher prior to coming to Harvard; not long after graduating, he started a life sciences company that he later sold for many millions of dollars. Or take Stig Leschly's example; it was his interest in collecting vinyl records that led him to start the company that eventually became exchange.com. Or the case of another Section A classmate of Marc's and Marla's, a woman named Sheila Marcelo. Sheila and her husband were young parents when they attended HBS together. Finding child care was a difficult challenge. Does it surprise you to learn that a few years later Sheila launched Care.com?

Is this correlation perfect? Of course not. Entrepreneurs who have launched two or three businesses, for instance, are occasionally able to ignore this rule because they're highly skilled at identifying and exploiting promising new markets But less experienced entrepreneurs who followed the solution-first, problem-second model—the "me-too" crowd who launched Internet companies, for example—often didn't make it. Time and again, I encountered entrepreneurs who launched a company in a market they had no personal knowledge, interest, or experience in. Very few of their startups were successful.

And though it clearly makes sense to build a business around the solution to a problem experienced by many people, it's also true that some companies get lucky. On occasion, someone develops a product that solves a problem few people seem to have. The company languishes for a while, but then lightning strikes and all at once solving that particular problem matters to millions of people. Believe me, I hope you are one of those rare people who has exquisitely good luck. But for the rest of us, luck is not a plan, and you should do your utmost to remove it as a factor when deciding whether to launch a new venture.

THE BOTTOM LINE

Ask yourself again: who cares?

Or, if you prefer, ask the Harvard Business School version of this question. One of the constructs that HBS students use to evaluate any entrepreneurial opportunity is simply this: consider the people, the opportunity, the context, and the deal. With a critical eye, examine every aspect of your idea for a startup. Will customers care? Will investors care? Will the market care? Is there a ready market for the product or the solution to the problem you've chosen?

If you focus on an idea you personally care about, you're more likely to understand your customer. You're more likely to remain motivated and passionate. And you're also more likely to pivot quickly and successfully when, as usually happens, you realize that your solution to the problem you've chosen isn't precisely the right one.

As I'm sure you understand by now, it's surprisingly difficult to identify a problem that can provide the key to a successful startup. But it's even harder to come up with an innovative solution. As you begin to take on this new challenge, keep in mind the next lesson I learned from Marla, Chris, and Marc.

Think big. Think new. And think again.

CHAPTER 7

We are all in the gutter, but some of us are looking at the stars.

—OSCAR WILDE

MARC: MOVING CLOSER

As Marla and Chris identified the fields or industries in which they wanted to become entrepreneurs, Marc Cenedella was in the throes of a more basic search. After a months-long effort, during which he turned down several offers, he landed a promising job at a Manhattan investment firm called the Riverside Company. It met his criteria, he told friends: Riverside was big enough to handle interesting deals and employ smart people, but small enough so that he could have an impact.

But after a few months there, he had mixed feelings about the job. He was learning a lot, but he also realized that he'd overestimated his opportunity to improve the operations of the companies in which Riverside had invested. Any company stable enough to be considered for a leveraged buy-out investment, and thus liable to attract Riverside's interest, was by definition doing well enough that a guy armed with a one-year-old MBA was unlikely to have much impact.

Meanwhile, the Internet gold rush was in full swing, and in the HBS class a year behind Marc's, *everyone* seemed to be eager to launch something, or at least to join a new and nimble startup. It was not at all uncommon now for students at top business schools to come up with ideas for startups and then sign multimillion-dollar venture capital deals before they had even graduated. When *Time* magazine ran a cover story under the banner "GetRich.com," in September 1999, the profile included a story about four HBS graduates who were launching a Web-based company focused on the educational market. One of the cofounders was Amar Singh, the student who had saluted Chris Michel every morning during Chris's first semester at HBS.

Many newly minted MBAs who wanted to jump into the Internet game moved to California immediately after graduating. But Marc had no desire to leave New York. He loved his life outside of work—the parties he and Steve Perricone threw in their nineteenth-century brownstone were already becoming legendary. When he took time off, he was often traveling to countries he'd never been to, still a favorite diversion. And speaking of diversions: New York was full of beautiful women from all over the world, a major plus for a single guy like Marc.

Increasingly, though, he harbored a nagging feeling that he was missing out.

New York City's tech center was known as "Silicon Alley," and though it was smaller than the hotbed in northern California that had inspired its name, it was still extremely active. Marc, analytical as always, carefully approached the question of where he should go if he left Riverside. He was fascinated by the power of the Internet, and he was persuaded that it could be a transformative tool for many industries. But he had little patience for hype and the extreme valuations that many young firms were attracting. The core advantage of the Internet over brick-and-mortar ventures, Marc concluded, involved the flow of information. Using the Internet, you could collect, review, and categorize large amounts of data much faster than by traditional means. Following this logic, Marc decided to focus on firms that traded in information products, as opposed to firms that created or sold tangible products and then used the Internet to attract customers or deliver goods.

He started putting out feelers, applying for positions and networking with many of the Web startups that populated the lower end of Manhattan. During the fall of 1999 and winter of 2000, he went on between forty and fifty job interviews.

Once again, Marc got several offers right away. But he turned them down, because there was always something about the opportunity—the industry, the size of the company, or his proposed role—that didn't quite work for him. Friends began wondering aloud why Marc didn't start something of his own. He'd already had the experience of launching Forbes Pacifica, and no one doubted that if he came up with the right idea and a good plan he could get funding and launch.

Marc listened to his friends' advice, and in some respects the idea of starting a new company was tempting. But two things held him back.

First, he was still intrigued by the notion that he could be a creative facilitator. At least for the moment, he wanted to be the person who seized upon someone else's idea and either greatly improved it or implemented it. And second, in his heart of hearts, he still wasn't ready to commit himself to becoming a full-fledged entrepreneur. Forbes Pacifica had been a seminal experience, but he wasn't particularly eager to run that difficult gauntlet again. Inevitably, launching a company meant uncertainty, pressure, and wild swings of emotion. Besides, he felt that with each interview he was learning something new, and he was certain that the cumulative knowledge would ultimately help him make the right decision. In his view, these companies weren't interviewing him so much as he was interviewing them.

A little more than a year after he started at Riverside, Marc was invited to interview with a young company called Online Retail Partners, which had raised more than $60 million in venture capital. Traditional brick-and-mortar retailers were scrambling to get online, and the company's main business was consulting and helping them get there. Marc walked into a small outer office in the company's New York headquarters and met with the head of Human Resources, a young man about Marc's age named Dave Carvajal.

"Carvajal," Marc repeated thoughtfully as Dave introduced himself. "What is that, Portuguese?"

Marc had no way of knowing this, but there was probably no question that could have irritated Dave more. His parents were Ecuadoran immigrants, and lately he had grown very proud, almost defensive, about his heritage.

Despite that inauspicious opening, Dave was surprised to find that he was impressed by Marc and enjoyed talking to him. Among other things, Marc was clearly one of the smartest people Dave had ever interviewed. Toward the end of the conversation, Dave made it clear that if

Marc wanted a job at Online Retail Partners, it would almost certainly be there for him.

Marc liked Dave as well, but he was underwhelmed by his firm.

"Look," Marc told Dave, "Online Retail Partners works as a concept. But there are a thousand other companies doing the same thing. And only one or two are going to win. Those just don't strike me as good odds."

Dave sat back in his chair. Smiling, he changed the subject and began describing his own background. He had started his career as a corporate headhunter, and then gone on to become one of the first employees at the Internet job board HotJobs—a firm then known as much for a giant marketing gamble as for its business. In early 1999, HotJobs had spent more than $1.5 million—half its annual revenue—to buy an ad on the Super Bowl broadcast. The risk had paid off: overnight, HotJobs had become one of the two best-known job boards, right behind Monster.com.

Dave had picked the right startup to join, and when HotJobs went public in late 1999 he had done very well. Then Online Retail Partners came calling, and he had jumped at the chance to get in on the ground floor of another new company. But now he was wondering if he'd made the right move. As it happened, he thought Marc's calculation of the odds of Online Retail Partners' success was dead-on, and in fact he was thinking seriously about returning to his former company. For the moment, though, he decided to do Marc a favor: since Marc clearly had no interest in working for Online Retail Partners, Dave offered to set up meetings for him with the top executives at HotJobs. He made the calls and sent Marc over for an interview.

Almost as soon as he arrived at HotJobs, Marc realized that this was exactly the kind of opportunity he was looking for. The company was growing rapidly, and its business was all about collecting and trading information rather than physical products. Less than a month after meeting Dave Carvajal, Marc accepted an offer as a vice president at HotJobs. He sat down with his bosses at Riverside, told them the news, and gave them the standard two weeks' notice. They worked him hard during those last days, but that was fine with Marc, since he wanted to leave under the best possible circumstances. You never knew when your paths might cross again.

MARLA: THE LAUNCH AND RELAUNCH
OF BLUEMERCURY

For the first time in her working life, Marla Malcolm was her own boss, responsible for setting her own agenda and paying her own salary. Bluemercury wasn't much yet—a plan, a flush bank account—but she and Barry Beck celebrated its official birth on May 14, 1999. Their world headquarters consisted of Marla's house in Georgetown and a small cubicle in a back section of the office from which Barry was still running the Washington, D.C., region of Tower Systems.

They had two immediate priorities. First, they had to reach out to the premium cosmetics companies whose products she hoped to sell on her Web site. Second, they had to hire a Web development firm to design and build the site's infrastructure. Once they had a prototype in place—ideally in just two or three months—they could approach a handful of venture capital firms and quickly raise the kind of money they would need to grow very big very fast, before anyone else got the same idea.

The next several weeks were filled with tense negotiations. Marla learned that it would cost $800,000—four-fifths of the money they'd raised so far—just to build an inviting, functional bluemercury.com Web site. A couple of weeks later, she was shocked to find that the company she had hired to build the site hadn't even started its work. Frustrating as that was, however, she and Barry soon realized they had much bigger problems.

They had moved quickly, but now they discovered that bluemercury was coming late to the game. Several other, better-funded competitors were already out there, all operating semistealthily, all seeking to move the cosmetics industry to the Internet. Marla was badly shaken when she learned that Beauty.com, Eve.com, and Gloss.com were all starting with similar plans and targeting the exact same arena as bluemercury—but each of those companies had raised $20 million in venture capital. Another site, BeautyJungle.com, had $20 million in marketing money alone. Then, in summer 1999, Marla heard that Eve.com had entered into a $5 million advertising deal with Yahoo!.

Because Marla had successfully pitched her idea only to Ledecky and a couple of other investors, she had never worried about raising enough money to launch. But there had been an opportunity cost she'd never considered. Because she and Barry had never made the rounds of venture capital firms, they'd never learned about the many other firms that were simultaneously pitching similar ideas. Instead of competing solely with department stores and a few specialty retailers—an assertion Marla had made on nearly every other page of her business plan—she and Barry would now be launching in direct competition with nearly a dozen well-funded Internet beauty sites, none of which she'd even heard of a few weeks before.

All the competition could obviously prove fatal to bluemercury. Marla was confident that the idea of an online cosmetics hub would work, but she also knew that it couldn't possibly work for even half of the companies that were now racing to get a piece of this new market. True, the intense competition validated her sense that she had identified a very promising business, but this was cold comfort indeed. Suddenly, bluemercury's relatively meager funding made it almost impossible to imagine that they could become the "Neiman Marcus of the Internet." And that, in turn, made it less likely that they could attract the high-end brands their company needed.

Worried that bluemercury might be in real jeopardy unless she could compete with Beauty.com and the others, Marla went back to Ledecky and tried to raise more money. But that well was now dry. E2enet hadn't gone public yet, and it wasn't clear when or if the company ever would. By this point, the company had a formal board of directors, and its members were none too pleased that Marla and Barry were asking for more funding so quickly. Meanwhile, although the market for Internet startups was still booming, investors were starting to become more cautious. Frantic, Marla started making overtures to venture capital funds and private equity investors, and then flew out to Silicon Valley to pitch the idea. But even there, the atmosphere was entirely different than it had been just a few months before. Inevitably, when she got to the part of her presentation where she outlined the competition, the potential investors all saw the same thing: bluemercury was dead meat.

It was the most strenuous summer of Marla's life. She pitched to every potential angel she could find—even HBS classmates like Marc Cenedella and Steve Perricone—trying to lock up additional investments in $10,000 and $20,000 chunks. But virtually everyone turned her down. Marc, for one, thought she was valuing the company too high; he wasn't convinced that he would get enough equity for his investment, and Steve followed his lead. In her most difficult moments, Marla wondered whether bluemercury simply wasn't meant to be. Maybe she should have waited, she told Barry. Maybe she should have worked for Ledecky for a few years before going out on her own. She might have had a better chance of successfully launching a company if she'd had more seasoning.

"Seasoning?" Barry replied. He'd been through these kinds of difficult times before. If it were easy, everyone would launch their own firms. Besides, you only got so many years on this earth. What would a few more years with Ledecky have taught her that she hadn't learned already?

"Seasoning," Barry told Marla, "is when you take a piece of meat and beat it with a cleaver. Then, when it's good and beaten, you rub salt in it. Then you're seasoned. This is what it's like to be an entrepreneur. You get beaten up pretty bad."

It was time to rethink the plan for bluemercury. For Marla and Barry, the Internet might as well have evaporated. That was the old opportunity, and it was gone. But Marla had already taken the $1 million, and she was consumed by fear of failure. The idea of shutting down her company before it had even sold its first product was unbearable.

Marla thought back to EFX, the two-store chain in D.C. that had inspired her to think of launching bluemercury in the first place. Even now, she remained a loyal EFX customer. She loved both the variety of products and the stores' atmosphere. Maybe, she realized, the key to her idea wasn't the Web site—it was the cosmetics. And if Eve.com, Beauty .com, and the others were totally focused on the Internet, maybe her smart move was to follow the advice of baseball great Willie Keeler: rather than going head to head with the competition, she could "hit 'em where they ain't."

In July 1999, Marla sat down and completely rewrote the bluemercury business plan. She recast the company as a bricks-and-clicks enterprise—she would open retail stores, and the Web site would be a companion channel.

This shift in focus meant Marla and Barry had to do one of two things. They could start their own retail stores or they could partner with an existing boutique. Every day as she walked through Georgetown, Marla saw the potentially perfect model or partner: EFX.

Barry wasted no time. He cold-called EFX's founder and persuaded her to meet with him and Marla in Ledecky's office in downtown Washington. At first, they talked about a joint venture or partnership. But soon it became clear that the vision he and Marla had for the company was wildly different from the one that EFX's founder had. Barry and Marla kept after her, showing her all the online competition she'd soon be facing, and convincing her that she was going to be swamped. EFX's sales were about $1.8 million a year, but the company was carrying a lot of debt and they argued that it simply didn't have the resources to compete with all the well-financed competition. Finally, Barry and Marla made a concrete offer: bluemercury proposed to buy EFX outright.

EFX's founder was open to the idea, so Marla rushed back to the E2Enet board and asked them to fund the deal. But the response was even more negative than when she'd asked for money to market the bluemercury Web site.

"Absolutely not," one of the investors told her. Another member of the board said buying EFX would be an "idiotic move." After all, E2Enet's mission was to invest in Internet companies; adding a brick-and-mortar cosmetics chain to the mix seemed a foolish distraction.

Frustrated and scared, Marla was now convinced that bluemercury would not survive unless they bought EFX. She made a decision. She owned a town house and she had saved a little bit of money. She was hardly flush, but she figured her position was at least as good as Jon Ledecky's had been when he'd started U.S. Office Products with a quarter-of-a-million-dollar cash advance on his credit cards. She knew it in her gut. Now was the time to think big, to bet on herself. This was the moment to be bold.

Barry handled the negotiations. To fund the purchase agreement to buy EFX, Marla had to remortgage her home and sign a personal guarantee to cover all of the company's outstanding obligations. By the time the deal was done, Marla owned two retail stores and a half-finished Web site—and she was now carrying half a million dollars in debt.

But she had saved bluemercury. And if it was no longer the business she had originally imagined, it was now a real, live company. In short order, Marla and Barry hired a cosmetics executive who'd been working at the Barney's chain of department stores; they also rebranded the EFX shops in Georgetown and Dupont Circle as bluemercury stores. EFX brought with it the purchase records of its twenty thousand customers. More important, the company had a long history of dealing with the most prestigious vendors in the cosmetics industry, the ones Marla needed to ensure that bluemercury—both the Web site and the stores—could grow to become a high-end destination. Meanwhile, Marla pushed the programmers she'd hired to complete the Web site. On November 1, 1999, six months after she had set out on her own, bluemercury.com went live for the first time.

Marla hadn't worked in retail since her part-time jobs in high school and college. She hadn't consulted for retail clients at McKinsey, and she hadn't studied retail with any particular attention at HBS. Even so, she was confident that she could run the EFX stores and succeed. She considered herself bluemercury's prototypical customer, so she rebuilt the stores based on what she found most enjoyable and appealing.

Hiring the right people mattered enormously. The first question she would ask prospective employees was usually, "What is your favorite brand of beauty product and why?" Any applicant who couldn't answer that question with passion and intelligence certainly wasn't a "beauty junkie" like Marla—and so she clearly wouldn't be well suited to work for bluemercury. Marla hired only full-time workers and paid them full-time salaries with benefits rather than commissions. Thirty-something women who came into the store thinking of buying $50 lipsticks or $100 tubes of face cream, Marla reasoned, would expect salespeople to know their merchandise. Equally important, her customers should know that the salesperson didn't have a financial incentive to steer them toward a particular line of beauty products.

So much of Marla's success now depended on her confidence and her ability to make things happen. At the moment, she owned only two stores and a Web site, but Marla still thought big. She was determined to become not only a successful CEO but the face of the beauty industry. (One of her investors, Ed Mathias, half-jokingly called her "Marla Stewart.") She hired a public relations firm that did an effective job of getting ink for her new enterprise. Marla and her company were written up in Oprah Winfrey's new magazine *O*, and the *Washington Post* did a feature article on the official bluemercury launch in late 1999. Another article in the *Washington Times* reported on Marla's plans to open a second headquarters in New York City—one to go along with "its Washington headquarters at 1229 29th St. NW." (That, of course, was the address of Marla's town house in Georgetown.) A writer for *Inc.* magazine interviewed Marla about how she and Barry had decided which computers and other tech products to purchase when they started the company. Months passed and they never heard another thing from *Inc.* But then one day she and Barry were in a grocery store and Barry spotted the front cover of the current issue of the magazine. On it was a giant photo of Marla.

That was a good day, but there were plenty of bad ones. Less than a month after Marla bought EFX, Sephora—a French cosmetics chain backed by the giant conglomerate LVMH—opened a store right next to the larger of her two bluemercury outlets. Even more daunting, Sephora announced plans to open more than seven hundred new stores in the next several years. With that kind of competition, Marla once again wondered how she could possibly survive. But she was in so deep now that she had no choice but to continue. She put blinders on and drove forward.

CHRIS: THINKING BIG

By early summer 1999, Chris Michel had written a thirty-five-page business plan for the company he was now calling MilitaryAdvantage. He prepared to quit his job at Mercer; though he had no money and a mountain of education debt, he was also possessed by an unbridled optimism. And his plan for MilitaryAdvantage was nothing if not ambitious: its goal was to organize *everybody* in the armed forces. Chris assembled a PowerPoint presentation about his new venture, and the first slide communicated the company's scope. "A vertical portal serving the military community is a big idea," the slide announced. Then, using bullet points, it described the demographic Chris was targeting:

- The military market is large and attractive
- 30 million current/former military members
- Another 40 million adults with close ties to the military

The military, Chris wrote, was "online and buying." In fact, he asserted, members of the military and their families were more likely than civilians to make online purchases. In the late 1990s, broadband Internet service was still a thing of the future for most Americans, but all military computers were due to be connected to high-speed connections within two years. MilitaryAdvantage would be able to reach its market easily and efficiently. Perhaps most important, he wrote, no one else had yet focused on using the Internet to serve the military market.

Chris's unofficial partner in this enterprise was Anne Dwane, who had wholeheartedly embraced the concept. But she wasn't ready to work on MilitaryAdvantage full-time—she loved her work at Interval, and she was reluctant to quit before they had raised enough money to launch. For the near term, Chris recruited a young Mercer associate named Steve Echikson to join him, but he soon recognized that he had to bring in someone else as well. Chris knew he was more of a "big idea" guy than a "get things done" guy, and he needed a complement. As it happened, Echikson thought he knew the perfect person: his mentor and adviser at Mercer, a partner by the name of Brad Clark.

Clark was a couple of years younger than Chris, but he'd climbed higher up the ladder at Mercer. He had joined the firm straight out of college, gotten his MBA at Stanford, and returned to Mercer in 1996. That made him a six-year veteran, and he was starting to burn out. Like Chris, he worried that he'd missed the golden opportunities right in front of him. He could almost laugh about it: he had graduated from a top business school in the heart of Silicon Valley in the mid-1990s, settled in San Francisco, and had gone into consulting, working on oil and gas projects a thousand miles away.

Chris, still working at Mercer, walked into Brad Clark's office one day in late July, carrying a printout of the MilitaryAdvantage presentation. The two men had met only once or twice before, and Clark had never served in the military. But Chris was so enthusiastic and his plan so impressive that within minutes Clark had made a private decision that he would leave Mercer to join Chris's startup.

Negotiations proceeded quickly. Clark wanted a significant stake in the company. He acknowledged that Chris had come up with the idea, developed the plan, and targeted a very promising market. Further, Chris's background as a navy officer and his passion for the company's mission gave the venture an obvious edge. Clark worried that he was being impulsive, but he was restless and ready to take a risk. He even offered to put up some seed money to make it happen. Within a couple of days, he and Chris had a deal.

Chris timed his departure from Mercer so he wouldn't have to repay his first-year signing bonus, but by mid-September he was at last ready to strike out on his own. He would be CEO of the new company, Brad Clark would be VP of business development, and Steve Echikson would be a director working under him. Once they had VC-level funding, Anne Dwane would come aboard as VP of marketing.

During those first few weeks, the team worked out of Chris's tiny apartment, crowded around tables at Starbucks, and sat in the living room of the San Francisco house Clark shared with several other friends. Chris started leveraging his contacts from the navy and his time as an admiral's aide. He recruited several retired military officers and a couple of well-known people to serve on the new company's board of advisers. His former boss in the navy, the now retired Admiral Tom Hall, signed on, as did Professor Ed Zschau from Harvard Business School. He also persuaded Carl Mundy, a former commandant of the U.S. Marine Corps, and Stephen Ambrose, the noted military author and historian, to join the board. He invited General Norman Schwarzkopf as well, still a hero from his Persian Gulf War days. But the general sent a letter declining, saying he was already on the boards of too many other Internet startups.

Chris tried to persuade several contractors to work for the company on a contingency basis until they received funding. And he hired a lawyer, who in turn was able to use his contacts to get appointments with VC firms. Chris had never asked anyone for funding, but he'd taken Entrepreneurial Finance at HBS and read about the process in various HBS cases. He could speak the language, so he figured he'd be fine.

But then he, Anne, and Brad Clark walked into their first pitch meeting at a prestigious venture capital firm called Sigma Partners—and their presentation fell on deaf ears. The VC partners simply didn't believe that Chris was selling something of value, and his passion left them cold. In the following weeks, Chris made presentations to six more VC firms; nobody bit. In the late 1990s, the conventional wisdom was that any entrepreneur pitching to a venture capital firm needed to present a credible plan to reach $50 million in revenue by the fifth year of operations. Chris's plan projected that and more, but the investors just didn't buy it. A few expressed deep skepticism that the military was a good demographic.

"How much does an army sergeant or a navy lieutenant even make, anyway?" one partner at a venture capital firm asked. Chris started to wonder if some of the partners came to the meeting just to meet a guy who was crazy enough to pitch a military site to VCs in northern California.

Other investors were skeptical because they felt the domain name—MilitaryAdvantage.com—wasn't especially striking. At least one asked why Chris's plan didn't include the purchase of the domain military.com.

To all these objections, Chris replied that MilitaryAdvantage could be a lifelong channel, serving members of the military from the day they first began thinking about joining the armed forces all the way through their careers, personal milestones, and eventual separation from the military. He spoke about the natural affinity that soldiers have for one another; about the military as a kind of family; about the urgent need for a way to share a huge amount of information within that family. But no matter what he said or how he said it, the venture capital firms wouldn't bite.

Chris tried to maintain an optimistic facade, but he was beginning to have doubts. Packed into Brad Clark's old Toyota, Chris, Anne, and Brad drove from one VC shop to another, up and down Sand Hill Road in Palo Alto. After several weeks and more than a dozen pitches, Chris was almost ready to throw in the towel. They had a Web development firm lined up, and they'd found office space they wanted to lease in San Francisco, but they couldn't raise the money to pay for any of it. Maybe they'd miscalculated, Chris thought. Perhaps he should let Clark off the hook and give him back his seed money; then they could all go find jobs with existing startups.

One afternoon in early October, the team assembled at Clark's house and Chris leveled with them. He knew they all believed in the cause as much as he did, but maybe the problem wasn't finding the right backers;

maybe it was finding a better plan. He admitted his own frustration and told them he didn't want to string them along.

"There comes a time when you have to ask yourself if maybe the market is right," he said somberly.

They went around the table, and each had his or her say. Brad Clark voted to keep going. He'd left a six-year career at Mercer for this, and as the only one to commit any serious cash so far, he felt his opinion should carry extra weight. Anne was also convinced they should keep at it awhile longer—although she acknowledged that since she still hadn't left her full-time job while they started, she had less to lose than they did.

But it was Steve Echikson who pushed back the hardest. Where was the fire and drive, he wanted to know. Where was the determination he had seen in Chris when they started out? Besides, they'd worked on the project for only a short while, even if it had felt like years. He was adamant: they should continue.

"If this was a great idea two months ago," he said, "it's a great idea now."

Chris had never seen Echikson so animated, and his words had a strong impact. Chris realized that as CEO of the fledgling company, he was obligated not to give up. He didn't need to protect his team by giving them an out when things got tough. His job was to keep his promise. He would lead them forward.

Chris stepped back from the edge. He and his little team had no more resources or leads now than they had had at the start of the conversation. But they had renewed resolve. Chris hoped it would be enough.

In the second or third week of October 1999, Chris's lawyer sent the MilitaryAdvantage proposal to a partner at a venture capital firm called Mayfield Partners. There, it caught the attention of Mike Levinthal, a Stanford MBA and engineer who had been with the firm for close to twenty years. Levinthal had no military background, but he liked these sorts of business ideas. They were profit-seeking and potentially category-killing—but they were also, as one of his colleagues put it, "dot-coms with a dot-org vibe." In fact, Mayfield had just invested in a new education startup called edu.com, founded by another 1998 HBS grad named

Adam Kanner. Why not give Chris Michel and MilitaryAdvantage.com a shot as well? Levinthal wondered.

When Chris, Anne, and Brad Clark sat down in the Mayfield conference room, Chris did all the talking. By now he had the pitch down pat—the PowerPoint presentation was well honed, and he was able to anticipate most of the questions that Levinthal and his partners had. He'd heard it all before at the other VC firms.

For his part, Mike Levinthal had sat through many, many presentations from would-be dot-com millionaires, yet Chris's passion made the idea stand out. Here was someone who understood the business side, but he also seemed to understand the military community better than anyone else in Silicon Valley. The market MilitaryAdvantage had targeted was wide open, and Levinthal believed that MilitaryAdvantage could dominate it.

Levinthal stepped outside and pulled several other Mayfield partners into the room. The more Chris talked, the more intrigued Levinthal and his colleagues grew. And though they were of course drawn to the venture's potential for making serious money, they also liked the idea that investing in MilitaryAdvantage would be a way of serving the military and thus the country.

In the days that followed, Levinthal put a team of analysts together to perform due diligence on the claims that Chris had made in his presentation. They checked out Chris's background, and those of Anne and Brad Clark. They called their references, including Ed Zschau, who of course gave Chris his highest recommendation.

On October 31, 1999, late in the afternoon, a courier arrived at Brad Clark's house. Clark tore open the hand-delivered envelope. Inside was a check for $5 million, made payable to MilitaryAdvantage.com, Inc. They were officially in business.

During his presentations, Chris had often talked about the need to raise money so that he could "lock up scarce assets." Now that they were funded, he raced to do as much of this as possible. If he could negotiate partnerships with some of the nonprofit organizations and companies that veterans already trusted, for example, he would not only improve his company's position, but make it harder for anyone else to launch later and compete. Early on, Chris was thrilled when they became America Online's exclusive military partner—a big deal at the time—and so provided news and information about the armed forces for AOL's captive Internet audience. And even when his initiatives didn't work out precisely as Chris hoped, he felt that the waves were beginning to break his way. In one instance, he sought out the best image-making and publicity team he could find, and a colleague recommended that he make every effort to hire Abigail Johnson, who ran a Silicon Valley PR firm. Though she felt MilitaryAdvantage wasn't a great fit for the kind of work she did, Johnson soon became an informal adviser and important sounding board for Chris and Anne.

The asset they really wanted was the domain name, military.com. News reports were full of stories about Internet speculators who had scored hundreds of thousands or even millions of dollars by selling domains they had registered. Wine.com sold for $1 million, Drugs .com went for more than $800,000, Business.com had been sold for $150,000 in 1998—and then sold again in 1999 for $7.5 million. Chris and Brad Clark tracked down the owner of the military.com domain—a college professor in Florida—and learned that acquiring it was going to cost them several hundred thousand dollars. It was the most difficult financial decision Chris had ever made, but he was convinced they had to dominate the market they were targeting and get big fast. And rebranding the company would give them a substantial strategic advantage.

From now on, MilitaryAdvantage would be known as Military. com. After writing the check to the college professor, Chris noted wryly that at least somebody had already made a big profit as a result of his idea.

They hired the best Web development firm they could find and built their Web site. The site had hundreds of sections so that veterans associated with specific military units or ships would have pages of their own. And now that Mayfield had invested and they'd launched a Web site that was beginning to attract a substantial number of visitors, the company had enough credibility to raise a lot more money. Within months, Chris had raised another $20 million in venture capital, but the company spent money almost as fast as it came in. Their official launch party in March

2000, with a VIP reception on the USS *Hornet* in San Francisco Bay, cost them $100,000 alone.

The worldwide Web, meanwhile, was quickly becoming a big part of people's lives. But there were also signs that the Internet gold rush might be peaking. In January of that year, America Online and Time Warner announced that they would merge, and analysts noted with amazement that under the terms of the deal, AOL—the Internet upstart—bought the much older publishing and broadcasting giant. And although the outcome of that year's Super Bowl was in doubt until the last play, the game would be best remembered for the seventeen Internet startups that spent more than $40 million to broadcast television commercials during the program. Pets.com, which offered free shipping on orders for 25-pound bags of dog food, paid $2.4 million for a thirty-second spot starring a sock puppet. Another ad featured a company's investors pleading with viewers to visit their Web site, computer.com. ("Sweet mother, I hope this works," one character in the ad begged, as a graphic below his image proclaimed: "Invested Life Savings.") Barely two months later, reality returned: the NASDAQ dove and the Internet bubble burst.

But for Chris and his team, it was hard to know whether this was really the end of the boom. The industry had been through rough patches before, and deals were still being made. Traffic on their Web site was increasing, their brand was building, and they still had a substantial amount of capital. But then they experienced their own little crash in the form of an article in the *Wall Street Journal*, which appeared not long after their launch. The first two sentences of the piece turned their world upside down.

> Only three weeks ago, not one commercial Web site catered to U.S. military personnel and veterans. In the next week, four major sites—each boasting deep pockets and enough retired four-star generals to fight a major war—will begin fighting it out for the military audience.

Even Ross Perot planned a venture, called militaryhub.com. Perot said his goal was to take the company public at a very high valuation, and that he planned to ensure that all pre-IPO stock went to veterans and active-duty military members so that thousands of soldiers, sailors, and marines could become millionaires. All this time, Chris had believed that he would be first to the fight. Now he knew that the idea wasn't unique at all.

This wasn't just business anymore. As the *Journal* article predicted, Chris and military.com were about to go into full-on combat.

CHAPTER 8

THINK BIG, THINK NEW, THINK AGAIN

It's not what you look at that matters, it's what you see.

—HENRY DAVID THOREAU

A real opportunity consists of both a problem and a proposed solution. And as I got to know Marla, Chris, and Marc—along with so many other successful entrepreneurs—it struck me that once they identified problems that needed to be solved, they thought big, thought new, and then thought again.

What do I mean by this? "Thinking big" can mean coming up with ideas that have scale and scope, as well as aiming for huge financial returns. At the very least, it means pursuing ideas with enough potential to make them worth your time—not to mention your investors' and customers' time. Venture capital firms, as you have no doubt come to understand, are rarely willing to fund companies that do not project revenues in the tens of millions of dollars. But thinking big refers to more than just money. We get only one life, and the successful entrepreneurs I interviewed were determined to spend their limited time on this earth wisely by pursuing plans that would make it possible for them to have as much impact as possible.

Since the era covered by this story was dominated by the explosive growth of the Internet and high-technology companies, it's tempting to presume that "thinking new" means employing new technology. But that's not necessarily true. More fundamentally, it means bringing your outsider's perspective to bear in an industry where people have always done something a certain way.

And finally, "thinking again" means recognizing that almost no one comes up with both a great problem and the perfect solution right out of the gate. The successful founders I got to know while writing this book may or may not have been interested in becoming serial entrepreneurs— but without exception they understood that they had to become serial innovators.

THINK BIG

I'm a firm believer in asking for help when I need it. And so, not long after meeting Marla Malcolm for the first time, I sat down with a colleague at the *Washington Post* named Ylan Mui, who had interviewed Marla for the paper. I thought Ylan might have some insights into whether Marla had the heart of a true entrepreneur, and whether I should consider writing about her as one of the main characters in this book. What was it that struck you most about her? I asked.

Ylan thought for a minute, and then replied that it was the scope of the business Marla had set out to build. From the earliest days, even when bluemercury was brand new and tiny, Ylan sensed that Marla had never believed that she was starting a small specialty retailer. Instead, she was always determined to build a category-killing cosmetics colossus.

I told Marla about this conversation the next time I talked with her, and Ylan's observation struck her as entirely unremarkable.

"I always thought big," she said. "I don't know why, but I was never going to go out and do just a couple of little stores."

It's hard for me to convey the tone of voice with which Marla said that—suffice it to say that she scoffed at the notion that she ever would have done anything other than think big. It never occurred to her to scale down her vision or to be "realistic," even when she was facing daunting competition and had little to show for her efforts besides an idea, a couple of stores, and a mountain of debt.

The truth is, the scope of what many of us would call success is dwarfed by what high-percentage entrepreneurs consider success. Reading my descriptions of Marla's, Chris's, and (later) Marc's business plans will give you a sense for the scale of their ambitions. But their tendency to think big wasn't predetermined. Attending Harvard Business School and learning about the sort of opportunities that awaited them after graduation played a part, but it wasn't the only impetus, and it probably wasn't even the dominant one. Why do I say this? Because the majority of HBS graduates don't start successful companies—and when they do start companies, they usually wait much longer after graduation than Marla, Chris, and (to a lesser extent) Marc did.

It's easy to lose sight of this point in the context of a book like this one. If not for the fact that our three entrepreneurs thought big, it's highly unlikely that I would have met them, researched their stories, and included them here. But consider Chris Michel, for example. Rather than conjuring up a large-scale enterprise, he might have imagined a Web site with a simple tool that would tackle the immediate problem he had identified, which was how to streamline the tangle of benefits available to veterans. Instead, within minutes he was thinking about the entire universe of problems that active and former members of the military face—everything from finding the right moving company to searching out old army buddies, from navigating the GI Bill to deciding what to do with their lives when they got out of the military. Marla did something quite similar. From the earliest days, as she sat in her town house in Georgetown and began sketching out what became bluemercury, she saw her company not simply as a way to sell cosmetics online, but to create a Nieman Marcus of the Internet.

As I researched their stories, I often wondered what conditioned Marla, Chris, and Marc to think big. In fact, I was sometimes frustrated when I asked them directly about where this trait came from. Their answers were less than helpful, perhaps because they had never even considered the question before. The sun rose in the east, water was wet, and they thought they could build big companies and change the world.

But as I got to know their stories better, I decided that they hadn't just been born with outsized ambitions. They had *learned* how to think big. I realized that, intentionally or not, all three had trained themselves over time to scale up their ideas about what they could accomplish in life. And that led me to believe that the rest of us can do the same thing.

———

Chris is a good example of my point that people aren't always naturally ambitious. When I asked him when he first began to think big, he didn't know quite how to respond. "I have to say," he said, "I was doing really well in the navy. I mean, I don't think that my career could've been going any better, at least not on paper. But for whatever reason, I was not satisfied. I love the navy, but the navy did not seem enough."

Chris permitted me to read the journals he kept while in the navy, and they include descriptions of feeling overwhelmed, even intimidated by some of the high-ranking officers he met early in his career. In one entry, written not long after he graduated from flight school, he mentions shaking hands with the top admiral in the navy. He described the admiral as "one of the few men I've met that truly projects an aura of greatness."

Reflecting on the question of when he became legitimately ambitious, Chris suggested that it might have happened after he moved to Washington. Every day, he interacted with top military and political leaders—people he'd seen only from afar up until then. Gradually, he came to understand that they were human beings, too. Or, as he put it, he "got close enough to see the wizard." And if they could climb so high up the ladder, why couldn't he?

Marc Cenedella told me that when he was in fourth grade, he had to write a report on what he thought he would do when he grew up. He wrote that he planned to go to Harvard, play wide receiver in the NFL, and then run for Congress.

"I've just always felt that way," he told me. "It seemed like my peers were as much the people I read about in books as the actual people in my classes or workplace."

But it's one thing to feel that way as a kid, and quite another to continue to do so years later, when most of us scale down our dreams and aim to accomplish goals that seem "reasonable." Marc, for one, found himself thinking in a much more ambitious way about his future during his college years when he worked as a bartender at official university events. Many of his friends aspired to work someday for the big investment banks, consulting firms, and law firms. To a kid from Buffalo, New York, those opportunities at first seemed as high as anyone might ever hope to climb. But later, as he poured drinks at reunions and listened to the stories told by alumni who had spent decades working in exactly those types of firms, he grew to see those kinds of ambitions as ordinary and pedestrian. Marc began to believe that he could never be satisfied with that which his friends aspired to, and that someday he might accomplish something far more remarkable.

As for Marla Malcolm, it's possible that she inherited her penchant for thinking big from her dad and built on it. I knew that her father had been an entrepreneur, and one day I asked if she thought he had passed his entrepreneurial tendencies on to her.

"Relative to his parents he was incredibly successful," Marla replied, "but he's gone through the booms and busts that all small business owners go through. He's never, ever had a boss. He bought his first piece of property when he was twenty-six. He tells a story about convincing a bank to give him a loan to put up a building in Oakland—an apartment building. So he was pretty entrepreneurial, just on a smaller scale."

Marla told me another story that spoke volumes about how she imagined her future when she was young. Shortly before Marla left home for college, the regional representative for one of the insurance companies her father worked for told her that his company had big plans for her. Flattering her, he said that after working for the company all through high school, she knew the business almost as well as he did. He had spoken to his bosses about her, he said, and he knew they hoped that one day she would take over her father's business.

Marla said little in reply, but privately she was mortified. "Is this what they think of me?" she remembered thinking. "It's way too small."

My own theory about the origin of Marla's considerable ambition is that she learned to think bigger and bigger because she surrounded herself with people who aimed very high. They pushed her to take on greater challenges, and to envision ever broader definitions of success. HBS contributed to this awakening, as did working for Jonathan Ledecky. But the person who really encouraged her to expand her horizons was Barry Beck. Barry had already learned to redefine the scope of his own dreams—in fact, one of the real impetuses for him to do so was meeting

Marla and Jon Ledecky, back when he had hoped Ledecky would buy his maintenance business.

"In my mind," he told me one afternoon, "I was a very successful guy. Then I met these people, and I was like, oh my God—I get it. There's a whole other level."

To illustrate his point, Barry explained that in the winter his maintenance company would hire smaller companies to take on such things as snow removal. But after meeting with Jon Ledecky, he realized that Ledecky looked at him the way he looked at a lone guy with a snowplow.

"I was just a tool for them," Barry explained. "They're taking these assets and buying and selling them as if I'm a checker on a checkerboard. The truth is that I hadn't really been exposed to that before. It was exciting and exhilarating—but a little depressing, too."

Learning to think big is a process that never stops—and, while that's a blessing, it can also be something of a curse. Most of the entrepreneurs I interviewed were justifiably proud of what they had created, but they also often seemed to be battling a fear that they hadn't set their sights high enough. There's little worse than spending your life trying to achieve something that, deep in your gut, you don't truly believe is worth doing. One antidote to that is to think huge at the outset—and to force yourself to think hard about whether your ambitions are truly big enough.

The first time Barry Beck and I talked, we went on for close to two hours. I barely had to ask any questions. He had strong feelings about a lot of the challenges faced by entrepreneurs. But he grew most passionate when he said: "Don't go out there and look for experiences. Experience is what you get when you don't achieve what you want. Go out there and do what you want to do and succeed at it."

I looked down at my notebook as I wrote, and suddenly Barry became silent. Then, he resumed speaking, even more intently this time.

"And be careful which mountain you climb. God forbid that you climb a mountain, plant your flag at the top, and then look around and realize—What was I thinking? I climbed the wrong mountain."

THINK NEW

Thinking new is what gives the intelligent entrepreneur a shot at slaying the dominant, entrenched competitors. Why? Because if coming up with an innovative idea is difficult, doing so again and again is much harder. Corporate history is littered with once-innovative companies that stopped seeing new problems and discovering new solutions.

Many of the entrepreneurs I talked with told me that because they didn't share their competitors' preconceptions about how business was supposed to be done, their thinking was much more innovative. Innovation usually comes from either bringing a new technology to an industry or coming up with a new business model. We see both of these factors in the cases of Marla, Chris, and Marc.

Take bluemercury, for example. Marla identified a lot of things she disliked about how cosmetics were sold in America before she launched her company. Department store products were locked away in cabinets, and because salespeople were employed by brands, they would push clients only toward the products that earned them the best commissions. But what she didn't realize until she sat down and studied the industry was *why* it was set up that way. The answer that ultimately came to her was that the business model had been designed to serve the needs and preferences of cosmetics manufacturers—not the needs and preferences of customers.

And so, when she bought EFX and opened her stores, Marla built her operation around the mantra of "honest, friendly, expert advice." She had her employees display products in a way that encouraged customers to pick them up and try them out. And she insisted on hiring full-time salespeople, employees who wanted what she wanted out of her work—not just an hourly job, but a real career.

It's more than possible that none of this would ever have occurred to Marla if she'd worked in retail or cosmetics before. But she hadn't, and thus she didn't identify with retail managers or cosmetics vendors. She identified with the people who shopped in her stores. She built the bluemercury's business model around providing the greatest possible benefit to her customers, which was both a simple and a profound innovation.

Think of Marc Cenedella, peddling puppy kibble to the Japanese. He'd been selling pet food for just a few months, and he was still new to selling to Asia by the time he launched Forbes Pacifica. Combining the two was a simple innovation, but Marc took advantage of a new market and created an entire company based on it.

Or think about Chris Michel's innovation. It's tempting to think that he simply employed new technology—the Internet—to inform and bring together the community of armed forces veterans. Although that's part of the key to his success, it's hardly all of it. And here I can speak from personal experience. As it happens, I was in the Army Reserve at the same time that Chris was dreaming up Military.com during a Naval Reserve drill. Like everyone who was serving in the armed forces, I was frustrated by how difficult it was to get accurate information about benefits that were available to me and my fellow soldiers. But Chris's unusual perspective—a military veteran with an MBA who desperately wanted to become an entrepreneur—enabled him to see the potential in a huge market that was right in front me and everyone else in the military. He had the ability to think new and then see how an emerging technology could serve as the engine for a business that would solve problems shared by millions.

THINK AGAIN

It's funny, but almost nobody seems to find the right innovative solution to a problem the first time. I often heard from HBS grads and other entrepreneurs that they'd launched businesses with entirely the wrong idea—and succeeded later only because they recognized their mistake, slammed on the brakes, and tried something different. Stig Leschly told me he blew through $100,000—money that he had borrowed from his family, no less—in his first attempt to start the company that became exchange.com. Even before he attended HBS, Marc Cenedella had to reevaluate the way he was running Forbes Pacifica and work harder and smarter just to turn a profit. And as the story of our three entrepreneurs unfolds in this book, you'll notice that before they succeeded all of them had to revamp and redo, again and again.

"The funny thing about bluemercury," Marla Malcolm told me one day, "is that I was able to raise the capital for what I'm doing now only because the company began as an Internet play. But we had to quickly change our strategy. I had a bad first idea but then found a way to transform it."

If Marla hadn't started out with that big, new, ultimately wrong idea, she would never have been in a position to pivot and improve. But keep in mind that she had begun by focusing on a problem she knew something about. Then, when she realized that she had come up with the wrong solution, she changed her approach almost overnight. Would she have been able to move so quickly and confidently if she had launched the certified e-mail company with Barry and then discovered that the original solution wasn't the right one? We can't know for sure, of course, but it seems less likely. And it's obvious that her admirable ability to think again greatly improved her odds of success.

SMALL VERSUS BIG

As I explored these insights with various professors at HBS, I was frequently reminded that thinking big doesn't necessarily mean thinking complicated. "Some of the best ideas are simple," Ed Zschau reminded me. And he rattled off examples—Starbucks was founded on a pretty simple idea; so was FedEx, and yet nobody believed in it at first.

But as I dug deeper, I found myself trying to untangle the importance of this focus on scale and novelty. Are entrepreneurs substantively different from small businesspeople? Are they doing the same thing, only on a larger scale? Or are they doing something qualitatively different?

Professor Noam Wasserman offered an interesting perspective on this question. "Entrepreneurship researchers break down into categories," he told me. "There are the finance guys who study venture capital, and there are the small business researchers. If you did a poll of the small business researchers they would probably say overwhelmingly that small businesspeople are entrepreneurs. My definition is different. The types of issues that entrepreneurs face the most, the problems that are the toughest for them and that I focus on in my case writing and in my research—well, small businesspeople simply don't fit the bill. It's the people who are trying to build the next Google or the next big biotech that I consider the entrepreneurs. But small business academia disagree with that."

One of the central issues in Wasserman's research involves what he calls the dilemma of "Rich vs. King." Entrepreneurs, he believes, almost inevitably face a difficult decision: Do they care more about controlling the growth of their enterprise, even when maintaining control means putting limits on how large it can grow? Or do they care more about maximizing their venture's scale, even when doing so means giving up some control to make it happen?

To guide the classroom discussion in his Founders Dilemmas course at HBS, Wasserman wrote a case about an entrepreneur named Evan Williams, best known today as the CEO and founder of Twitter. A few years younger than Marla, Chris, and Marc, Williams dropped out of college after three semesters and started several companies that eventually failed. When he came to the end of that string, he had little to show for his efforts beyond an overdue tax bill.

As Williams once explained in an interview, "I didn't know how to deal with people, I lacked focus, and I had no discipline. I'd start new projects without finishing old ones, and I didn't keep track of money. . . . I made a lot of employees mad."

Wasserman says that one of the lessons illustrated by the case is that Williams began to succeed only once he truly learned what it meant to think big and think new. After his first company failed, Williams relocated from Nebraska to California and cofounded a small technology consulting company called Pyra Labs. As a side project, Williams and a coworker developed a simple, automated system that would let them share their work and collaborate easily via the Internet. The project was called Blogger—Williams is sometimes credited with coining the term *blog*—and it quickly grew to become a popular Web application, if not an especially profitable one.

But Pyra Labs had a difficult life. Bills went unpaid and ultimately all of Williams's employees quit. Deliverance came in 2003 when Google purchased the company in order to get its hands on Blogger. Although Williams worked at Google for only a year and a half, his experience there taught him to envision the world and see what was possible in an entirely new way. As he put it in an interview:

> I was continually impressed by their ability to question everything and think bigger than anyone else would have done. "Why can't we index the whole Web better than anyone else?" They approached everything like that. It's healthy to plan for bigness.

Two years later, Google went public. Soon thereafter, Williams cashed out some stock and launched a new company, Odeo. By the time he began building that company—which eventually launched the micro-blogging service Twitter—his mind-set had completely changed. He thought big and moved aggressively forward—raising $5 million in venture capital, scrapping and revising the company's original product (a podcasting service), and even personally buying out his investors by making whole their $5 million investment when they soured on the company.

As I write, Twitter is growing exponentially—it currently has about twenty million users, although it doesn't generate much revenue yet. But the company has now raised $57 million in venture capital, and it is without question a big, new idea.

Of course, most entrepreneurs won't raise tens of millions of dollars, but thinking new about your venture is just as vital. Wasserman and I talked about an informal case study we'd both read, about a sole-proprietor cart vendor who sold coffee to rush hour commuters. Instead of following the traditional model of running such a business, which entailed little more than taking a customer's order, making his change, and filling the order, this vendor decided to leave some money on the counter of his cart and allow his customers to make their own change. Although he was occasionally stiffed by customers who paid less than they should have, he found that his increased efficiency in churning out cups of coffee more than made up for the difference.

While the scale of the cart vendor's business isn't particularly impressive, Wasserman agreed that he should be considered something of an entrepreneur. He introduced something new, and ultimately useful, to the business model.

Wasserman then made a comparison to the founders he studied. "Some of the best entrepreneurs enter into a brand-new industry, and they see a better way to do things than the people who are steeped within that industry. As outsiders with different experiences, they have broader thinking, and they often see how to adapt a model from another industry to this new industry where things haven't changed in a while. They can see other ways to do things because their perspective isn't based on those unstated assumptions about how things have to be done."

THE NEXT RULE

Of course, thinking big and new, and then thinking again, is not your ultimate goal. In the end, you've got to figure out how to deliver products and services to customers at a profit. As we'll see, in the late 1990s many entrepreneurs lost sight of this obvious point; too often, they focused on novelty and scale at the expense of a sound business model, and ultimately their ventures failed. But some founders like Marla, Chris, and Marc understood that if thinking big, thinking new, and thinking again was essential to successful entrepreneurship, other factors were just as important.

As you undoubtedly understand by now, starting up a new venture can be a daunting challenge. What often keeps you going, I'm sure, is knowing that your venture is your baby. It's your dream. Sometimes, though, what it will take to realize that dream seems to be much more than one person can possibly handle. But that's okay—you don't have to accomplish everything by yourself. In fact, you probably shouldn't even try. Because if there's one thing I heard over and over from the entrepreneurs I interviewed, it's that you can't do it alone.

CHAPTER 9

It's not who you know. It's who you get to know.

—CHRIS MATTHEWS

MARC: MEETING ANDREW AND ALEX

HotJobs turned out to be everything Marc Cenedella hoped it would be. The company had already been through its IPO, but it still had the kind of chaotic environment he liked and expected at a startup. The company was hiring like crazy. There wasn't even enough furniture; for Marc's first week, he didn't have a desk. He'd arrive early each morning, find out who was sick or on vacation, and take that person's spot for the day. Bursting at the seams, the company held department meetings on the fire escape. Still, Marc was having a blast. The business model—which was virtually identical to the company's bigger competitor, Monster Worldwide—was simple, and it worked. Employers paid to post ads on the Web site; applicants then browsed through them and applied to appealing jobs for free. And HotJobs was growing: more users, more money, and in 2000 a $40 million advertising budget, three times what it had spent the year before.

One morning in May 2000, a couple of months into his tenure, Marc came out of the elevator in the HotJobs offices on West Fortieth Street to find a well-dressed, college-age man sitting in the lobby. Andrew Koch, a rising senior at Brown University, had interned in the HotJobs marketing department the summer before. He introduced himself, shook Marc's hand, and explained that he was back for another summer. This time he would be interning in business development.

"That's interesting," Marc replied. "I'm the VP of business development, and I had no idea you were coming." He took Andrew into his office and gave him his copy of the *Wall Street Journal* to read while he figured out what to do with him.

In the weeks that followed, Marc and Andrew became good friends and forged a great working relationship. Almost immediately, Marc treated Andrew a bit like a junior partner; without thinking about it, he duplicated the role that several important mentors had played for him at a similar young age. When Marc had decided to move to San Diego after college, for example, he'd sought out an older Yale alumnus and entrepreneur named Tim Wollaeger. Wollaeger had encouraged him to trust his instincts and head west; later, he'd encouraged him to start Forbes Pacifica. And when Marc worked in Japan, an older businessman had taken Marc under his wing in a traditional Japanese business relationship called senpai-kohai—meaning roughly, "big brother/little brother." Marc had taken to calling his Japanese mentor "senpai," and now he was acting as a kind of senpai to Andrew.

He took Andrew almost everywhere he went at work, and he let him know he was free to chime in whenever he felt he had something to say. Andrew's candid comments raised a few eyebrows that summer: during pitch meetings with potential business development partners, he sometimes played the role of the kid pointing out that the emperor had no clothes. But Marc found this amusing, and also useful. He was sorry to see Andrew go when summer ended and it was time for him to return to Brown.

That fall, a few weeks after Andrew left, Marc got another call from Dave Carvajal, who was still working at Online Retail Partners. Dave said he'd met someone Marc ought to interview, a French-born Internet marketing expert named Alex Douzet. Dave had tried to recruit Alex, but Alex—just like Marc—had doubts about Online Retail Partners and its business model. Instead of being offended, Dave told Alex he should interview at HotJobs.

Alex had nodded, but he hadn't been convinced. "What's the job, exactly?" he asked.

"There is no job," Dave replied. "It's open enrollment. If they like you, I'm sure there will be a job for you."

Marc took to Alex immediately, in part because their conversation quickly moved well beyond the usual meet-and-greet patter. One of the questions that Marc had been wrestling with lately was how much revenue an Internet company should be willing to spend on marketing. HotJobs, Marc had long since come to understand, had a chicken-and-egg problem: from an employer's point of view, paying for ads only made sense if enough qualified applicants actually used the site. But the applicants would only visit the site if the jobs were there to begin with. HotJobs spent gobs of money in an effort to attract new applicants, and part of Marc's job was to reduce that cost. At the outset, nobody at HotJobs was even tracking how much they spent to persuade a new user to register with the site. Recently, Marc had worked the numbers and was shocked when he discovered that HotJobs was spending about $700 for each new applicant. He knew there had to be a better way.

Now that he had Alex—this supposed marketing genius—sitting in front of him, Marc put the question to him.

What percentage of annual revenue should a company like HotJobs devote to marketing? he asked. And how much do you think we should be spending to attract each user? $100, maybe?

No way, Alex replied. He didn't know what the exact number should be, but he thought it was much lower than that, maybe $5 to $25.

Marc and Alex talked the problem back and forth for most of the meeting, each of them getting more and more animated. Though Marc didn't make Alex an offer during that first conversation, he asked him back for a second interview. This time, Alex brought with him a three-page analysis of the cost-per-applicant issue. In great detail, he explained why he was sure he was right—and why Marc was wrong.

This was just the kind of spirit Marc was looking for, and he offered Alex a job right away. It was a wise move. Within three months, Alex helped Marc cut the amount HotJobs spent on luring each new applicant down to $50. Within another year it was down to $1.

HotJobs had bought its first Super Bowl ad in 1999; that same year, its larger competitor, Monster Worldwide, bought three. Outside analysts later estimated that because of the resulting publicity, HotJobs had turned a roughly $1.5 million ad buy into something like $25 million worth of exposure. And by going head-to-head with Monster, HotJobs's cofounders had done a great job of stoking their employees' sense of rivalry with its older, better-funded competitor. The combativeness reached a fever pitch in early 2001, when HotJobs's founder, Richard Johnson, wrote an open letter to Monster's CEO, Andy McKelvey, suggesting that both companies put their reputations on the line and allow a neutral third party to judge which firm's Web site was better. The challenge was declined.

A month later, Johnson stepped aside as HotJobs's CEO. Then, in June 2001, the two companies made a surprising announcement: Monster was acquiring HotJobs. This was like Coke buying Pepsi, or GM buying Toyota—in the employment industry, the merger was huge, unexpected, and potentially game changing.

The announcement had an immediate effect on Marc Cenedella's life. He spent the entire summer working with Monster's chief operating officer and a team of people from both companies, racing to get the deal ready for approval by the Federal Trade Commission. It was an exciting time. Marc couldn't talk much about his work with friends and family, though, since the acquisition of one public company by another triggered all kinds of SEC rules about what could and could not be disclosed. But it was clear his life would soon change.

CHRIS: GETTING BIG FAST

Military.com was now large and growing quickly. By mid-2000, barely a year after Chris had first come up with the idea for the company at a Naval Reserve drill, he now employed nearly seventy people, including a twenty-member team working out of Washington, D.C. Chris was spending more than half his time on the road now, much of it in Washington, trying to lock up more scarce assets. He negotiated advertising and content deals with the different branches of the military, though it wasn't always easy. (In one instance, for example, an official from the U.S. Marine Corps said the marines wanted to recruit via Military.com only if they could squeeze out the army, navy, and air force.) Chris also did everything he could to expand his portfolio, including making an ultimately unsuccessful attempt to buy the *Army Times* publications from Gannett. And knowing that it would help his company, Chris spent a lot of his time trying to become the unofficial booster-in-chief of the American military. He joined every veterans organization he could think of and attended every military-themed event he could get invited to. Meanwhile, he was still flying in the Navy Reserve—for example, he spent two weeks on a counterdrug mission in Belize in summer 2000.

If Chris worked at an almost manic pace, it was largely because he heard the startup clock ticking: Military.com had very high expenses, and it didn't have enough revenue coming in to sustain itself for too much longer. One young Military.com employee joked that while other companies' business models were being described as "b2c" (for "business to consumer") or "b2b" ("business to business"), Military.com's model was "ppt2vc"—PowerPoint presentation to venture capitalists.

Chris was slow to anger, but that kind of cynical joke really irked him. He lived and breathed Military.com: he was doing everything possible to make the company profitable, and when talking to Brad Clark and his other direct reports he hammered home the point that increasing revenue had to be one of their main goals. Yes, they had put together some significant advertising and marketing deals with AT&T, the Air National Guard, and several other businesses and organizations. They had also entered into a joint marketing agreement with the *Wall Street Journal* that was unusual at the time. Rather than simply running banner advertisements for the newspaper on their Web site, Military.com asked new members if they were interested in getting the *Journal* at a lower rate than they could elsewhere. Then they packaged the members who said yes and sold the chance to contact them to the *Wall Street Journal*. In this way, Military.com began providing qualified leads to their corporate clients, and to Chris it seemed a promising business.

Still, the company hadn't yet developed the kinds of reliable revenue streams they needed. Ultimately, the reason was simple: they hadn't yet found the right customers.

In September 2000, the *Industry Standard* magazine came out with an article comparing the six Web sites competing to become the dominant military and veterans' portal. Military.com was clearly in the lead—it had the most registered users and the most investment capital. Ross Perot's Miltaryhub.com was still listed, but an accompanying chart offered some withering comments: "No slogan, and wouldn't return phone calls" and "FUBAR. The site appears to be missing in action." By comparison, the chart's notes about Military.com were positive: "Has achieved air superiority. . . . Ground battle under way."

But although this kind of small victory was satisfying, the stress of launching a complex enterprise in an untested new market was beginning to take a toll. At first, Chris and Brad Clark had worked well together; now they were having a harder time getting along. Chris had an entrepreneur's natural optimism. He was also a born salesman. "People want to believe," he often said. He loved telling the story of Military.com, and his passion for the venture was obvious to everyone. So was his belief that it would succeed.

But Clark, who managed much of the day-to-day operations, was finding it increasingly difficult to share Chris's confidence. With each passing day it became more apparent to him that the company was not living up to expectations, and he began to lose heart. The burden of doubt he carried got a little heavier each time they created a financial forecast and failed to meet it, and heavier still every time they sat down at a board meeting and explained once again that they needed more time to find the right business model. Clark had never in his life failed to meet expectations—from Harvard to Stanford to Mercer—and the notion that they weren't delivering on their promises was extremely distressing.

Chris wasn't Pollyannaish—he knew that Military.com was trying to climb a very steep hill—but he also understood that as the CEO it was his job to be an optimist. Besides, the company was doing exactly what the VCs had wanted them to do: get big fast. VCs expected nine out of ten of their companies to fail, Chris knew, but they counted on that tenth company to return ten, twenty, or fifty times their investment. That was the VC game: you put your $5 or $10 or $20 million on the table for a shot at a billion-dollar opportunity. But the VCs also understood that generating major revenues and profits takes time. Look at the old media brands that had become titans of the industry, Chris told some of his employees. *USA Today* was the number one newspaper in the country by circulation, but it had taken a full decade for it to become profitable.

By now Military.com employed eighty-five people. They were still growing, but finally Chris acknowledged to Clark that they were throwing money at the wall and hoping that it would bounce back as revenue. Their extravagant launch party had cost $150,000 or more. They had purchased back-cover advertisements in armed-forces-themed publications and put up billboards outside major U.S. military bases. They were clearly the market leaders—in one board meeting, Chris compared the company to an F-14 taking off at full-throttle on an aircraft carrier, ready to rocket away and dominate the competition.

"An F-14?" one of the directors replied. "You're more like a humvee in the desert. And you might want to think about the burn rate."

Military.com was churning through its investment with frightening speed. Optimist though he was, Chris had days now when he feared his company might not survive.

In early fall 2001, Chris flew to Washington, D.C., for a meeting of the board of directors of the Navy Memorial, one of the dozens of organizations he'd joined as booster-in-chief at Military.com. The Ritz-Carlton in Pentagon City was almost his second home, and as a navy reservist he was able to stay at the hotel for the government rate. He used the hotel almost like an office: it wasn't unusual for him to have two or three breakfast get-togethers, followed by a string of meetings.

But on this September morning, Chris went into D.C. for his board meeting. He arrived early, made his way to the Navy Memorial offices, and settled down for a cup of coffee in the break room as he waited. A muted television in the corner was tuned to CNN, and gradually Chris and some of the others in the room became aware of the breaking story out of New York. It seemed a plane had accidently crashed into one of the towers of the World Trade Center.

As they watched the live images of a second plane flying into the second tower, the horrible truth became apparent. Chris ran outside to Pennsylvania Avenue and stood with a retired admiral who served on the board with him. Hundreds of people ran by them, heading down the wide street in near-panic. It was like a bad Godzilla movie, Chris thought. Rumors were rampant that the White House, just a few blocks away, had been attacked. Chris realized that if he were going to die now, he would never know what hit him.

Three thousand miles away in San Francisco, Anne Dwane had seen the initial report about the first plane. She logged on to her computer, went on the Military.com Web site, and put out the first "breaking news alert" that the company had ever sent to its members, reporting that there had been some kind of attack on New York City. Then she rushed downtown to Military.com's office, fielding calls on the way from reporters who couldn't reach the Pentagon or other government sources, and who figured that her company might have some insight into what was happening.

"Do you know anything about the towers coming down?" one reporter asked Anne while she was still walking to the office. This was her first indication of the scope of the tragic event.

By now, Chris had made his way back across the Potomac River to the Ritz-Carlton. He saw smoke rising just a few blocks from the hotel and realized that the Pentagon had also been hit. Pulling out his Naval Reserve identification card, he ran to the building to see if there was anything he could do to help.

As he approached the Pentagon, it was instantly apparent that an airplane had smashed into the building very near where his old office had been. Someone told him that the death toll inside was now in the hundreds. Chris finally reached Anne on his cell phone, and she put him in touch with some of the reporters who had been calling. One of the television programs put Chris's cell phone report on live. A friend later told him that he was identified on-screen as "Christopher Michel, Terrorism Expert."

A few weeks after 9/11, Chris and Anne got an e-mail from a navy officer at the Pentagon. He had been working in the Naval Command Center, which had been destroyed when the highjacked airliner had hit. Almost all of his coworkers had been killed, but when he had read Anne's "breaking news alert" on Military.com, he had gotten up from his desk and walked down the hall to a room with a television to see what had happened. Were it not for Military.com, he wrote, he would have perished.

After 9/11, the entire country rallied around the armed forces, but the sudden change of focus didn't give a significant lift to Military.com. By November, the company's situation was dire. Mayfield was like the rest of VC firms in Silicon Valley and San Francisco—the economy had already turned sour, and after 9/11 their portfolio of once-promising investments seemed seriously at risk. In case after case, their companies were run by young management teams who had never been through a crisis before. Military.com, of course, was no different. At one board meeting, a director looked at the company's numbers and leaned back in his chair, his body language a clear indication of his pessimism.

"This company might have social value," he said. "But it has no commercial value. This is really a nonprofit."

A lot of companies were struggling that fall, and some of those that had advertised with Military.com stopped paying their bills. In some cases, Chris and Anne Dwane concluded, their advertisers had made a cynical calculation: they figured there was no reason to pay a company that wouldn't exist much longer.

The hole grew deeper. Chris felt horrible: he still believed in the idea behind the company, but he had enticed friends and colleagues to work with him, and now Military.com was on the brink of failure. They went through one harrowing round of layoffs and then another; morale plummeted. Walking to the office every morning, Chris and Anne saw the visible evidence of the mass extinctions in the Internet world. "For Rent" signs adorned the windows of office buildings nearby. The *Industry Standard*—the Internet-themed magazine that had proclaimed Military .com the winner of the "Air War" among armed-forces Web sites—was located just a few blocks away, and now its doors were closed as well.

The Military.com board thought that perhaps an experienced, "gray-haired" CEO might be able to turn things around, and Chris was open to the idea. He was willing to do anything to save the company, even replace himself. Chris and the board settled on a veteran executive and former Ohio State football player named Lad Burgin, who had come in as a crisis CEO and turned around a public medical device company a few years before. The only obvious drawback on Burgin's résumé was that he'd never been involved with an Internet company before.

One of their VC investors thanked Chris for handling the transition so graciously; the investor had been through similar disruptions with other companies, and the CEOs often put up a big fight. But that wasn't really in Chris's nature. In fact, when some of the Military.com employees heard the news about Chris's departure and told him he should insist on staying in place, he pushed back.

"Support the new guy," he told them. "Suck it up."

Chris stepped aside just before the end of 2001. He tried to stay away from the office as much as possible so that Burgin could work without interference. It was an odd, very difficult time. He and Anne were still dating; they'd started a company together, and now only she—not he—still worked there. He felt lost, and he began swimming every day just to keep his life organized and his spirits up. But at Military.com the problems only got bigger. There didn't seem to be much that Burgin or anyone could do in such a deteriorating environment. The Internet world was melting down, and the investors who had once been so bullish on the Web were now convinced that the whole thing had been little more than a fad.

Throughout his first two years at Military.com, Chris had stayed in touch with Abigail Johnson, the PR expert he'd met early on and unsuccessfully tried to hire. Abigail described herself as a "rah-rah American," and she believed that Chris's company had an important mission beyond simply making money. Chris could always count on her to give him advice as an objective observer. Over time he and Anne Dwane had forged a close friendship with Abigail and her husband, Steve, who was her business partner and had been an executive at several Silicon Valley companies.

Now Chris needed her counsel once again. In February 2002, he drove down to her office in San Carlos, California. They sat in her little conference room at a small round table, and Chris told her the whole sorry story of his resignation. "This is terrible," Chris said. "It's like witnessing a slow-motion train wreck. I just want to move to China so I don't have to watch the company die."

It was obvious to Abigail that Chris was as passionate as ever about his company. But though he still served on the board, he'd tied his own hands by stepping down. Burgin was in charge now, yet his effort to turn the company around was no more successful. Unless Chris took drastic action, Military.com would die.

Abigail believed in Chris and she believed in his company. She decided she would make it her business to persuade him to get off the sidelines. Military.com faced the same challenges that every struggling Internet company in the world was facing, but she was convinced that it still had value and could be successful.

"You need to get back in the game," she told him. "You need to go back to *your* company and run it. And you need to do it immediately." True, she added, he might not succeed. "But frankly, if anyone is going to shoot Old Yeller, it should be you."

MARLA: THE DINNER CLUB

In Washington, D.C., Marla Malcolm was watching the fallout from the dot-com bust and counting her blessings. What if she'd been successful and raised many millions of dollars in private equity investment or venture capital back in late 1999? She would likely have doubled down on her Web site strategy, and her company might well have flamed out by now. Instead, bluemercury had enjoyed positive cash flow throughout 2000, and the revenues generated by the retail stores far outpaced what came in through the Internet portal. She didn't think of bluemercury as an Internet company at all now; it was a chain of stores that happened to have a complementary Web site. And she was happy and proud that she had never appended the faddish ".com" suffix to the end of her company's name.

Her mentor Jon Ledecky, meanwhile, had negotiated his way out of E2Enet, the Internet incubator and investor that Marla had helped him found less than two years before. In March 2000, E2Enet had been acquired by U.S. Technologies, a company that had, of all things, spent the past decade contracting the labor of inmates at state and federal prisons. As a consequence, U.S. Technologies now owned a significant stake in bluemercury, and when Marla met with the company's CEO, Gregory Earls, over breakfast one morning, she came back shaken. She'd never meet with Earls alone again, she told Barry; he'd been rude and obnoxious, and he'd browbeaten her for supposedly doing a terrible job of running bluemercury.

Marla was sure that Earls didn't get it at all. She felt like a genius for having given up on the Internet strategy, mortgaged her home, and bought EFX. Moreover, it was clear to her in retrospect that cosmetics hadn't been that great a Web business to begin with. It now seemed obvious, but part of the fun for customers who wanted to purchase cosmetics was testing and trying products in the store; otherwise, how would they know what they were getting? Maybe eventually customers will become so accustomed to buying things online that an Internet business selling high-end beauty products might work, she thought. But in the short term, in the early 2000s, it wasn't a winning concept.

One by one, the better-funded, Internet-only competitors Marla had feared either shut their doors or were acquired and absorbed into larger companies. Even Sephora, the richly funded chain that had opened next door to the flagship bluemercury store in Georgetown, turned out to be a blessing in disguise, for two reasons. First, although Sephora and bluemercury targeted slightly different demographics, any customer visiting Sephora was likely to check out bluemercury as well. And second, having a Sephora store so close by had sharpened Marla's ability to compete. With a ready barometer right next door, she constantly compared her operation to what her competition did. It forced her to be innovative and helped her set bluemercury apart.

Marla and Barry spent a good part of 2000 trying to decide where they should open their third store. Barry thought they should strengthen their presence in metro D.C. by going across the Potomac River to an upscale neighborhood in Alexandria, Virginia. But Marla was convinced that they needed to spread to another region. Her view prevailed, and in early 2001 they opened their third bluemercury store in Barry's native Philadelphia, on Walnut Street near Rittenhouse Square. The new store was a success from the start, and by the end of the year it was on track to earn $1.2 million, while the two D.C. stores made $1.5 million and $770,000, respectively. In the meantime, Marla had continued to burnish her image—she was now seen as an up-and-coming face in the beauty industry, and she was often featured in women's magazines, local media, and national publications. In August 2001, she achieved an ego-boosting milestone when a front-page story in the *Wall Street Journal* about the increasing prevalence of the color blue in business highlighted Marla's experience.

Thanks in part to Ledecky, Marla had developed good relationships with some of the Washington region's most powerful financiers. She and Barry were careful to follow Ledecky's DROOM rule—Don't Run Out of Money—but they were also conservative in their approach to raising investment, since they didn't want to have to give up too much equity in return for funding. With the third bluemercury store up and running smoothly, they had a template in place, and now they wanted to expand further. The concept had worked in D.C. and Philadelphia; they could make it work elsewhere as well. But to pull it off, they would need more capital.

When Marla told her investor Ed Mathias of their plan to grow, he knew just where to take them. Mathias was a member of an elite Washington investment fund called Capital Investors. Comprised of virtually all of the top tech entrepreneurs in the D.C. area (including the cofounders of America Online, MicroStrategy, Nextel, and other local tech firms), the group met once a month for a great meal and a rigorous discussion of two potential investment opportunities each time. Washington was a small city from a business standpoint, but the members of Capital Investors were easily the biggest fish in the pond. And although the fund focused mostly on pure technology firms, Mathias wanted them to consider Marla and bluemercury.

Securing an invitation to pitch to the group required the support of the fund's president and manager, a twenty-eight-year-old former Morgan Stanley analyst named Andrew Sachs. Sachs, who in 1996 graduated from Georgetown University with both a bachelor's degree and an MBA, had landed at Capital Investments after a series of serendipitous meetings. He'd left Morgan Stanley to manage a new investment fund for his cousin, whose company had produced the musical *Rent* on Broadway. Through that experience, Sachs had met Mark Warner, a wealthy Virginian who had made his fortune in cellular phones and hoped to jump-start a film industry in Virginia. When Warner had initiated the effort to put together the Capital Investors fund, he reached out to Sachs to run it. (By the time Marla and Barry met Sachs in November 2001, Warner had just been elected governor of Virginia and was no longer active in the group.)

Sachs agreed to meet with Marla and Barry, and he was impressed by what they had built. So many of the entrepreneurs he talked to had little more than ambition and pie-in-the-sky predictions that their company was sure to be the next Yahoo! or AOL. But bluemercury was a real business already, and Marla could point to novel tangibles like revenue and an actual plan for growth. It didn't hurt that Marla was an attractive woman; she made a very different impression from the typical presenter, who was usually some nerdy young guy with a software package, or an older, more experienced professional who wanted to launch something in the tech world. Marla ran a conventional business, one that was not necessarily all that fascinating—but she herself might be.

Sachs met with Marla and Barry three or four times, and he did a bit of due diligence. The typical investment made by Capital Investors was about $250,000, so there was no need to research bluemercury as thoroughly as he would if he were looking at a company requiring, say, $10 million in funding. But Sachs liked what he saw. "This is like selling illegal drugs," he thought. "The business model is crazy. You pay $100 for a little tube of something and it goes down the drain every night."

Capital Investors, known in the D.C. press as "the dinner club," had funded about ten entrepreneurs by the time Marla and Barry showed up to pitch bluemercury in early December 2001 at The Caucus Room on Ninth Street NW. They waited outside a private room while the dozen or so members who showed up that night ate dinner.

After the meal, Sachs passed out copies of the short executive summary he'd prepared, and then Marla and Barry came in to give their fifteen-minute pitch. Marla briefly described the company and then spoke about the competition. There was only one national company in the same business—Sephora—and the chain had reached the United States only three years ago. Although bluemercury operated just three stores, its fourth was scheduled to open in a few months, and Marla told the investors that she was confident she could open more stores quickly if she and Barry could raise the necessary money. They had the formula worked out; they just needed the capital to put it in play.

Knowing that these investors weren't accustomed to investing in a traditional retail business, Marla emphasized some of the appealing aspects of the cosmetics industry. Their customers viewed their products as necessities, not pure luxuries. This wasn't the fashion business, she emphasized. There was no risk of getting stuck with bad or outdated inventory. If things didn't sell, the vendors took the products back.

Then Marla turned to the sales picture and showed a pleasing upward curve. Revenue in the smaller of the two D.C. stores had increased 29 percent from the year before, and sales in her larger D.C. store had almost doubled. Add the profitable new Philadelphia store to the mix and all the signs were pointing in the right direction.

Finally, Marla noted how many other companies in the beauty industry had been acquired by larger competitors—great news since every investor's ultimate goal was to put money into a company that would be bought out or go public. Companies like Kiehl's and Bliss Spa had been acquired by companies generating between four and ten times their annual revenue. The investors could do the math—at that rate, you could justify a current valuation of bluemercury at somewhere between $14 million and $34 million.

There were a few questions, then polite applause. Andrew escorted them back outside.

"I recuse myself," one of the investors said immediately after Marla and Barry left. "I'm in love."

They'd all been hugely impressed. Like many investors, they cared as much or more about the people behind a venture as the venture itself, and Marla presented a complete package. She was the right-brained idealist who knew what her clientele wanted because she was her own ideal customer. But she also had a driven, analytical mind-set. Even as she and Barry were asking for money to open their fourth store, the investors could see that Marla had a carefully considered plan to open the fifth, sixth, and seventh stores, all the way up to a dozen or more.

They also agreed that Marla might well have found the perfect complement in Barry. Although he had let Marla do most of the talking, he came across as an intense, driven zealot—a bull of a man who got things done no matter what. When one investor asked Sachs what he thought of Barry, Sachs replied, "Can you imagine being the contractor who had to finish work on a new store, with that guy breathing down your neck?"

It also helped that Ed Mathias had introduced them to Capital Fund in the first place. It would be hard for the group to vote against funding a company in which one of their own had already invested his money.

A few minutes after Marla and Barry left the private dining room,

Sachs stepped outside. The group had voted to fund. Though it would take several weeks to work out the details, they would have the money they needed to open more stores—and an entrée to more money when it was time to expand again. In a little over two years, Marla had gone from writing a business plan based on entirely the wrong idea to running a company with a real shot at greatness.

By now Marla and Barry had spent thousands of hours together, and they were no longer just business partners. Later, Barry liked to recall a dramatic moment not long after the Capital Investors pitch, when he and Marla were having dinner at the swanky Palm restaurant in Washington. He could no longer remember whether they were celebrating the opening of one of their stores or some other milestone, but he did recall stopping the conversation with a blunt announcement.

"Look," he remembered saying. "I gave up all this stuff—my career and my business and my life. And it's not just because I like bluemercury. It's because I love you. I love you—you know what I mean? I want to marry you. I'm done."

Marla would laugh when she heard Barry tell that story. For her part, she remembered no big out-of-the-blue moment. But once they became romantically involved, they moved as fast in love as they did in everything else. They got married in October 2002 in a ceremony on the roof of the Hay Adams Hotel in Washington. As it happened, the hotel stood next door to the building where Marla had worked for Jon Ledecky when she and Barry first met.

At the reception, Barry's sister declared that Marla and Barry must have been meant to be together from the beginning. After all, she pointed out, their company's name incorporated both of their initials. Marla Malcolm; Barry Beck; the M and the B—bluemercury.

MARC: THE DECISION

Eleven days after 9/11, Marc Cenedella and Steve Perricone threw one of their biggest parties ever.

Marc had witnessed the first jet that hit the World Trade Center flying overhead. He'd been walking to work at the time, cutting through Union Square Park, when he heard a huge roar and looked up to see the plane hurtling south. When he arrived at the office, he'd been immediately called into a meeting, at which it was decided to send everyone home, but not without confirming that all their employees had a way out of the city or a place to stay. HotJobs had a lot of young employees—kids, really, just out of college—so the company felt a special responsibility to ensure that everyone was okay. When they finally closed the office, Marc walked back to his apartment and found that he and Steve had responded identically: in light of a horrific act of terrorism, and given the danger of civil unrest and a possible power failure, they'd both made it their first priority to visit several ATMs. Each walked in the door with a few thousand dollars in cash and four one-gallon jugs of water.

The tragedy had a profound effect on everyone's attitude toward life and work, but in the days that followed the dominant feeling in the HotJobs headquarters was one of defiance—no one wanted to let nineteen despicable human beings achieve their ultimate goal of seriously disrupting the American economy. Meanwhile, Marc's thirty-first birthday happened to fall on the weekend after the attacks, and Marc and Steve had been planning to throw a big bash. They postponed the gathering for a week, scrapped the idea of a birthday party, and called it their I Love New York More Than Ever Party. To Marc and Steve, the only way to respond to such a barbaric act was to throw it back in their faces, and thus to show that they hadn't been successful in instilling anything other than determination in New Yorkers.

By now, Marc had a lot of great friends and colleagues at HotJobs. He and Alex Douzet got along very well, and Dave Carvajal had finally left Online Retail Partners and rejoined the firm. Andrew Koch had graduated from Brown and he was back as well. Although Andrew didn't report to Marc anymore, Marc rekindled their Senpai-Kohai relationship. During Andrew's first few months as a full-time employee, Marc arranged for Andrew to rotate through several different departments—product development, customer service, account management—so as to broaden his horizons and help him get a feel for how the entire company worked.

You need to learn finance, Marc told him, and he bought Andrew a copy of *Analysis for Financial Management*, a textbook that had been written by the father of one of Marc's college roommates. He immediately started assigning Andrew weekly problem sets from the book.

That fall, Marc was still working primarily on the deal that would allow Monster to acquire HotJobs. It was a frustrating series of negotiations, and it didn't help that most HotJobs employees weren't all that excited about the idea of being acquired by a company they considered their archrival—the supervillain in the online recruiting world. By late 2001, the deal still hadn't closed.

Then, midway through December, a new suitor suddenly appeared. The CEO of Yahoo! faxed an unsolicited letter to the new CEO of HotJobs, offering to step in front of Monster and buy the company for $436 million. (Monster had offered an all-stock deal that had been valued at $460 million back in June, but the company's stock had fallen over the past few months and the bid was now worth considerably less.) The following Sunday evening, the top executives of both companies met with their investment bankers at Rockefeller Center in a room facing north high above Central Park. On the HotJobs side of the deal, Marc was playing a crucial role, and he brought Andrew Koch with him as a way to further his horizon-broadening plan for his young friend.

Andrew looked around the room. He saw Marc, the CEOs of both companies, a few other top executives from Yahoo!, several investment bankers, and he realized that with the exception of a couple of young bankers he was by far the most junior person there. But, unlike the others, he hadn't been up all night preparing pitch books, nor did he spend the meeting scurrying around, getting coffee. His only task was to watch, listen, and learn.

The next day, the accountants and IT people from both companies met to see how well their financial and internal technology systems would match up. All the lights were green, so later that week HotJobs went back to Monster and gave them seventy-two hours to beat Yahoo!'s bid.

"We do not see a financial or strategic rationale for modifying our bid," was the official reply from Monster. The deal with Yahoo! was done. By February 2002, the lawyers and bankers signed off, and now HotJobs was part of a giant company.

For Marc, the acquisition came as a huge relief, but it was followed almost immediately by an equally large letdown. Some of his closest colleagues left Hotjobs to pursue new opportunities. Alex Douzet left to get his MBA. Dave Carvajal wanted to leave as well; he had decided he wanted to work in real estate. Only Andrew Koch planned to remain at the company, at least for the time being. Almost overnight, HotJobs seemed to lose its entrepreneurial spirit—no surprise, perhaps, given that it was now a relatively small piece of a conglomerate that was head-quartered three thousand miles away. Marc tried to put a good face on all the changes, but privately he was deeply discouraged.

He disliked the more bureaucratic new regime—he was reminded of that recruiter from GE Capital who came to HBS and asked him to fill out a ten-page form. Maybe it's time, he thought. He'd been resisting the notion for years, but he was beginning to believe it was finally time to start his own company. At the very least, it was time to leave HotJobs.

Marc negotiated a severance package that would allow him to leave the company and start over somewhere else. His last day was April 19, 2002, and his last official act was to send an impassioned 583-word e-mail to everyone at HotJobs. He kept every shred of his discontent to him-self; instead he thanked everyone for the opportunity to work with them over the preceding two years, and told them how proud he was of what they'd accomplished.

After he hit the send button, Marc walked out of the HotJobs office for the last time. He had no specific plan for his future. His first inclina-tion was to try to land a job as a CEO or high-level executive at another company that he thought he could kickstart into a higher gear. He'd met an executive running something called the Center for American Jobs, which focused on helping companies recruit semiskilled and unskilled workers via telephone. By advertising "1-800-TRUCKERJOBS" or "1-800-NOW-HIRING," for example, the organization could quickly categorize every applicant.

Do you have your Class A License? Press one for yes; two for no.

How many years of experience do you have?

Do you have any felony convictions? Press one for yes; two for no.

Marc was tempted to jump on board, but then he had another idea. At the time, the highest-traffic Web site focusing on tech jobs was Dice .com, and Marc spent several weeks trying to put together an investment group to buy them out. But the deal fell apart.

After nearly a year of intense work on the HotJobs merger, Marc was burned out. He explored the streets and restaurants of New York for another month or so, and met Andrew Koch for drinks at the Half King Bar on Twenty-third Street. Andrew noticed that Marc was a bit more emotional than usual. He also seemed all but certain that he had to start a company of his own.

"I don't know where and I don't know when," he told Andrew, "but you and I will be working together again."

As spring turned to summer, Marc decided to return to another passion—travel. Leaving New York behind, he took off, with a plan to be on the road for six months and see as much of the world as he could.

CHAPTER 10

YOU CAN'T DO IT ALONE

Change creates unprecedented opportunity. But to take full advantage of those opportunities, focus on the team. Teams win.

—JOHN DOERR

THE KEY TO FINDING KEY PEOPLE

They wanted to be entrepreneurs, and even before they had any real plan or knew what business they wanted to enter, it was important for Marla, Chris, and Marc to surround themselves with the right people. By this point in our story, Marla and Chris had already made and leveraged relationships that were crucial to their success. Meanwhile, Marc— although he didn't know it yet—had already developed relationships with most of the key people who would help him make his dream a reality.

Virtually all of the highly successful entrepreneurs I got to know while researching this book leaned heavily on what academics call "social capital" to build their businesses. First, they developed networks that would help them to identify and pursue opportunity. Second, they did a remarkably good job of recognizing their own personal strengths and weaknesses, which led them to put together startup teams that complemented their talents and experience. Could Marla have started bluemercury without Barry Beck? Could Chris have launched Military .com without Anne Dwane? I don't think so. Like many other experiences in life, successful entrepreneurship teaches us that you can't do it alone.

AN ACCIDENTAL NETWORK (ON PURPOSE)

"Somehow I always attach myself to the people that get me to the next step," Marla Malcolm told me one day. "It's different from networking. I hate networking. Networking to me means going to these big events and meeting a lot of different people. Barry always says, 'Oh, you're so good at networking.' But the truth is I can't stand it."

You may well feel the same way. Networking, as Marla uses the word, can seem awkward and insincere. Even so, she realizes that she "somehow" built a top-tier network. In my view, her natural introversion actually helps her to build relationships. Perhaps because she's never glib or chatty, Marla doesn't come across as a superficial or obviously ambitious person who is interested in others only for what they can do for her. But still, with foresight and concerted effort, she had a knack for putting herself in the right places and developing relationships with the people she found interesting.

Here's an early example. Back in 1993, on her first day at McKinsey & Co., Marla was the only new business analyst in the San Francisco office with the gumption to introduce herself to the forty-one-year-old senior partner, an intimidating man named Bill Meehan. While researching this book a decade and a half later, I sought out Meehan and others who had worked at McKinsey with Marla. Meehan told me he'd lost touch with her since she left for HBS, and he hadn't known that she had gone on to start a company until I contacted him. But he distinctly remembered meeting her that first day.

"She didn't have a commanding physical presence," Meehan recalled. "But you think, 'wow,' this is a completely natural person, not pushy, not arrogant. It's what you wish your kids would do. It's how to distinguish yourself in ways that are attractive."

In fact, Meehan told me he still tells "The Marla Story" in speeches. The anecdote wasn't inherently dramatic, and Meehan said he couldn't remember what they'd talked about during that first conversation. But he still uses that story as an example of how young businesspeople can push past their boundaries, make contacts, and build relationships.

"I seem to find people that lead me to the next level," Marla explained in another conversation. "I remember in high school, my math teacher,

Mrs. Kubicek—I used to hang out with her and have coffee in between class, and she pushed me along. I think she helped me become comfortable with the idea of being friends with older people. So in high school and college, I sought out advisers. I had three in particular that were helpful to me. It was a kind of mentoring, even if it wasn't the sort of thing where you call them for advice on everything."

She continued: "Another great example is Ed Mathias. I got to know him when I worked at U.S. Office Products that one summer. And then when I was looking for jobs during my second year at HBS, I came down to D.C. and met with him. I spent a day in his office reading business plans. I got to know him without having any certain end in mind, but he was very helpful later."

Helpful indeed—he put up part of the seed money for bluemercury and later introduced Marla and Barry to other investors. The key point, though, is that Marla got to know him before she was looking for any particular favor or help. They had a relationship based on respect, and he was therefore more likely to help her when she later needed it.

If you ask Chris Michel how and why he became successful as an entrepreneur, don't expect him to list his best personality traits or analyze his business. Instead, he'll talk about serendipity, about how he met the right people at the right moments in his life, and they helped him to make good choices. People like Anne Dwane and HBS's Ed Zschau are on this list, along with others you'll get to know in the coming pages. And Chris often singled out Abigail Johnson, especially because of the advice she gave him in the "Old Yeller" conversation.

But even before Chris met Anne and the others, he had displayed a knack for getting to know the interesting people around him. When he became an admiral's aide in the navy, for instance, he made it his first job to get to know everyone. And at HBS, once he got over his initial fear of academic failure, he went out of his way to introduce himself to unusually interesting people. As just one example, he developed good relationships with the people who ran MIT's design lab, just because he was fascinated by what they did. That led, in part, to the field study he, Anne Dwane, and Tom Goundry did for Initio Pharmaceuticals.

Marc Cenedella displayed the same ability to meet and get to know a wide variety of people. Years later, people in Marc's class at HBS remembered him as Section A's organizer and friend to all. Intentionally or not, he was building a network, but I'm quite certain that a genuine interest in people—not a mercenary motive—was the most fundamental driver of his social behavior. Yes, he did eventually come to understand that the friends he ate dinner with, went to parties with, and went to class with could be the core of an important business network, but that came later. In the beginning, he just wanted to spend time around people he enjoyed. And after HBS, Marc showed a talent for managing his exits well. Whenever he left a company, he always tried to do it gracefully and leave the best possible final impression. Remember how he put in two hard weeks at Riverside after he'd already given his notice? And when he left HotJobs, he sent everyone a long, inspiring e-mail, one that a number of people remembered years later.

All of these examples suggest the importance of getting to know lots of interesting people before you know how they could ever help you. In fact, it's more than likely that in the end you'll ask only a small percentage of the people you know for help. But if you have a sincere affinity for interesting people, that hardly matters, since the pleasure of getting to know them is an end in itself.

That said, it's also worth pointing out that our highly successful entrepreneurs never hesitated to introduce themselves to people who might prove useful or to leverage well-developed contacts when they had a specific end in mind. An especially good example of this boldness is Marla Malcolm's determined effort to land a job at U.S. Office Products. This is a lesson for any of us who has ever casually applied for a job and grown discouraged after not hearing back, or who chose a career path based on what we had been told was reasonable, rather than what truly inspired us. While her classmates waited for the top employers of the day to visit the HBS campus, Marla buried herself in the library, trying to identify the most interesting people in the business world and then, once she'd done so, reaching out to them.

"I went at it every different which way," she told me. "John Quelch was on the board of U.S. Office Products, and he was a professor at Harvard Business School. He won't remember the meeting—I met with him only once—but he put in a good word for me with Jon Ledecky. And I cold-called Jon Ledecky numerous times and sent my résumé to just about everyone at USOP. I called everybody on the senior team—people like Don Platt, the CFO, and Mark Director, his chief legal counsel. I just kept calling until I got that job. And that job changed my life."

RECRUITING THE RIGHT TEAM

Time and again, the highly successful entrepreneurs I got to know told me that success requires a team. At the founding stages, it usually consists of two or three people. Generally, that means making sure you have what I think of as a Big Idea Person and a Get Stuff Done Person. Ideally, of course, a founder excels in both of these roles. But very few of us do, and successful founders are honest about what areas they need help in.

"The truth is, there's always a second person," Barry Beck told me in one conversation. "Steve Wozniak and Steve Jobs. Bill Gates and Paul Allen. It's very, very rare that one guy ever brings it all to the party. Even when you think that's the case—the truth is it's not. You look at any successful entrepreneur and there's always someone."

"Marla never would have gone out on her own without me," he said. "I still feel a little guilty about pushing Marla so hard to leave Jon Ledecky behind. Early on, I said to her, 'Why are you still working for Jon? Leave.' But that opened a whole new world to her."

Barry also clearly understood their different roles. Marla's job was to be the company's front person and focus on the big picture. His job was to get things done behind the scenes and cut deals.

As we'll soon see, Marc Cenedella presents a somewhat different picture, in that he was without question the driving force behind the venture he eventually started. Marc exhibits no false modesty on this point—he is identified as the venture's founder on its Web site, while his cofounders are listed as . . . well, as cofounders. But during the course of my research, he reminded me again and again to focus on his cofounders' contributions.

In one early conversation, I told him—probably too flippantly in retrospect—that I was having a hard time figuring out who was "Robin" to his "Batman." Marc gently chided me for using the metaphor—he didn't buy the idea that he or anyone in his story was "Batman"—and he then insisted on the importance of understanding the roles played by people like Alex Douzet and Andrew Koch in launching the company you'll be reading about over the next few chapters.

Chris Michel also went out of his way to talk about the contributions made by others to the success of Military.com. You might presume that a CEO or founder might push some of the credit to his cofounders out of self-deprecation or for comity's sake. But Chris was very specific, and his stories rang true. He needed someone like Brad Clark to complement him; even more, he said, he needed Anne Dwane.

"There is no way that Military.com would be what it is today without Anne," Chris said. "She was not the product person, but she was the execution powerhouse.

"Remember," he continued, "five other people had the same friggin' idea. And *Army Times* was definitely better positioned than anyone. So I think it's all about the people, and their ability to execute."

In 1997, HBS professor Bill Sahlman wrote a now-oft-quoted article in the *Harvard Business Review* called "How to Write a Great Business Plan." Given the article's title, it's perhaps surprising that Sahlman made a point of minimizing the importance of business plans; their effect on the prospects of any new venture's likelihood of success, he wrote, rated about a 2 on a scale of 1 to 10. Instead, he recommended focusing on the "interdependent factors critical to every new venture." First among these factors, he said, were "the men and women starting the venture, as well as the outside parties providing key services or important resources for it, such as its lawyers, accountants, and suppliers."

It's hard to predict the amount of revenue (never mind profit) that will be generated by any startup. Appropriately, investors assume that the financials included in the business plans written by most founders are wildly optimistic. But in a way, that doesn't matter. By Sahlman's estimate, the typical venture capital firm receives two thousand business plans a year. Reading all of them thoroughly would take up a great deal of the firm's time, and it wouldn't be sensible to do so in any case.

But what does make sense is to go right to the section on the venture's executive team.

I heard variations on this point over and over. "I invest in people, not ideas," says HBS alumnus Arthur Rock, for whom the entrepreneurship center at HBS is named. "Good people, if they're wrong about the product, they'll make a switch."

Another partner at a top-tier venture capital firm told me, "What makes a successful company? The strength of the management team. It's very important. We seek out entrepreneurs who are able to hire other outstanding people. We look for a founder/CEO who has exceptionally high intellectual horsepower, who understands the nature of competition and what will be required to win—for someone who is going to win. We look at all ingredients—the size, the business model, the competition. But 50 to 75 percent is the caliber of the people."

If you're fortunate enough to attend HBS, you'll get an excellent education, and the confidence-building experience of studying two hundred cases will have you believing, almost by osmosis, that you can handle exactly the kinds of challenges our protagonists faced. When you graduate, you'll have the equivalent of a "certified smart guy stamp of approval" on your résumé. But you'll also receive what every HBS alumnus told me was a huge bonus: access to the HBS network.

At first I couldn't quite grasp how this worked. My overactive imagination envisioned a twenty-first-century version of a smoke-filled room where the Powers that Be in Business decided who to support and promote, who to invite into their world. Of course, that's a pretty cynical view, nor is it accurate. But if you scale back the melodramatic flourishes, the image does contain a kernel of truth. HBS goes out of its way, for example, to link up new graduates with accomplished alumni, who in turn agree to serve as official mentors to them.

But what I didn't originally understand was the importance of a different opportunity. At HBS, the students actively network with one another, and this is at least as important as the opportunity to network with professors or other potential mentors.

This student-to-student networking is strongly encouraged by HBS.

The school suggests that students join study groups, for example, and I heard of a number of companies that were later started by founders who'd been in these study groups together. Students can also go to the HBS Web site and find a clearinghouse for anyone who wants to seek out other students eager to take part in the annual HBS Business Plan competition—students can even categorize themselves as "no idea, looking for idea," or "have idea, looking for team." But the emphasis on networking at HBS is most evident in the way the school structures the student body. Each MBA candidate is assigned to an eighty-member section, and everyone in the section goes through the entire first-year curriculum together. As the official HBS Web site puts it:

> Students quickly discover that the section experience gets them fully engaged during their first year at HBS and beyond, helping to forge lasting friendships and invaluable contacts for life. In effect, the section becomes a safe and intimate haven where, under the encouragement of mutual support, students can apply newly acquired skills and leadership abilities. It's one of the most formative and defining experiences at HBS.

As its approach to the importance of networking suggests, the school takes an almost proprietary interest in its students. There's no better illustration of this attitude than an apocryphal story about an HBS student who gets into an argument with a member of the school's administration. As the debate grows heated, the student exclaims, "Why are you treating me like this? I'm the customer!" Shaking his head, the administrator soberly replies, "No you're not. You're the product."

In fact, HBS's operating philosophy bears some resemblance to the business strategy that became known as qualified lead development. Just as Military.com generated revenue in its early years by specializing in deals such as the one the company negotiated with the *Wall Street Journal*, HBS presents a "package" of good leads to the business world. Investment banks, consulting firms, and corporations all look to HBS to provide them with first-rate employees. Prospective students know this, of course, which is a primary reason why it's so difficult to win admission to the school. In a way, then, HBS's ability to develop qualified leads is its most valuable asset.

As Stig Leschly pointed out to me, almost everything HBS does is designed to prepare students to pursue opportunities. Unlike many academic institutions, the school has little interest in ranking them one against the other. Virtually nobody flunks out of HBS (Chris Michel's original fears notwithstanding). Beyond that, Leschly said, "recruiters are not allowed to ask for grades. You're not allowed on campus if you ask students their GPA. Everything is pass/fail. You've got the best, most elite institution in the country, and we're basically acknowledging that we can't grade these people. And how do we decide who to admit? Not based on grades. We didn't even require the GMAT until *U.S. News & World Report* started counting it. What's really going on is that we look at the recommendations of people who work with our applicants."

HBS looks for people with character, intelligence, leadership ability, and ambition. And after having brought them all together, sometimes the best thing HBS or any other institution can do is step out of the way.

HOW BIG A TEAM DO YOU NEED
(AND HOW DO YOU FIND THE TEAM MEMBERS)?

Some of the academic research in the area of entrepreneurial team building seems devoted to proving, as empirically as possible, what might otherwise be known as common sense. For instance, it doesn't come as a shock to learn that most entrepreneurs draw on "resources available to people through their social connections."

Noam Wasserman explained, "In terms of learning to network, there is a bunch of research done on social capital . . . but almost all of it is focused on small businesses. In my research, I focus on the high-potential venture types, as opposed to the mom-and-pop shops and the corner groceries and cleaners."

Why, I asked Wasserman, is there a dearth of research on how to assemble a top-flight team—especially since investors, entrepreneurs, and academics all seem to agree that building a great team is perhaps the most crucial part of any business plan?

"There is a little bit of early research," Wasserman replied. "I've seen a couple of working papers that try to pull apart the question of what is a good size of a startup team. And there's some academic research that looks at whether or not it's good to have a bigger founding team. What's clear, though, is that founding teams with two or three people tend to be more stable."

As it happens, several startups that grew out of the HBS classes of the late 1990s had four, five, or a half dozen or more cofounders. Most of them failed. Since all the founders of these ventures had MBAs and were roughly the same age, they often didn't get along and had real trouble dividing the work and responsibility. Everyone thought he or she should be calling the shots. But Wasserman also told me that solo founders rarely succeed, either. In fact, he directed me to a 2006 Web article by Paul Graham of YCombinator entitled "The 18 Mistakes that Kill Startups." Number one on the list was "single founder."

But of course it's not just a matter of knowing how many people should be on a venture's founding team—much more difficult is meeting and recruiting the people you need to be successful. Especially if you haven't attended an elite business school, it's not easy to develop robust business networks like the ones comprised of HBS alumni. So what can you do?

I asked Marc Cenedella how he would answer this question, and here's what he said. "The number one rule is to be passionate about something. Your passion is your best means of meeting people. There's so little of it in the world, and people are drawn to the excitement of somebody who is really alive, really on fire about something. Everything else follows."

Pretty good advice, yes? And here's some more.

Use Your Existing Networks. Did you go to college or graduate school? Are you a member of a church group? Do you have family and friends you can lean on? Are there organized networking events in your area? Remember, the key isn't just to get to know people; it's to get to know interesting people. In the same way that it's important to take an inventory of your own interests when trying to come up with an idea for a startup, when you're building a network it's a good idea to think about who you find interesting. And be both patient and persistent. When budding writers ask me for advice on how to find an agent or a publisher, I've learned to say that you have to get through at least one hundred no's before you're likely to hear yes. If you are willing to send a hundred manuscripts, you're obviously serious about getting in the game for the long run and you have a shot at succeeding. It's the same thing in entrepreneurship and building a network.

Decide where you want to work. If you want to start a tech firm in Silicon Valley, move to Silicon Valley. If you want to start a restaurant chain, get a job working in restaurants. Whatever interests you, go and do it, or get as close to it as you possibly can. Not only will you learn a lot about a particular business or industry, you will also increase your chances of meeting your future cofounders and team members. And if you've worked with someone before, there's a much better chance that you'll know whether he or she is a likely business partner or employee.

Use Technology. It's much easier to build a network now than it was even a few years ago. A good example, in fact, is this book. I didn't go to Harvard Business School, nor did I know any HBS professors or alumni at the start of this project. So I had no choice but to do a lot of cold calling. After committing myself to the idea, my first step was to use Facebook, LinkedIn, and other online networks to find late 1990s HBS graduates. I ran Google searches for phrases like "graduated from Harvard Business School in 1998," and "earned her MBA at Harvard." I began to collect profiles and contact information for a number of HBS graduates. When I contacted them directly, not everyone wanted to help, but enough did. And when several people agreed to put me in touch with their classmates and friends, my research network began to come together. It didn't happen overnight, and I encountered a lot of dead ends. But eventually I found Marla, Chris, and Marc, and I built the network I needed. And I had a lot of fun in the process.

Don't waste time building useless networks. Subscribe to a few Internet groups or attend a few formal networking events, and you'll encounter a lot of people for whom networking seems to have become an end in itself. If you spend any time at all on LinkedIn, Facebook, or other social networking sites, you'll come across hordes of people who apparently collect contacts and friends just so they can prove that they're tremendously important and popular. But building a good network isn't about quantity; it's about quality. You might have a network of about a dozen people, but if each one of those people cares about helping you and can make a real contribution as you become serious about starting a new business, that's a lot more valuable than having several thousand friends on Facebook.

The good news, then, is that you don't need to go to HBS or another prestigious business school to meet and get to know the people who will someday help you pursue your entrepreneurial dream. It's worth keeping in mind that a majority of the people on the *Forbes* magazine list of the four hundred richest Americans who created their own wealth either went to state universities and lesser-known colleges or dropped out of college before graduating. Think Bill Gates (Harvard dropout), Steve Jobs (Reed College dropout), Larry Ellison (University of Chicago dropout), Michael Dell (University of Texas dropout), and Warren Buffett (who attended University of Nebraska as an undergraduate—although he did later go to Columbia Business School). Without the help of an institution like HBS, they met a wide range of smart and interesting people, built a great network, and succeeded at the very highest level. There is no reason why you can't do the same thing.

THE NEXT RULE

The truth is that whether you draw on a network of hundreds of people or just a few dozen key colleagues to build your team and launch your own company, in the end it'll be your name on the door. All of those people you recruit? At some point—probably at a lot of points—they'll be looking to you for leadership, direction, and inspiration. It's your company, and in the end you bear the ultimate responsibility for not only launching it, but growing it into a thriving, successful business.

Which is why the entrepreneurial life can sometimes be a lonely one. No matter how many good people you've recruited, no matter how strong your team, it's ultimately your baby and so you carry the heaviest burden. You have to be prepared for that, and you have to steel yourself against the uninformed naysayers—some of them well intentioned, some not—who will try to break your spirit, bring you down, or just give you flat-out bad advice.

It's your dream, and finally it's up to you to make it happen. As the successful entrepreneurs I interviewed made so clear, sometimes there's simply no other choice. You must do it alone.

CHAPTER 11

To be a champ you have to believe in yourself when nobody else will.

—SUGAR RAY ROBINSON

CHRIS: THE REBOOT

Chris Michel kept thinking about Old Yeller. Changing CEOs at Military .com hadn't solved the company's problems, and their backers now seemed on the verge of writing off their investment as a loss. Chris and his original booster within Mayfield, Mike Levinthal, talked often about what a shame it all was. Maybe, they wondered, it might be possible to raise a comparatively small amount of money and buy the whole thing back. Levinthal couldn't be involved in such a plan—given his position at Mayfield, it would be a clear conflict of interest—but he got Chris thinking. Was there a company out there willing to buy Military.com for a dollar, someone with deep-enough pockets just to keep the venture going for a while? At least his remaining employees wouldn't lose their jobs, and they'd have a chance to guide the company to safe harbor. It also might be the only way to save the company.

In February 2002, after thinking about this approach for a few days, Chris set up a conference call with Military.com's board of directors. Summoning all of his courage, he announced that he planned to return as CEO. He didn't ask permission, although he needed their approval;

he simply told them that this is what he wanted. By then, the venture was floundering to the point that the board could hardly object. Even Lad Burgin was more than willing to step aside—he'd come aboard hoping to lead a cutting-edge Internet company and instead he'd spent his time laying people off.

Military.com had burned through more than $30 million since late 1999, and by the time of Chris's return the company was down to its last $50,000—not even enough money to pay that month's expenses. With no prospect of raising any additional capital, Chris initiated another aggressive schedule of layoffs, the company's third in as many years. Steve Echikson departed, first to travel the world and then to join another startup. Brad Clark left as well, heading off to get married and find another opportunity. Chris and Anne Dwane were still romantically involved, and the crisis tested their personal and professional partnership as never before. Within weeks of Chris's return, they had winnowed the staff to fewer than a dozen people.

To outsiders and Military.com members, however, the company didn't miss a beat. The Web site functioned as well as ever. When one of Chris's former navy commanders, Anthony Winns, stopped by on his way through San Francisco after being selected for promotion to admiral, he was amazed at how busy their tiny offices seemed. Another old friend, named Ernie Phillips—he had been Chris's sponsor in the navy and was now a student at the Naval Postgraduate Institute in Monterey—took Chris out to dinner around this time. Phillips walked away from the evening with no inkling of Chris's difficulties; in fact, his friend seemed not to have a care in the world.

Fortunately for Chris, however, he could let his guard down and express some of the anxiety he felt with a small number of people, Anne first among them. Several other HBS classmates were also running Internet startups in the Bay Area, and most of them were in trouble, too. From time to time, Chris would run into his section mate Amar Singh, he of the morning salutes and the educational software startup that was featured in *Time*. Singh's company had been through some very rough times as well; fortunately, he and his partners were eventually able to sell the firm. But the sale was a "single," Singh told Chris, not a home run.

Recently, Chris had become particularly close to another fellow

HBS alumnus, named James Currier. They had met only once during their time at Harvard, and Chris didn't even recall that encounter. James had been a member of Section H in the class of 1999, and in January 1998 Chris had been one of a handful of "Old H" members who came by to welcome and warn them.

Inspired by their HBS classmates' reaction to the Myers-Briggs test, James and a cofounder named Rick Marini had created eMode, a company that designed personality tests and Internet games. They'd raised $9 million in venture capital within months of graduating—and blown through almost everything before finally figuring out how to attract users and make money. At the nadir, James had been so anxious that he barely slept four hours a night—or only as long as the dose of Nyquil he'd take to knock himself out would last.

Now, one of Chris's investors reintroduced them. James and Chris were physical opposites. Where Chris seemed to have seamlessly traded his navy uniform for a business uniform, with a miniature of the navy "Wings of Gold" pinned on the lapel of his sports coat, James usually had longish hair and several days' growth of beard. He wore T-shirts and slacks. He was married with young kids, and even when eMode began to make money he still didn't get much sleep while trying to raise a growing family.

Despite their differences, the two became great friends. Chris found James wonderfully straightforward and authentic; he never had a hidden agenda. And James knew how hard and lonely it was to run a company that was in trouble; he had even offered to step aside as CEO when he felt that his leadership might be causing eMode to fail. It didn't take long for Chris to realize that it would benefit them both to have a true colleague—he relished the prospect of talking with someone who was going through similar ups and downs, and with whom he could be completely honest.

Chris and James worked on separate islands, each trying to find enough coconuts to live. They shared the dream of becoming successful entrepreneurs, and the feeling of immense responsibility for all the money they'd raised and all the employees they'd recruited to the cause. But despite their friendship, they both understood that in the end they were alone. Only Chris and James could improve their companies' fortunes and lead them to sustained growth and profitability.

Eight years had passed since Chris's old P-3 Orion had nearly crashed over the Atlantic Ocean. Now he felt like the pilot that day, doing everything he could to find a safe place to land and keep the company from crashing. Military.com had closed its office in the nation's capital to cut costs, but Chris once again made a trip to Washington. A year before he'd wanted to buy Gannett's military publications; now the combat boot was on the other foot and he was trying to convince Gannett to acquire Military.com. He also arranged to meet with Ross Perot, in the hope that the billionaire who had tried to launch the unsuccessful militaryhub three years before might prove willing to buy his company. And he pitched the business to one of the top executives at Monster Worldwide. But no one was interested in buying.

By the end of 2002, Chris had stabilized the company by radically cutting costs, but it was barely hanging on. Chris, Anne, and their small group of employees now held meetings in a tiny conference room—the entire staff was able to fit in a room that would have been one person's office just a few months before. They charted out the flameout date on a whiteboard, counting down to the day when they would be completely out of cash. They talked about orderly shutdowns, consulted with bankruptcy lawyers, and tried not to think about how close they were to the edge.

Then, they had yet another problem. Among Military.com's investors was the television network A&E. Chris had especially coveted the deal, because A&E owned the History Channel, which was popular with the kinds of people who would be interested in an armed-forces-themed Web site. But A&E's investment had been structured as a convertible debenture, a type of corporate bond that gave A&E the right to convert its investment into Military.com stock in the future—or, alternatively, into a loan that Military.com would have to repay. With the company's future in doubt, A&E chose the latter option, but Military.com simply didn't have the money to cover the loan.

Chris was both embarrassed and frustrated. Although A&E had the legal right to call in its note, in Chris's view they were violating the unofficial rules of Silicon Valley. Chris argued his case as best as he could; he even suggested that if A&E pulled the plug on Military.com it would be like publicly declaring that they didn't support the men and women of the armed forces. Much to Chris's relief, he was ultimately able to negotiate a repayment plan. For the moment, he'd saved Military.com from collapse, but each month they now had to come up with a check for A&E, in addition to meeting all their other obligations. The company was so close to the edge that Chris felt like every decision, no matter how small, could make the difference between life or death.

In early 2003, the American economy improved a bit, and the United States prepared to invade Iraq—two factors that combined to improve the fortunes of any company that catered to the American military. Finally, Military.com started making a little money. And though the improving economy did put a breeze at their backs, Chris knew that what had really made the difference was the creative thinking of Anne Dwane.

In their earliest research, before they even raised enough money to start Military.com, Anne and Chris had learned that only a small portion of the military veterans who were eligible to receive college tuition under the GI Bill actually used their benefits. This was surprising, in part because the military had made education benefits a cornerstone of its recruitment campaigns in the 1980s and 1990s. Furthermore, soldiers and sailors had to give up part of their paychecks each month while they were in the service in order to take advantage of the benefit later.

The failure to use the benefit was a loss for the veterans, of course. But as Anne pointed out, it was also a loss for the colleges that those veterans might otherwise have attended. She saw an underserved market: qualified lead development for the education industry.

Imagine, she said to Chris: You're the head of admissions at a college or vocational school and you're trying to fill your classes. What if you could find a steady stream of students who were capable of doing the course work, who would add value to your student body, and whose tuition would be paid by the federal government? Anne proposed that Military .com offer educational institutions a simple deal. First, the company would add a check box to its registration form and its communications with its members, asking if they wanted to hear from "military-friendly colleges." Next, Military.com would sell the contact information they collected to colleges and vocational schools.

Surprisingly, few colleges actively targeted veterans. So each side of the equation—the potential students and the colleges—had a problem, and neither reached out effectively to the other.

When Anne and Chris began this initiative, they were careful to keep the quality of the contact information high. If a Military.com member checked the box saying, "Yes, I'd like to hear from veteran-friendly schools," he or she would be taken to another screen with a second message, reading something along the lines of, "Confirm: by clicking on this link, you will be contacted by colleges that want to recruit you." The leads the company provided to the schools were thus doubly or triply qualified.

The new program wasn't an immediate success. Among other challenges, it proved difficult to get nonprofit educational institutions to think analytically and precisely about how they attracted prospective students. It didn't help that Military.com was offering a digital solution to many schools and colleges that, in the early 2000s, still operated in an analog world. In some cases, Anne also had to combat the perception that people who joined the military did so precisely because they were not college material. She and Chris would insist, "Military students are a perfect fit—mature, motivated, and supported by government funding."

But several newer, for-profit educational institutions—including the University of Phoenix, Kaplan University, and DeVry University—were already pursuing robust Internet strategies and were predisposed to using an online solution to meet the challenge of attracting new students. And because they had to make money, they had a stronger incentive to track their recruitment costs. Many of these schools and colleges understood exactly how Military.com could benefit them. Soon they began signing on in ever increasing numbers.

This was an important lesson, Anne realized. Thinking new was important, but they needed customers who could think new as well. Cutting-edge companies became the suppliers and customers of other cutting-edge companies.

Chris was thrilled to see this new source of revenue begin to grow significantly—and he found it ironic as well. After all, it was a conversation about the GI Bill that had given him the idea to start Military.com in the first place. For that matter, it had been the GI Bill that in 1947 had spurred Professor Myles Mace to develop the first entrepreneurship course at HBS, after he realized that many of the servicemen returning from World War II wanted to learn how to start their own businesses.

Throughout late 2002 and early 2003, Anne and Chris ramped up the business of educational lead generation. In addition, other companies started taking Military.com more seriously. For example, the Fortune 500 insurance company USAA, which catered primarily to veterans and their families, entered into an increasing number of deals with them. By the summer of 2003, Military.com could look back on a full year of solid operating results. True, no one was suggesting that the company would someday become a half-billion-dollar venture, as Chris Michel had confidently predicted in the original business plan. But Military.com had survived. Chris and Anne were making a difference in people's lives. Like the pilot of Chris's P-3 Orion nearly a decade before, they had survived their near crash, taken control, and were now headed in the right direction.

MARC: THE IDEA

Marc Cenedella came home to the United States from his round-the-world trip in September 2002, just in time for the Burning Man festival in northern Nevada's Black Rock Desert. After leaving HotJobs, he had flown to France for his nephew's christening, caught a plane to Moscow for another friend's bachelor party, and then taken a red-eye to Mongolia in time for Nadaam, a three-day religious festival and rodeo. He spent months traveling throughout China, Laos, Japan, and Thailand. By the time he reached New York City again, his hair reached his shoulders. His mind was clear and his spirit was free.

He was also hungry for his next challenge. Marc moved back into his old apartment with Steve Perricone. He spent a lot of time at the Half King Bar on Twenty-third Street, where he and Andrew Koch would drink beer and engage in intense discussions about everything from the books Marc was reading to the businesses he was thinking of starting. The two were often joined by their former colleague Alex Douzet, who had returned to New York after having earned his MBA at INSEAD in Europe.

Andrew was still working at HotJobs and not at all enthused about continuing. Alex, meanwhile, had interned in London as an investment banker and fielded a job offer from Google, but neither of those business cultures appealed to him. He wanted to jump into a truly entrepreneurial enterprise, but he had come back to the city in the midst of one of the toughest job markets in years. Half his MBA class seemed to be unemployed—most of the people with jobs were those who had worked for banks and consulting firms before school and returned to those same employers afterward.

All three friends were a bit unsettled; they were eager for the next chapter in their professional lives but didn't know what it might be. Marc seemed to have the clearest vision: he was all but convinced that it was time to start his own business, though he hadn't yet committed himself to any one idea. Both Alex and Andrew were eager to see what Marc would come up with; for his part, Marc counted his friends as the first two people he'd want to recruit into any new venture.

Every time they met for drinks, Marc seemed to have a different idea in mind. He talked about trying to raise money for a fund that would buy Internet stocks. He suspected now that the investment pendulum had swung too far, and that the market was undervaluing firms it had overvalued just a few years earlier. He also talked about launching an executive search firm that would leverage the power of the Internet and scale it far beyond anything the existing headhunters were doing. He believed he could make it a national or even a global business, and that the new technology made it possible to overcome the limitation that had led him to reject the industry when he was in business school—the fact that headhunters were usually tied to one city.

As the weeks went on, Marc renewed the relationship he'd had with the Center for American Jobs. He began negotiating a deal that would require him to raise venture capital for the firm in exchange for a position as one of the company's top executives and a good amount of equity; he also brought Alex on board. They spent a lot of time traveling back and forth to the Midwest trying to work out all the details. But in the end the company's president balked because the structure of the deal would leave his initial investors—including friends and family who had put up money early on—completely high and dry.

With nothing to show for several months of work, Marc and Alex were frustrated. They both began to think it might be time to bend all their efforts toward landing a "real job." And if he had to look for a corporate job, Marc decided that Monster.com might be the best place to start.

During Monster's unsuccessful attempt to buy HotJobs, Marc had gotten to know the company's CEO, Andy McKelvey. Marc liked and respected McKelvey; he also believed that he could help McKelvey realize the full potential of a division of his company that wasn't doing particularly well.

Monster offered a service called ChiefMonster that was aimed at the highest end of the job market—including the so-called C-level positions and those of other senior executives. ChiefMonster wasn't gaining much market share, and Marc asked McKelvey if he could meet with him to pitch a new approach.

"ChiefMonster is a dog," Marc told McKelvey at the meeting. "It's not getting any traction at all. Hire me, let me take it over, and I'll make it work. What do you have to lose?"

McKelvey liked Marc's spirit, but he wasn't inclined to bring him in at that level. Still, he thought Marc could be a valuable member of his team and offered him a job as the head of mergers and acquisitions.

Marc was tempted, but he didn't want to be a finance guy—he wanted to run something. He turned McKelvey down.

It was now spring 2003, and Marc had gone for more than a year without a paycheck. He couldn't seem to work up any real enthusiasm for taking a job at someone else's company. He'd been there, done that, got the severance package, and he was now certain that he wanted to be an entrepreneur again. But though he still didn't have his Big Idea, he was confident that it would have something to do with the online recruiting business. Marc knew the industry and had grown passionate about it.

Marc wasn't like his roommate, Steve Perricone, who was now closing in on five years with Deutsche Bank, the same company he'd started with right after their postgraduation trip to Spain. Sometimes Marc felt as if he'd been looking for jobs most of his life. When he counted all the positions he'd held over the years, he realized that he was now embarked on his twenty-seventh job search. He'd worked a myriad of jobs—everything from paperboy to janitor at a day care center in high school to senior vice president at a company that was sold for more than $400 million. He'd been interviewed hundreds of times, and he'd also spent a lot of time on the hiring side of the interview desk. No wonder he was so drawn to the field, he thought. He was a poster child for an age-old question: how do you figure out what to do with your professional life?

He'd become fascinated by a difficult problem, and Marc was increasingly certain that the Internet could provide a new solution. He thought back to one of the major complaints made by the companies that posted ads on HotJobs. The ads were virtually guaranteed to get hundreds or thousands of replies, but only a small portion of them were worthy of consideration. The matchups were sometimes truly absurd: a forklift operator would apply for a position as director of marketing, and a would-be career switcher with no relevant experience would apply for a job as chief technology officer. You might ultimately find your candidate, but the ads were expensive and you had to cull through a ton of chaff to find the few kernels of wheat.

Marc wondered: what if a job board could sort through the applicants ahead of time and somehow prequalify people before they applied? As he thought this through, a possible profit-making solution presented itself. What if the easiest way to prequalify applicants was to charge them to apply? Wouldn't that induce job seekers to evaluate carefully whether they were qualified, and self-select out if they weren't?

Marc didn't have sisters growing up, but now that he lived in New York City he developed a closer relationship with two of his female cousins, Loraine and Jennifer, who lived in the city as well. He'd introduced Loraine to his HBS friend and classmate Tom Morgan, and now, five years later, Loraine and Tom were married. Both of his cousins worked in sales, and neither was thrilled with her current job situation.

When Marc saw them one day in June, he started asking them all kinds of questions about how they were approaching their job search.

"Tell me, do you ever use Monster?" he asked at one point. And then, "Do you ever use HotJobs?"

Both Loraine and Jennifer said they didn't use either service. Instead, they networked informally. They went to industry events. They heard through friends who was hiring, and where.

Marc and Loraine had a bit of a running joke going—Loraine had a habit of calling Marc and asking him to look things up for her on the Internet, rather than simply doing so herself, and Marc would tease her about how computer illiterate she was. So now, a few days after their conversation about job hunting, Marc decided to send both cousins an e-mail.

From: Marc Cenedella
Sent: Tuesday, June 10, 2003 3:49 PM
To: Loraine Cenedella; Jennifer Cenedella
Subject: your job genie

This is off the WSJ Online edition:

Global Account Manager
Location: Stamford, Connecticut
As a successful salesperson, do you want to walk into the offices of
C-level executives and be thought of as a strategic partner rather than
a salesperson? Would you like to represent the leading brand in IT and
be able to offer products & services that provide insight into how to
solve an enterprise's most troubling issues? Are top level training and
being handsomely rewarded for overachieving important to you? If so,
join Gartner and begin to collaborate with the best minds in IT . . .

Less than a week later, he sent them another lead. Every day now, between trading stocks online, visiting his favorite bars and restaurants, and exploring his adopted hometown of Manhattan, Marc would spend an hour or two searching for jobs he knew he would never apply for, in a field he had no intention of entering. He started turning up amazing leads, positions that Loraine and Jennifer found very intriguing and that they knew they never would have come across otherwise.

He enjoyed helping them out, but he was also trying to flesh out his idea for a job board where the applicants would be prescreened.

Marc realized he had a huge chicken-and-egg problem. In a way, it was even bigger than the one HotJobs and Monster had originally faced. Compiling jobs from other Web sites seemed like a low-level solution; to break through and succeed in a big way, he would have to be able to list jobs that people couldn't find anywhere else. But without a solid core of job seekers, how could he persuade employers to post ads?

It didn't help that the online job board market was already crowded. Even if his idea worked, Marc was certain that his potential competitors would respond quickly and undercut him. What was to prevent competitors from simply launching better-funded versions of the same idea?

The answer came to him on the morning of July 1, 2003, a Tuesday. Marc had heard about an HBS video that was supposed to be worth watching—it was a presentation by Clayton Christensen, an HBS professor and the author of a book called *The Innovator's Dilemma*. Christensen's thesis was that market leaders tended to be conservative and focus on making incremental progress, rather than taking giant leaps forward either in technology or business processes.

As he listened to Christensen, Marc had a eureka moment. Almost by definition, big companies often didn't respond to or even recognize radically different approaches to their business models. It was a paradox, but it made sense. If Marc built a job board that imitated the big players' model but offered only marginally better performance, the established companies would know exactly how to compete. But if his business model were audacious and unconventional, they might not know how to respond at all. This was especially likely, Marc reasoned, if his model involved charging job seekers rather than employers. He would completely upend his competitors' model. And they would never try to compete with him by giving their product away to their clients—that would be suicidal.

Marc shut off his computer and called Alex Douzet.

Alex was always happy to listen to any proposal or concept Marc came up with, and he found this idea intriguing. Assuming the underlying product was good—assuming, in other words, that the leads Marc turned up were truly valuable—Alex was confident he could put together an inexpensive plan to recruit job seekers who would be willing to pay for the service.

But Alex was both excited and wary. His last collaboration with Marc—the months-long effort to get involved with the Center for American Jobs—had yielded nothing, and he'd now gone a year and a half without a steady paycheck. Moreover, he believed that the company would have to start by giving its product away for free, so as to entice job seekers to try it and build it to scale quickly. Still, he and his wife were leaving on a two-week trip to his native France the next day— and Marc had certainly given him something to think about.

Around lunchtime, Marc opened a computer file containing a business plan he'd played around with over the years. He'd use it as a template now. He gave his new company a name—Upper Keep—and began drafting a presentation for potential investors.

The problem

Recruitment is a $30 billion industry in which companies pay to ask "hey, who wants this job?"

For $100,000 jobs, the answer is: everybody

Which creates the catch-22—everybody apples for these jobs when posted, so they're rarely posted

Upper Keep changes that equation . . .

July 1, 2003   2

He went on to list the benefits provided by his imaginary company.

- Solves mutual screening problem for highly compensated jobs
- Job seekers pay to receive comprehensive, targeted job listings newsletters
- Employers get difficult-to-find high-quality candidates

By late afternoon, Marc was finished. He called Andrew Koch and asked him to meet at the Half King again. Over several Guinnesses, Marc pitched his idea to Andrew and talked it back and forth with him.

As it happened, Andrew had participated in several discussions at HotJobs about the difficulty of recruiting people for highly compensated positions. He'd even been involved in meetings where some people had talked about wanting to try to charge job seekers. But no one at HotJobs thought it would work.

It might not ever work for a broad-based jobs Web site, Marc agreed, but it could work if his company focused on a narrow portion of the job market. "If we're only accepting the highest-paying sales jobs," he said, "people will pay for those leads."

On July 17, Marc met up again with the two cousins who had inadvertently gotten him started on this idea. Over lunch at a Turkish restaurant on Third Avenue, Loraine and Jen asked Marc how his mother was doing, and then Loraine asked him what was up on the dating front. He liked to joke that Loraine owed him one since he'd introduced her to her husband.

But as the lunch went on, Marc kept steering the conversation back to questions about their careers and asking them what they thought of the job leads he'd been sending them.

"I'm thinking of starting a company that does this," he told them. He had tried out a number of different names, and now he was calling it SalesLadder.com. They were good representatives of his ideal customers, he told them, and once again he wanted to ask them a crucial question: would they consider paying for such a service?

Maybe, they replied. Maybe they would.

For the rest of July, Marc seemed almost to disappear. Steve Perricone would come home from work and find Marc sitting at his computer, reading intently or typing away furiously. He didn't go out much at all, but he talked with Alex and Andrew, and he e-mailed Loraine and Jennifer. He got in touch with other people he'd gotten to know while working at HotJobs, as well as a few people he knew at other companies in the recruiting field. He asked all of them whether they thought his business model might work. The response was overwhelmingly negative.

Marc continued to focus on developing and improving his product. He also began thinking about how he could raise the capital he'd need to launch his venture. The investment world had changed profoundly in the past few years. At the height of the dot-com fever, people like Chris Michel could raise millions or even tens of millions of dollars based on PowerPoint presentations. Now, VCs were much more cautious. As he continued discussing the idea with Alex, Marc realized that he'd need to develop a prototype, a working business model—maybe even one that generated revenue. He'd come face-to-face with yet another chicken-and-egg problem. Without revenue, he couldn't attract capital investment. But without capital investment, he couldn't produce revenue.

The realization that the venture would have to be self-funded and bootstrapped tested Marc's commitment like nothing else. But he had one advantage—his confidence. No matter what anybody said, he was absolutely convinced that his idea was viable. Marc had been intrigued by several opportunities he'd considered since leaving HotJobs—his plan to buy Dice, for instance, and even trying to run ChiefMonster for Andy McKelvey. But this was palpably different. Maybe that was because he had come up with the idea himself. And maybe the negative responses he'd been receiving somehow spurred him on. Whatever the case, he understood that if he didn't truly believe in this idea, the venture would never be more than a forgotten computer file.

This will solve a real human need, Marc told himself as he worked alone in the apartment on East Twelfth Street. Most workers, he reasoned, weren't entrepreneurs. If they wanted to get ahead, if they wanted to earn more money and find greater job satisfaction, they had to keep thinking about who they were working for, what they were making, and whether they might do better somewhere else. By targeting the top of the job market, his company—Upper Keep, SalesLadder, or whatever else he decided to call it—could argue that anyone who didn't subscribe was potentially giving up thousands of dollars each month. Even the fact that job seekers would be paying for his service might allow them to satisfy some basic desire to know that they were making every possible effort to improve their lot in life.

For now, his new company would follow Alex's model, producing a weekly e-mail newsletter that anyone could subscribe to for free. Knowing that they also would need a Web site so that job seekers could eventually become paying customers, Marc started interviewing programmers and Web site designers. The costs astonished him. Even the simplest interface would cost many thousands of dollars. Marc simply couldn't justify an investment of $30,000 or more so early, even if he'd had the money on hand.

Marc thought back to middle school and high school, when he'd been a bit of a computer geek. He'd especially enjoyed playing around with a Commodore 64, and he'd been pretty good at programming back then. How hard could this be? he wondered. He researched and experimented with several out-of-the-box design programs, such as Dreamweaver and FrontPage, but he found them disappointing. It would take nearly as long to learn how to use them as it would to learn how to program on his own. He went to a bookstore, dropped $50 on a dense tome called *PHP and MySQL Web Development*, buried himself inside the apartment once again, and learned the basics.

He designed a Web site that was at best rudimentary, but he figured it didn't have to be pretty at this stage. It just had to work. Three weeks or so later, he came up for air and launched the first version of the site. Basic and bare, the site was a single page, and its design flourishes were limited to a few slightly different colored blocks of text. Nevertheless, it had the one crucial feature. When you filled in your name, e-mail address, and zip code and clicked the button that said, "Yes, please send me your $100K+ jobs newsletter," it captured your information, so that Marc could e-mail you the following Monday.

In late August, Marc started running a few ads on Craigslist. Looking for help finding $100,000-plus jobs? If so, the ads promised, SalesLadder would send along a free newsletter. Marc also launched a simple viral marketing campaign, asking his cousin Loraine to e-mail all her colleagues in the sales industry and ask them to take a look at the Web site. A few days later, Marc was thrilled when he got his first three subscribers. He took Steve Higgins, his old Yale roommate, out to an expensive lunch to celebrate. And then, on September 9, Marc invited Andrew and Alex to join him at a Manhattan Starbucks.

There, amid a crowd of caffeine addicts and the whoosh of the espresso machine, he told them he was going to incorporate the company. They would be his cofounders and first employees—if, that is, they wanted to be a part of his venture.

Marc almost didn't even have to ask. They had both been waiting for this moment for a long time.

CHAPTER 12

YOU MUST DO IT ALONE

It is not the critic who counts; not the man who points out how the strong man stumbles, or where the doer of deeds could have done them better. The credit belongs to the man who is actually in the arena, whose face is marred by dust and sweat and blood; who strives valiantly; who errs, who comes short again and again, because there is no effort without error and shortcoming; but who does actually strive to do the deeds; who knows great enthusiasms, the great devotions; who spends himself in a worthy cause; who at the best knows in the end the triumph of high achievement, and who at the worst, if he fails, at least fails while daring greatly, so that his place shall never be with those cold and timid souls who neither know victory nor defeat.

—TEDDY ROOSEVELT

IT'S ALL ABOUT YOU, ISN'T IT?

Actually, kinda, yes. You're the one who's reading this book. You're the one who wants to be an entrepreneur. You're the one who will likely come up with the right idea and recruit the team, and you're the one who will ultimately reap the most substantial rewards. So although you absolutely must work with others to achieve your dream, in the end it's very much about you.

Exciting as this is, it's also terribly daunting. The highly successful entrepreneurs I got to know while researching this book endured enormous, spirit-crushing, confidence-testing challenges. When they achieved their early milestones, sometimes there was nobody around to cheer them on. True, most of them had shown a willingness to work alone before launching their companies. Marc had flown to Japan on his own to build Forbes Pacifica. Marla had buried herself in the HBS library, combing the archives for information about possible employers. Chris had spent most of his childhood learning how to be the new kid in virtually every school he attended. But all three also proved adept at working with a wide range of people and collaborating closely with their peers.

They all learned the hard way that a scary, central, and unavoidable part of being an entrepreneur is that it's sometimes very lonely. They came to understand that starting your company means that much of the time you have to do the difficult work and make the hard decisions alone.

ALONE IN A ROOM

"The first two months," Marc Cenedella recalled during one of our interviews, "it was just me. Solo."

Marc spent the summer of 2003 alone in his apartment. He had no income, no job, very little encouragement—and yet he came up with the idea for the company that would become TheLadders.com. He believed in his vision and made it happen. Talk about individual commitment and believing in an idea: he even learned how to write computer code so he could create the first version of his company's Web site.

In many respects, Marc embodied the classic image of the creative entrepreneur. He was the iconoclastic innovator, the heroic loner defying convention and building what nobody else thought would work. All true enough, but to hear Marc tell the story, those early days were actually quite enjoyable.

"It was exciting and fun," he said. "I wasn't bringing in any money, but I knew there was something there. So I focused on coding, getting the thing up and running, working to get the test version up by early August and send out the full test version to Loraine and Jen. And when I sent it to them, they were like, Whoa, I didn't realize you'd actually get the thing going!"

Where does this kind of self-confidence and persistence come from? If you've analyzed two hundred different case studies at a place like HBS, is it then inevitable that you'll believe that you, too, can accomplish what the protagonists of those case studies did?

Marc didn't think so. "Stubbornness," he told me, "that's the secret." He attributed his success to the fact that he "had a strong sense of my own opinions. I think to a certain extent you're born with that. Being an entrepreneur is about saying, I know this doesn't exist. This segment isn't being addressed. But I can go do it. I suppose some people might call that arrogance. To me, it's a matter of self-assurance."

Long before she attended HBS, Marla Malcolm proved that she had no shortage of self-confidence. Even as a teenager, she set her sights high and believed she was destined to achieve great things. Later, when she decided to open a chain of retail cosmetics stores and apothecaries, Marla was undaunted by the fact that she had no significant professional experience in either retail or cosmetics. Some things about starting up bluemercury did scare her, but I never got the sense that her lack of experience in her chosen industry was one of them.

"That didn't bother me," she told me. "I'd worked in a clothing boutique when I was in high school, called Ibis. I worked every Saturday until I got really active in volleyball and had to drop out because of our weekend tournaments. And I always worked. I worked at my dad's office as a bookkeeper. So retail didn't scare me."

Marla laughed, and then said, "Once I figure out where I want to go, I'm dangerous. Do you know what I mean? Because I'm positive I can get there. For me it's always about figuring out where I want to go and what I want to do. Once I know that, the rest of it comes naturally."

Of my three protagonists, Chris Michel was perhaps the least likely to become a highly successful entrepreneur. He traveled the longest distance—his work at age twenty-five was so different from his professional life at age thirty-five that it's sometimes difficult to comprehend how he made the transition. Attending HBS certainly helped, but it goes far beyond attending an elite business school for two years. Reflecting on how his confidence and tolerance for risk increased over the years, he pointed to evidence that the seeds of his entrepreneurial nature were always there.

"When I look back, I think I was always kind of an entrepreneur—in a way. I am not one of these people that started a dozen little businesses as a kid, but I did love to create. I've always liked to solve problems and try new things."

In the navy, for instance, Chris built a service project for his squadron essentially from scratch. He wasn't the first to come up with the idea. Over the years, a number of officers had approached the principal of a school in Brunswick, Maine, and offered to create a program in which sailors would volunteer to provide various kinds of help to the school. But the programs always fell by the wayside after a while, as officers transferred to new bases and people lost interest. Chris, however, was driven and organized, and he created a program on a completely different scale. Sailors worked at the school every day, doing everything from cleaning and painting the building to helping teachers in the classroom. The program was so successful that it endured for years. Nearly two decades after Chris left the navy, in fact, the school's principal was still talking about the program and remembered Chris by name.

"I look back at that school program, for example," Chris said. "I always found a lot of joy in creating. And I found that by doing things like that program, I changed the rules of the game. Rather than competing with everyone in the squadron to become the best guy in the airplane, I built my reputation creating things. It's become a success strategy for me: I don't play by other people's rules. In the navy, I made up my own set of rules. And that worked, or at least as much as it could work given that I was in the military. And that's been my approach ever since."

As a boy, Chris moved around a lot and spent many hours on his own. He enjoyed working on science projects and programming on an old Sinclair ZX80. Long before Harvard Business School, he got used to doing things alone and going his own way. In retrospect, the loneliest moment of his life probably occurred in early 2002, just after he'd handed the reins of Military.com to Lad Burgin. It was also quite possibly the most important moment in the company's history. If Chris Michel hadn't sucked it up and summoned the courage to return to Military.com, the company almost certainly wouldn't exist today. Chris, meanwhile, might well have gone back to consulting or joined someone else's company. And he might never have become a successful entrepreneur.

———

Interestingly, Marla, Chris, and Marc often had trouble remembering how hard the difficult parts had been. It was as if they'd simply blocked out the trauma. I was reminded of the theory that if human beings truly recalled pain in detail, no woman would ever be willing to go through childbirth twice. Time and again, Chris Michel would send me to Anne, or to company records, or to others he'd worked with who could fill in the gaps in his memory and so tell me what exactly had happened at Military.com in the early years when the going was rough. Marla, too, would pull records from her files and be surprised to see how bad things had been.

"I don't remember the numbers—I've got to look them up," she told me one day when were talking about bluemercury's perilous launch as a dot-com enterprise. "Once things work out, you put the bad stuff behind you."

Another successful HBS entrepreneur I interviewed told me about a psychologist friend who told him that he seemed to have aged ten years during the first, very difficult year after he started his business. Or consider James Currier, sleeping no more than four hours a night because the only way he could get any rest at all was to knock himself unconscious with a dose of Nyquil. From others, I heard stories of weight gain and strained marriages—and of playing a shell game with credit cards, using one to pay off another when the money wasn't coming in.

For these entrepreneurs, surviving—not to mention launching a successful company—meant having an iron will, a deep-seated tenacity, and the self-confidence to ignore those who told them they should give up their dream. Without those traits, most or all of them surely would have quit.

"You have to believe," Anne Dwane summarized. "You have to be the kind of person who perseveres. You have to have ingenuity to come up with a great idea. You have to have audacity to think you can actually do it. You have to be industrious and really work it hard. You have to have serendipity, and a lot of tenacity. This is not for everyone. But when I go to an entrepreneurship event now, even in this down market, there is still a lot of entrepreneurial energy. What's different now, though, is that all the poseurs are gone. Those that remain are the true entrepreneurs, the kind of people who will not be fazed by the environment. Now, you might be more realistic. You might be more cautious. But you will have the fire in the belly—the fire in the belly to build."

To the extent that academics study entrepreneurial psychology, the importance of confidence, persistence, and the ability to go it alone are borne out by the research.

"One of *the* tough tensions that good founders face is how to be solo players," Noam Wasserman agreed, "but at the same time, still be team players. The combination of the two is the critical element. It's easy to do one; it's easy to do the other; it's tough to do them both together."

You've also got to trust your gut, because no matter how closely you study a market, no matter how meticulously you build your business model, you will always have to accept a certain level of risk and vulnerability. Analytics can take you only so far; past that point, instinct has to take over. Interestingly, many HBS alumni told me they thought their classmates were often ill-suited for entrepreneurship for precisely this reason.

"Sometimes I think HBS folks are so analytical they get paralyzed," Anne Dwane explained. "Because if you look at most business models for successful companies, and you ask questions and look for holes in them, you can always find them. You can always say, 'Well, this competitor could get more active.' Or, 'Will consumers adopt the product?' Or, 'Is the market for this thing really big enough?' "

And because pretty much all of the MBA students at a place like Harvard are highly analytical, they will almost certainly ask all the tough questions about any potential venture. They'll see most of the risks but, ironically, miss the risk that overanalyzing a good opportunity might make them too cautious to seize it.

"A lot of these Harvard guys aren't used to the level of risk that you've got to accept," said Barry Beck—who is quick to point out that he did not go to business school. "I've met a lot of them. Not all of them have—I think Tom Wolfe called it 'the right stuff.' Whatever the right stuff is, you've got to have it."

Another successful entrepreneur from the class behind Marla, Chris, and Marc agreed. He'd first applied to HBS expecting to go to school with what he called the Masters of the Universe, after a line in another Tom Wolfe book, *The Bonfire of the Vanities.*

"At Harvard, there were a lot of overachieving but insecure people who were just trying to do the best they could in life," he explained. "In fact, the true masters of the universe weren't at HBS. The true masters of the universe realize that they don't need any help. They're just going off and doing it."

A true entrepreneur—someone, in other words, who comes up with an innovative idea, has the courage to launch a business built around that idea, and then executes with both passion and a high level of competence—is uncommon if not exceedingly rare. Look at the two HBS classes that followed the 1998 cohort: only 5 percent of the class of 1999 and 11 percent of the class of 2000 tried to become entrepreneurs within a year of graduating, despite the frenzy of positive reinforcement and easy capital.

Stig Leschly looked back on his own experience as both a student and an instructor and told me the following: "Why do at least 80 percent of our graduates decide not to start their own businesses when money's lying around? Primarily, I think it's because they don't have an idea. But it's also the psychology of the thing. Maybe Mommy and Daddy are getting nervous—after so many years in school, isn't it time to get a high-paying job? Or it's fear of being seen as a failure: 'I'll show up at my fifth-year reunion and be unemployed.' Business school students can be a pretty conservative bunch—many of them aren't willing to go off into the wilderness, work in solitary confinement, and tolerate the fact that if they fail they will make no money and everyone will think that they're a leper."

It must be said, though, that HBS does an excellent job of instilling confidence in its students. As we've seen, the school works hard to ensure that the students will learn a lot from both their professors and their peers, and it also provides a superb opportunity to network with an all-star team of overachievers. Further, the students' experience of analyzing about two hundred case studies and thus putting themselves in the shoes of so many different business leaders is unquestionably valuable.

Ed Zschau, who left HBS not long after Chris Michel and the rest of the class of 1998 graduated, took the case study approach one step further. While teaching at HBS, he'd also been teaching an undergraduate course in high-tech entrepreneurship at Princeton. When HBS ended its experiment with the accelerated, seventeen-month program that Chris, Anne, and James Currier attended, Ed had to choose between the two programs. He picked Princeton, he told me, because whereas many professors were teaching entrepreneurship at HBS, he was the only one teaching the subject at Princeton. But soon after choosing to teach at Princeton, he decided that in addition to requiring his students to study many of the same cases they teach at HBS, he would also require them to interview founders of successful startups and spend a semester writing a paper that demonstrates what they've learned. Why? To give them direct exposure to entrepreneurial minds and help give them the confidence that maybe, someday, they could start a company themselves.

Chris Michel, for one, is a full-fledged believer in that teaching method. "The beauty of the case method," he told me, "is that you are role-playing hundreds and hundreds of CEOs. You believe—without any factual basis—that you could be a CEO because almost every day you studied and reenacted the challenges they faced." There is no question, he said, that all that role playing helped him believe that he could fill those big shoes someday.

If there's one drawback to studying entrepreneurs who launched their companies in the late 1990s, it's that this was a moment in time when would-be founders had access to so much ready capital investment that the risk and loneliness that are inevitably a big part of becoming an entrepreneur were somewhat obscured—at least at the outset. As a consequence, many people who had nowhere near the necessary self-confidence and tolerance for risk were absolutely certain that they could succeed. And why not? After all, for a couple of years during that feverish time, it seemed that just about anyone with a big idea for a new venture could get rich quickly. But soon that fairy tale yielded to a new reality, and we all remember the stories about one twenty-two-year-old CEO or another who raised $10 million in venture capital during the dot-com bubble only to see it all gone a few years later.

"That period brought people who should not be entrepreneurs into the market," Anne Dwane said. "Entrepreneurship is characterized by a lot of highs and lows. When you're a small company, you have these great days—like, hey, we closed this deal! Then the next day something bad happens, and you're like, Whoa! No question, this roller-coaster ride is not for everyone."

Stig Leschly made a related point. "You're studying a moment in time when the risk variable was masked. Starting a business in 1998 became the equivalent of taking a job with Procter & Gamble. It was too easy. The capital was there. At HBS, there were clubs for students who wanted to become entrepreneurs—it was the thing to do. In 1998, if you were going to be a contrarian, you would go to work for Bain Capital or somebody. It's funny, too, because when I showed up at HBS in '94 and wanted to start a club for entrepreneurs, we couldn't get anybody to show up."

Some of the faculty at HBS got caught up in the fever, too. Perhaps rashly, they sometimes encouraged students to start companies even before graduating. One day, as Howard Stevenson and I were discussing this unique moment in the school's history, he got up from the table in his office at the Rock Center and opened the door to a cluttered closet at the far end of the room. After rummaging around a bit, he pulled out a baseball cap that had a cartoon dinosaur and the words RAPTOR TRAINER emblazoned on the front.

"This was produced by one of our proud faculty members," Stevenson said, "but I keep it in a closet. As the cap suggests—and I don't think this was a joke—he believed that we were training a pack of raptors to go out and destroy existing businesses, training them to take over the world."

HOW DO YOU DEVELOP A HEALTHY CONFIDENCE?

Raptor or no, it's critical that you believe in your entrepreneurial idea and your ability to start up and run a new company. My hope, of course, is that the stories about Marla, Chris, and Marc and the advice offered by teachers like Stig Leschly and Howard Stevenson will help you gain the self-confidence you'll need to make your entrepreneurial vision a reality. Inevitably, though, you will have to endure many moments of loneliness and self-doubt. At those moments, your well of confidence can never be too deep, so here are a few additional thoughts about how to ensure that it's as full as possible.

Get to know other entrepreneurs. As you've no doubt begun to recognize, people like Marla, Marc, and Chris—impressive as they are—are at their core not so different from the rest of us. Successful entrepreneurs are not comic-book heroes or cartoon dinosaurs, they are human beings who do their best to take full advantages of their strengths and mitigate their weaknesses. Ed Zschau now insists that all his students go out and meet living, breathing, and very human entrepreneurs; it's very important that you do the same.

We've already discussed how to build a network. Now that you have one, use it. Identify the people you'd like to emulate and then call or e-mail them. You may find that it takes fifty or one hundred calls and e-mails before you find someone you respect who is willing to have a cup of coffee with you, but hearing about their experiences—their successes and their failures—will prove invaluable.

Inventory your own successes. Think about what you've accomplished in life—especially when you've achieved something that others believed you could never do. What unexpected success did you have in sports? Did you get an A in the toughest college class you ever took? Did you convince the girl or boy of your dreams to date or even marry you? This isn't a silly self-esteem building exercise. It's about developing a reservoir of confidence, about believing that you have what it takes to build a business, about never selling yourself short.

Read about the great entrepreneurs and their successes. In one of our conversations, Marc Cenedella talked about being inspired by the story of Ben Franklin; he also recommended reading about successful entrepreneurs such as Michael Dell, Michael Bloomberg, and Ray Kroc. Enough founders have written memoirs to fill a very full shelf of any good bookstore. Read as many as you can get your hands on. But read them with a grain of salt, and remember that no matter how shiny their legend, these men and women are more like us than they are different.

Remember, too, that a lot of what you need to know cannot really be taught—you'll have to learn it on your own. Can a professor teach you how to be courageous enough not to worry about losing everything, as can sometimes happen to failed entrepreneurs? Can a book teach you how to be self-sufficient enough to travel the entrepreneurial road alone, as you so often must do? Of course not. But I do believe that this book can show you how, by adhering to its ten rules, you can substantially increase your chances of succeeding.

THE NEXT RULE

True entrepreneurship is rare. When you take the plunge—especially when you've done your homework ahead of time and identified a compelling solution to a real problem—you should be extremely proud of yourself just for trying. You've chosen not just to dream, but to take full responsibility for making your dream a reality. Doing so sets you apart. It's an inherently admirable thing to be the man or the woman in what Teddy Roosevelt called "the arena."

Of course, that doesn't mean you shouldn't do everything you can to minimize your downside and maximize your possible returns. As the highly successful entrepreneurs I interviewed and studied told me over and over again, true entrepreneurs work extremely hard to take as little risk as possible. They don't cultivate a large appetite for risk. Instead, they *manage* risk. That's something very different indeed.

CHAPTER 13

The men who have done big things are those who were not afraid to attempt big things, who were not afraid to risk failure in order to gain success.

—B. C. FORBES

In fall 2003, Marc Cenedella's SalesLadder.com was still little more than a step stool, but he had visions of an enterprise that would go sky-high and ultimately change the recruiting industry. He had only a few subscribers and not a penny in revenue or investment. But after the company's first organizational meeting at Starbucks in early September, Alex had come aboard as cofounder and vice president of marketing. He was willing to work for free for now—his wife had finally landed a job, so they were staying afloat financially—but starting in January he would have to pay off student loans from his MBA program. Andrew was still at HotJobs, the only company he'd ever worked for in his professional life, but he'd signed on unofficially as the unpaid director of strategic planning. For the moment, of course, they were just three guys working out of Marc's living room, so the titles meant little. But giving some structure to the company was important, especially since they all assumed that their venture would soon get off the ground.

Carefully, parsimoniously, Marc and Alex launched a campaign to attract visitors to the new SalesLadder.com. They signed up for Google AdWords, paying $50 a day to drive traffic to the site, and Alex peppered

Craigslist and other free and cheap Web sites with ads. They sent e-mails to friends and family, asking them to sign up—and then to ask *their* friends and family to sign up as well. All three friends spent their free hours scouring the Web for more sales job ads, adding content to the weekly newsletter that was the fledgling company's only product.

Meanwhile, Marc decided to lay the groundwork for future investment, using every possible low-cost tactic to build excitement. In addition to sending out the SalesLadder e-mails each week, he sent updates to anyone he considered a potential angel investor. He kept his messages short and to the point so that people would actually read them.

THE WEEK AT A LEAP: 9/23/2003

- We doubled our subscriber base to 800 unpaid subscribers.

- We sent 314 great, high-paying, open sales jobs to our subscribers.

- Our test marketing campaigns have proven that our CPA (cost per acquisition) is significantly below our budgeted $1.25.

- Rolling out several new CPC (Cost Per Click) and direct acquisition campaigns this week.

- What our subscribers are saying: "This is the best service I have seen. . . . For a profession as important as sales it seemed bizarre that the few job search sites never seemed to make it or take off."

The e-mails were part of a long-term project, and Marc was swamped with near-term deadlines. It wasn't immediately obvious how these updates would help his cause. A friend asked him why he took the time to write them. "People need excitement and adventure in their lives," Marc replied. "A guy starting a company from his East Village apartment? Even if we fail, it will be exciting to watch."

Marc, Alex, and Andrew were all working independently now, searching for job listings, drumming up subscribers, and trying various experiments that they hoped would build the company. But at least one evening a week, they all got together at Marc's apartment. Marc and Alex would start early, and when Andrew showed up after leaving Hot-Jobs for the day, they'd talk and strategize until ten or eleven p.m. Then the group would head out to the King's Head Tavern or the Telephone Bar and Grill on Second Avenue, where Marc would pick up the tab since he considered it a cost of doing business. Back home afterward, Marc would be up half the night, finding more job listings, teaching himself to program, tweaking the Web site.

The SalesLadder.com weekly newsletter was now the most important thing in Marc's life. He would go out with friends on occasion, but even on weekend nights he would head home early, saying he had to keep a clear head so he could write. He often looked a little haggard, and sometimes he would tell friends that he hadn't been to bed in thirty-six hours. But he could feel momentum building, and it gave him almost boundless energy. Each week more subscribers joined; Marc guessed that twenty-five thousand would be the magic number, at which point they could make a subtle switch and turn the weekly newsletters into a simple advertising circular. They'd still list the jobs, but at some point they would start charging the subscribers who wanted to access the contact information and get the other details they'd need in order to apply.

The Web site Marc had built was admittedly amateurish, and he laughed—almost proudly—at how limited his coding skills were. But it was quickly becoming clear that he needed a more professional-looking design. He ran ads on Monster and Craigslist for a chief technology officer. Of the résumés that came in, the most promising was from Richard Safran, a veteran programmer who had been working on computers since the 1980s. Marc interviewed Safran five or six times over several weeks before hiring him—equity only, no salary for now—to redesign the site.

Safran was passionate about programming. He was older, too—he'd written code on mainframes back when Marc was riding the swim team bus. He'd worked for a number of startups since 1999 or so, while also running a consulting business on the side to pay the rent. His hope was that at least one of the fledgling companies he'd signed on with would make it big someday.

Safran believed that Marc was launching SalesLadders as intelligently as he'd ever seen anyone start a company. And the group that crowded into Marc's living room each week had a special energy. Safran had known a lot of confident young CEOs, but Marc was the first one who seemed capable of actually predicting the future. The company was developing almost exactly as Marc had outlined it in his business plan. During their meetings, Marc would predict how many people were going to sign up that week, or how many jobs they'd find—and almost without fail it would happen.

Until now, the venture had been funded by little more than a combination of sweat equity and Marc's credit cards. But with four of them working on the project and most of the work being done in Marc's apartment or at the Starbucks at Union Square, it had become clear that they needed full-time office space. Marc explored a number of options and finally decided that the most economical solution in the short term was to rent a small, temporary office at the Select Office Suites at 116 West Twenty-third Street, about a twenty-minute walk from his apartment. But even that would require that he fork over about $7,000 in cash up front.

Marc took a deep breath and cashed out everything in his 401(k) and other retirement accounts. That produced enough money to cover the deposit and rent for the SOS office space; it also ensured that he would have something to live on in the months ahead if the company didn't make money as soon as he hoped. It pained him to know that he would take a major tax hit owing to the early withdrawal from his 401(k), but he consoled himself by promising that he would never be in such a low tax bracket again.

As he signed the paperwork and cashed out his account, he reflected that he finally, truly considered himself to be a real entrepreneur. He had started up and sold Forbes Pacifica, worked in investment banking and private equity, and helped close a deal to sell HotJobs for more than $400 million. He had traveled the world and explored different kinds of equity deals with several companies. But this was the first time in his life that he would be investing his own money in a venture of his own creation. He was betting on the combined talents of his cofounders, but in the end he was putting his own ability and his own future on the line—and his determination was the only thing he could really count on.

The others had known that most of the company's expenses were going on Marc's credit cards, but he tried not to make a big deal of it and didn't mention that he'd cashed out his retirement accounts. Besides, he didn't have to remind the others to drive the hardest possible bargains on everything that cost money. If any one of them needed a reminder of the importance of being frugal, all they had to do was look up from their computers and see three other guys taking no salaries and sharing one windowless office.

By Thanksgiving Marc renamed the venture again: SalesLadder.com was now simply The Ladders. He realized that he shouldn't limit the company's portfolio to sales positions, and he started registering a number of related domain names as well—financeladder.com, lawladder .com, and the like. He shifted into negotiation mode when he discovered that a group of Italian video game programmers had already registered theladders.com. The days of million-dollar domains were long gone, and now even the Italian programmers' asking price of a thousand euros was too high. Marc negotiated them down to 180 American dollars.

As their subscriber base continued to grow, Marc decided that they needed still more help, and soon he persuaded Steve Higgins—his Yale roommate and the son of the professor who had written the finance book Marc had bought Andrew two years earlier—to come aboard. Andrew still worked full-time at HotJobs, but in any given week he was often putting in more hours working for Marc. He'd get to HotJobs at about ten in the morning, work until six in the evening, and go straight to the little office on Twenty-third Street, where he'd work until midnight or one in the morning. His fiancée was finishing her degree at Brown University, so on weekends he would usually take the bus to Providence, work all day Saturday, go out to dinner with her on Saturday evening, and then return to New York and work most of Sunday night.

Richard Safran spent about forty hours a week on his consulting business, and he often put in another forty hours working for Marc. His busiest nights were Sundays, when Marc would send him the list of jobs that had to be included in the newsletter. On a good night, Richard would get Marc's list by ten p.m., but sometimes it didn't come until two in the morning. It was Richard's job to format the newsletter and have it ready to go out by four a.m. Inevitably, Monday mornings at his consulting business were rough.

Over time, Marc discovered that most of the nontechnical work wasn't difficult; it was simply a matter of breaking down the dozens of tasks into discrete action items, ensuring that they all got done, and then measuring the results. TheLadders ran banner advertisements on its competitors' Web sites—Monster and CareerBuilder, for example—and continually updated its free ads on Craigslist and other such sites. The hardest part of everyone's job was compiling the newsletters each week, which took an enormous amount of everyone's time because Marc had set a goal of including at least three hundred legitimate $100,000-a-year jobs in each issue.

Of those three hundred jobs, Andrew was responsible for coming up with seventy-five. One Sunday night, Andrew was about ten jobs short when he called Marc's cell phone and left a voice mail.

"Hey, I'm going to go meet up with friends," he said. "I didn't quite make it, but we're close."

Andrew knew that his shortfall would mean that they'd be listing only about 290 jobs this week. But really, he reasoned, who was counting?

He had shut off the computer and was about to walk out the door when Marc called back.

"No," he told Andrew. "It's just you. You have to go back and find those jobs or we won't hit our number."

Andrew cursed under his breath. But he hung up, turned his computer back on, and scoured the career sections of a few dozen more Web sites, looking for those last ten jobs.

CHRIS: THE FIRST WIN

The prospects for Chris Michel's company continued to brighten throughout 2003. Almost all of his efforts were now focused on selling qualified leads to colleges and other institutions. Chris sometimes felt as if Military.com had become a new company, and now he and Anne knew what they needed to do and how to do it. There was no single moment when they turned a corner, but the gradual uptick in the company's fortunes gave both of them a quiet confidence that they were on their way.

After spending the better part of a year trying to sell the company, by fall 2003 Chris had switched gears, and he now felt little urge to find a buyer. Although their numbers fluctuated, they now had a thriving, cash-flow positive business. In most cases, they were able to acquire Military.com members for about half to a third of the price they received for selling the contact information to other marketing partners. With that kind of margin, why rush to sell the company? As long as they survived, they were now beating expectations and positioning themselves to take advantage of new opportunities.

One November afternoon in 2003, however, Chris was sitting in his small office on Pacific Street in San Francisco when he got a call from a senior vice president at Monster Worldwide named Brad Baker. Baker was one of the executives Chris had met with when he'd tried to sell the company to Monster a year earlier. He was an entrepreneur himself; several years earlier Baker had founded an educational software company called Making It Count, but he'd ultimately sold it to Monster.

Over the past twelve months, Monster's business had picked up substantially. The company was now eager to acquire what it considered undervalued Internet companies, and as Baker pointed out during his phone conversation with Chris, Monster and Military.com overlapped in some interesting ways. Maybe Chris had been right when he had suggested in their meeting a year ago that a site like Military.com's, which brought together big affinity groups, could provide the "stickiness" that would keep people connected to Monster even when they weren't actively looking for a job. Additionally, Monster wanted to build its business with the federal government, and Chris's company clearly had a lot of good relationships inside the Pentagon. Baker remembered that the army, navy, and marines all had contracts with Military.com to refer potential recruits; besides, Baker joked, Chris's company had enough retired admirals and generals on its board of advisers to stage a coup.

Though Chris and Brad Baker hadn't talked in some time, they had liked each other when they'd first met and now they picked up right where they left off. Not only did Baker have firsthand experience with the trials of being an entrepreneur, he also enjoyed hearing Chris talk about his time in the navy, not least because his brother was a navy flier. And he admired Chris's tenacity—not everyone has the guts to cold-call a senior executive at a company like Monster and then talk his way in the door. So when Monster's CEO, Andy McKelvey—the same McKelvey that Marc

Cenedella had gotten to know during the company's failed attempt to buy HotJobs—had recently asked Baker for the names of companies he thought Monster should consider acquiring, Baker had immediately mentioned Chris Michel and Military.com.

"McKelvey will be in San Francisco next week," he told Chris. "Would you want to meet with him?"

As it happened, Chris had no idea who McKelvey was. He'd thought the head of Monster was Jeff Taylor, the man who had founded the Web site in 1994. But if Baker said McKelvey was worth meeting, Chris would of course sit down with him.

After the call, Chris did a few minutes of research and realized that he'd be meeting Monster's CEO. He also learned that McKelvey, now sixty-nine, had run a telephone marketing company for many years, and that he'd gotten into the recruiting business almost by accident. In 1995, soon after purchasing Jeff Taylor's marketing firm, McKelvey realized that Taylor's Web site—then called The Monster Board—had the potential to become a hugely successful company in its own right. It was another one of those stories about a company that thinks it's in one business only to discover that its biggest opportunity lies elsewhere.

The following Monday afternoon, the silver-haired McKelvey showed up at the modest offices of Military.com. He was alone, which surprised Chris, and very low-key. By now Chris had told the story of Military.com hundreds of times, but he'd never lost his enthusiasm for his original idea or his vision of what the company could become. He went on for ninety minutes; he began by describing the company's mission and its challenges, and then offered considerable detail about its cost structure and its growing revenue.

McKelvey paid close attention. When Chris finished, he asked only a few questions. Then he cut to the chase: Monster wanted to buy Military.com.

Chris was ecstatic. But as he began to think about what sort of deal he could negotiate, he also wondered whether he and the other principals at Military.com would actually see any money out of it. Two years ago, the situation was completely different: if McKelvey had come to him then, Chris would have sold Military.com for a dollar and nothing more than a promise to keep the company running. Now, though, the purchase price would have to be high enough to allow him to pay off his investors and provide some sort of windfall for the cofounders who had done so much to keep the company going through all the hard times.

McKelvey had bought and sold hundreds of companies over the years, and he understood Chris's position precisely. He also had most of the leverage: after all, no one else was making an offer to buy Military.com. Still, he thought the company had real value, and as he and Chris entered into serious negotiations, he offered repeated assurances that Military .com's management—Chris, Anne, and the others—would receive significant payouts.

As Chris's discussions with Monster proceeded, he had some related decisions to make. One was whether to ensure that founding employees who had since left the company—people like Brad Clark and Steve Echikson—get some of their equity converted into cash. He decided that this was the right thing to do, even though the company's contracts with these former employees didn't require it. Already, Chris had a sense he might want to start another company someday, and he knew that one's reputation had a lot to do with one's reception. But he also believed in what some people called karma. He was acutely aware that he had been incredibly fortunate at many points in his life. If he hadn't met Scott Leftwich at the P-3 Orion conference back in late 1995; if he hadn't driven Admiral White, Anne Dwane's uncle, to a meeting in 1996; if he hadn't bumped into Anne on the first day he arrived at HBS in January 1997; if he hadn't met Abigail Johnson—if all of these accidents of fate and so many others hadn't happened, there would be no company, no rebound, no sale. Chris was sure of it.

Sharing the money was the right thing to do, he decided. But he also didn't want to mess with fate.

Chris hadn't talked with Brad Clark in nearly two years, but he knew where to find him. After traveling the world with his new wife, Clark had settled in Washington, D.C., where he was now the chief marketing officer for the Motley Fool.

Chris picked up the phone and called him. After a few pleasantries, he got right to the point. "We have a verbal commitment to sell the company," he told Clark. "Your share is going to be $1 million."

Clark was floored. He had hoped that someday he might see the return of part of his initial $100,000 investment. A million dollars wasn't exactly retire-and-move-to-a-tropical-island money, but it was an outstanding five-year return.

Chris asked if Clark would be willing to help him persuade one of the other initial investors—another partner at Mercer—to sign off on the deal to sell the company; Clark immediately agreed. Meanwhile, negotiations with Monster went relatively smoothly, and by March 2004 they were done.

The final purchase price was $39.5 million. Four and a half years after coming up with the idea for the company that became Military .com, Chris walked away with a little over $5 million.

MARC: SWITCHING ON

Not long after they moved into their SOS office, Marc, Alex, Andrew, and Richard started laying the groundwork to charge subscribers for TheLadders' newsletter. Each week now, they advertised that they would soon start offering a premium level of service—the new President's Club—that would deliver the most value. People were clearly responding to their job listings, and they were earning a bit of revenue from running paid Google ads on the site that Richard Safran had designed. Recruiters and employers were even starting to submit jobs on their own, without Marc or the others having to look for them. They seemed to have come a long way toward solving their chicken-and-egg problem.

Almost all of their subscribers had signed on after hearing about the service through either word of mouth or low-cost Internet marketing. Marc got a great e-mail from his cousin Loraine one day, reporting that a colleague had just recommended the service to *her*—not knowing that she had anything to do with it or that she was related to its founder. One Monday morning when they ran into a last-minute bottleneck and had to delay sending out the weekly newsletter for a few hours, they started getting e-mails before nine a.m. from people asking, "What happened to TheLadders?"

We have enough traction, Marc announced shortly afterward. It's time to start the pay product.

Just after New Year's Day 2004, they changed the format of the newsletter and started charging for premium access. The first day, about fifty subscribers signed up. This was cause for celebration, but it was immediately followed by frustration when they realized that they had used such a high level of encryption on their credit card information that they couldn't access it themselves. Their first paying customers would actually get the premium product for free.

But others signed up, and though they weren't making scads of money, they could at least put together a spreadsheet now, showing how much they'd invested in advertising and how many jobs they'd found. They could also figure how much it cost to attract each new subscriber and how much money each subscriber brought into the venture. It was early, but they could point to real, solid data. Just as important, they felt a lot more confident that their venture was really going to work.

Marc started bringing on unpaid interns to help with the never-ending grunt work that he, Alex, Andrew, and Richard had been doing since the start. He also decided it was time to begin raising money. He called a consultant in the investment banking industry he'd met while trying to put together a deal for the telephone-oriented job board.

Warren Spar had been an executive at several top banks before starting an investment boutique called Sparring Partners Capital. He specialized in helping entrepreneurs hone their presentations and introducing them to investment firms who might be willing to put up money. He met Marc at yet another Starbucks—a detail Spar found amusing, as he had sworn off coffee years before.

Spar liked Marc's business model but he recognized that the company was still early-stage and quite risky. Still, he enjoyed this kind of challenge. Although he'd named his company after himself, Spar was proud of the name's pugilistic connotation. He thought of himself as someone who helped businesses prepare to get in the ring with heavyweight investors.

Thanks to Spar's introductions, Marc pitched his company to a handful of venture capital firms. It was quickly apparent, though, that the VCs wouldn't respond with any real interest until TheLadders could show more substantial revenue over a longer period of time. Marc did get some positive feedback from the meetings, however. One Silicon Valley firm suggested that it might be willing to offer terms if Marc would consider moving the entire operation to California; Marc declined. And when he pitched to a firm in New Jersey, the partners voted two to one not to invest, but the lone dissenter, Robert Chefitz, took out his personal checkbook and invested $50,000.

Still, Marc was disappointed that they hadn't been able to attract venture-level funding, which was generally defined as $2 million or more. Spar suggested they try an angel round. Over the next month or so, Marc and Alex went back to people they'd known at every stage of their careers. Marc had a hard and fast rule that he would not allow family members to invest; if the venture didn't fly, he didn't want to be responsible for losing his family's money. But otherwise they cast a very wide net.

Steve Perricone had been living with Marc for five years now, sharing a kitchen and a lot of good times. He'd long since decided that Marc was as smart as any person he'd ever known—and he could say that without putting himself down, because he saw a lot of daylight between the ordinarily brilliant and the Cenedella level. Even so, whenever Marc talked to him about his business model for TheLadders, Steve's reaction was always: *Makes sense, but what's the scale here? How much can you possibly do with this?*

Now that Marc was looking for significant funding, though, Steve thought hard about whether he should invest. He was doing fine financially, but he couldn't put $20,000 or more into a friend's business on a whim.

Still, he was tempted. As he put it to a friend, "I'm already taking part of the risk, because if this fails and Marc doesn't have any income, I'll be paying the rent myself for a while. I may as well put myself in a position to reap the benefits."

He was comfortable with investing $20,000. But then he thought, Why not raise it to $25,000? And after committing himself to reach that level, he asked himself, Why not go as high as $30,000? Before long, Steve had become one of the largest single individual investors in TheLadders.

Steve provided additional help by introducing Marc to some of his colleagues at Deutsche Bank. Within a day or two, eight of them had signed on. Meanwhile, one of Marc's old bosses at the Riverside Company, Bob Fitzsimmons, also invested in the venture. Leading the whole group was the largest angel investor, Kevin Ryan, the CEO of Internet marketing giant DoubleClick, who had been an early investor in HotJobs.

By the end of February 2004, Marc had raised $635,000, which was $135,000 more than he had actually sought. In barely half a year he'd gone from drafting a PowerPoint presentation in his apartment to running a legitimate, growing company.

The day after closing out the investment round, Marc sat down with Andrew Koch and asked him to make a firm commitment to TheLadders.

"When are you going to quit?" he asked Andrew, who still worked full-time for HotJobs. "When will you start with us?"

Andrew was torn, if not downright panicked. It was one thing to moonlight with Marc in an effort to help his friend get the company off the ground. But now he had to make a decision. True, he'd always believed that some day Marc would come up with the idea that could make them all rich, but was it really time to take the leap? Back in the fall, when they'd hoped to raise significant funding during a venture capital round, he and Marc had agreed that when the company formally launched Andrew would make $40,000 a year to start. That was already a lot less than he was making at HotJobs, and now Marc said his budget was even tighter.

"How low can you go?" Marc asked him. "We need to tighten the belt and make this money last. So how low can you go?"

Marc and Andrew ultimately settled on $30,000. And although Marc told Andrew and the others that he would increase everyone's salaries when the company reached various milestones as they grew, there was no written agreement. Excited but more than a little anxious, Andrew resigned his position at HotJobs. More than ever, he was putting his full faith and credit in the talented hands of Marc Cenedella.

CHRIS: "PAY TO THE ORDER"

Ten years to the month after his P-3 Orion had nearly crashed over the Atlantic Ocean, Chris Michel received a check from Monster Worldwide, the first of three installments. He found it amusing that it actually *was* a paper check—rather than wire him the money, Monster Worldwide apparently preferred to earn a couple of extra days of interest. He stood in his studio apartment on Davis Court and read: "Pay to the Order of: Michel, Christopher P. Two Million Four Hundred Sixteen Thousand Thirty-Seven Dollars and 59 Cents."

Chris could easily envision an alternative universe in which he had followed the safer path and stayed in the navy. By now he might be working in the Pentagon again, or perhaps commanding the sort of squadron he'd served in back in Maine a decade earlier.

And honestly? he thought. It would have been a good life.

Several friends who had met him since business school told him they couldn't imagine that he would have been happy as a career military man, but Chris wasn't so sure. Above all things, he was adaptable, and he knew he could be happy in many situations. That said, he realized that this single check for $2.4 million might well be as much as he would have earned during an entire twenty-year military career.

He signed the certificate of merger. And with that, Chris, Anne, and the remainder of the Military.com team were now employees and shareholders of Monster Worldwide.

Soon after closing the deal, Andy McKelvey sent Chris a cryptic text message on his cell phone: "Do you want to go to Papau New Guinea?" Not long after that, Chris was exploring the jungles of the South Pacific with his new boss, the 388th richest person in the world according to *Forbes* magazine. The two entrepreneurs would be working together, and McKelvey wanted to get to know Chris better than he had during the negotiations.

They talked about all manner of things as they traveled, and at one point their conversation turned to the price that Monster had paid for Military.com.

"You could have saved yourself $5 million," Chris confided, meaning that he would have been willing to forgo most or all of his personal payday if the deal had required it. Certainly he liked the idea of being wealthy—he wouldn't be traveling through an exotic land and staying at five-star hotels if it weren't for the windfall. But to Chris, it had truly been more important for the the company to chalk up a win than for him to win personally.

"Five million dollars?" McKelvey replied, in the tone of a man whose personal fortune was more than one hundred times that amount. "Doesn't matter."

Once he'd decided to buy the company, McKelvey explained, he was most interested in the people who had built it, run it, and rescued it. Big companies like Monster did this all the time, buying up small competitors for a few million dollars not so much because they wanted the business, but because they wanted the people.

Yes, McKelvey said, the idea behind Military.com was important, as were the ongoing revenues, the membership, and the intellectual property that had made the company what it was. But if they wanted to grow Military.com even more, they needed to acknowledge that in time they would almost certainly have to reinvent the company yet again. McKelvey was the embodiment of the point he was trying to make: he had taken a tiny Yellow Pages advertising firm and over forty years built it into the top recruiting service on the World Wide Web. When he'd started out, the field of human resources recruitment had barely been envisioned—not to mention the Internet.

"Besides," McKelvey said, "think about how many deals are done that leave the founders feeling screwed." To preserve the team that had built the venture into a company he wanted to acquire, McKelvey felt that $5 million was a small price to pay.

During their trip, McKelvey made it clear to Chris that he wasn't done, not by a long shot. In his opinion, lots of undervalued Internet companies were ripe for the plucking. Soon after returning from Papua New Guinea, he asked everyone at a board meeting to think of at least one company that might be a good fit with Monster.

Chris heard about the request, and he immediately followed up with a suggestion: Monster should buy Tickle, which was the new name for James Currier's company, eMode. "If you go on Alexa," Chris told McKelvey, referring to the Internet service that ranked different Web sites by traffic, "Tickle will always be near the top."

Like Military.com, Tickle had completely rebounded: it was now a very profitable, subscription-based service, with about eighteen million active users and annual revenues above $20 million. And in the past year or so, it had begun morphing into a social network—an emerging but already crowded marketplace dominated by companies like MySpace and Friendster. James hadn't experienced quite the same level of pressure from investors as Chris had, mainly because he'd taken only a single round of venture capital back in 1999. But he had been through his own ups and downs, and Chris thought he might be open to selling.

As it happened, McKelvey had already explored the possibility of acquiring Tickle once or twice when it was still called eMode. He'd thought highly of James, and Chris's mention of the company got him intrigued all over again. But Monster wasn't alone. In the past couple of years, James had engaged in an extended discussion with Women.com about a possible sale, and Match.com, the dating service, had also made an offer. But neither approach had panned out.

Now, as McKelvey got back in touch with James, selling wasn't James's only option. Investment bankers were now calling; they wanted to take the company public. And he had a term sheet in hand from a venture capital firm that wanted to invest tens of millions of dollars.

McKelvey made an aggressive offer for the company, but James hesitated. Then McKelvey sweetened the pot, raising his bid to $92 million. Now it was impossible for James to say no.

By May 2004, the deal was done. Both Chris Michel and James Currier, Section H veterans who had attended HBS a year apart, had started, built, and sold their companies to Monster Worldwide.

CHAPTER 14

MANAGE RISK

One of the great myths about entrepreneurs is that they are risk seekers. All sane people want to avoid risk.

—PROFESSOR WILLIAM SAHLMAN,
HARVARD BUSINESS SCHOOL

Money. For many of us, this seems to be the biggest obstacle to starting a company and pursuing our entrepreneurial dreams. We need it but we haven't got it. Or we've got some but not enough. And even if we're able to raise the money we need, we're afraid of losing it. Whichever, sinking money into a new venture is always a risk, and there's no denying that risk is inherent to entrepreneurship.

Or is it?

After getting to know a lot of highly successful entrepreneurs, I've concluded that the answer is . . . yes and no. (Can you tell that I was a lawyer before I started writing books?) Seriously, though, of course entrepreneurship involves risk, but so does every other choice you make in life. When viewed objectively and dispassionately, the decision to launch a company built on a solid business model might actually be less risky than a lot of other courses of action. Highly successful entrepreneurs like Marla, Chris, and Marc recognize this, and they consistently aim to strike advantageous deals and assemble teams of people who contribute essential assets. As I got to know my trio of entrepreneurs and their ilk, I came to understand that they don't take risks so much as they manage and minimize risk for everyone involved.

"THERE IS NO RISK"

Marla, you may recall, learned what she considers her most important personal lesson from Jon Ledecky: DROOM, or Don't Run Out of Money. Or, to put Ledecky's useful rule another way, Hedge Your Financial Risk. (Sorry, no catchy acronym available.) But hedging your risk doesn't mean that you should stay out of the entrepreneurial arena for lack of abundant funds. It means don't spend money when you don't need to. It means raise money before you need it, and focus relentlessly on growing your revenue and improving your bottom line.

Marla, for one, managed to hedge virtually all of her risks as she moved forward—no surprise, because despite her entrepreneurial nature she was a fundamentally cautious person. Her Harvard MBA certainly helped minimize her risk—she knew having the degree meant that she'd almost never have to worry about being out of work for long. Even before she went to work for USOP and Building One, she made sure she could return to McKinsey if those jobs didn't pan out. And she remained an employee at Building One until literally the day before Ledecky put up the first $500,000 of funding for her new company.

But securing sufficient money was the real risk, and Marla minimized it in two ways. First, she chose an ideal moment to look for her initial investment—the late 1990s was one of the most active investor climates in American history. Second, she sought capital for her own venture while working for one of the country's most aggressive and entrepreneurial financiers—someone with a huge appetite for risk and for whom the idea of investing lots of money was hardly risk at all. In fact, with some prodding from Marla, Ledecky came to believe that it was riskier *not* to get involved in Internet investments at the time.

Of course Marla is the first to admit that, in the beginning, she didn't do enough to adhere to the DROOM rule; almost before she knew it, she was running out of money and bluemercury was in trouble. Her company was puny compared to the other Internet cosmetics retailers at the time. She and Barry spent most of the million dollars they'd raised building their first Web site, and she was left with no option other than to buy EFX, primarily with her own money. Her risk increased substantially.

"After we bought EFX, I just put my head down and tried to figure out how to make money for the stores," Marla told me. "But it was scary. We had no money in bluemercury—nothing. We couldn't pay bills. I have to confess that I sometimes had those how-can-I-even-get-out-of-bed-today kinds of days. It's the stuff that most entrepreneurs go through. But thanks to that experience early on with bluemercury, we've been really, really careful about how we spend money.

"I even believe in saving money in ways a lot of people would consider silly," she continued. "For a long while we would not order paper clips. We would take paper clips off documents that came into the office. I can't help myself: I still take paper clips and binder clips off things and store them away."

That may sound like an extreme example, but so many entrepreneurs will tell you similar stories. And they're all making the same point. If you're truly afraid of running out of money—and no matter what your situation, you probably should be—do everything you can to mitigate that risk.

As I got to know Chris Michel, I was struck by the fact that despite the real estate mania that gripped San Francisco and the rest of the country in the years after he graduated from Harvard, he stayed in the same rented studio apartment for nearly a decade. Marc was similarly level-headed, and in fact he still rents an apartment. Not only did Chris and Marc both avoid the kinds of significant financial risks that have burdened so many of their contemporaries, they also were careful not to tie themselves to one location if opportunity arose elsewhere.

Like Marla, Chris had originally tried to raise money at almost the perfect time. While it took a number of pitches, he eventually found a venture capital firm that wanted to support his company, and he was able to raise a second round of investment almost immediately. Capital was plentiful in those days, and venture capitalists were especially interested in technology and Internet companies. In 1998, VCs invested a total of $21 billion in United States companies; in 1999, they invested $51 billion. A year later, the figure was $100 billion.

Chris took a very practical approach to risk. But he also tended not to get especially emotional about it: during and after his time at Harvard Business School, he developed an ability to analyze opportunities that others might consider highly suspect and conclude that they were in fact not particularly risky at all. It helped, of course, that he had a deep-seated faith in his abilities, even before he'd ever launched a company.

His own feeling is that he doesn't have a higher tolerance for risk than the average person. He also believes that this is true of most entrepreneurs. "There is no special, overarching level of risk tolerance among entrepreneurs," Chris told me. "But entrepreneurs do have an inflated sense of their own abilities. They absolutely believe that they can go out there and launch a successful company."

Marc Cenedella, like Marla and Chris, focused intently on limiting his exposure. He learned from his early mistakes and consistently hedged his bets.

"After that bad experience in San Diego," Marc said, "I learned my lesson: always get your deal in writing. And if it turns out that you do need to exit, make sure you manage the exit carefully."

Similarly, when he started the company that eventually became TheLadders, he funded it himself, and did so on a shoestring. He was almost unbelievably cheap. He learned to write code so that he could put up his initial Web site on his own. He worked out of his apartment; he brought in partners and employees for equity rather than pay; he and Alex used every guerrilla marketing tactic they could think of to reduce expenses.

"I went without a paycheck for two years," Marc said. "At the end of 2003, when I looked at my financial situation, I was a little concerned. I had cashed out all of my 401(k) and my IRAs so I could put together the money I needed to launch. Coming into '04 I was naked and unprotected. I had all my assets involved, and if the venture went south, it was going to be difficult. So yeah, I think you do have to have a slightly higher appetite for risk. But believe me, I did everything I could to limit my exposure. I never wanted the threat of an empty bank account hanging over my head."

The best possible business, Professor Howard Stevenson declares, is a post office box to which others send cashier's checks. He's clearly got his tongue firmly planted in his cheek when he says this, but his joke gets the point across. The one point virtually all entrepreneurial researchers and academics agree on is that successful entrepreneurs are always extremely smart about managing risk.

"I say this as a quasi-outsider," explained Stig Leschly, "but it's not exactly a Nobel Prize–winning conceptual breakthrough. It's pretty straightforward: by carefully managing risk, you preserve as many options as possible. This is one thing HBS is really good at. We're clinical, and our students become very good at analyzing all the elements of a venture, all the variables, so that if they do decide to ever start a company, their exposure is as limited as it can be."

Noam Wasserman agreed. "The underlying point—and you could call it a theoretical perspective that goes back to the foundation of the first-year course—is that entrepreneurs manage risk rather than take risk. Focus on the bottom line; raise money; be frugal. Here's what we try to drive home to students: You might walk into class thinking entrepreneurs take risks. But no, what entrepreneurs do is manage the risk they take, in part by allocating the risk to other players who are better able to manage it. That, by the way, is what Bob Reese does in R&R."

R&R

R&R: it's perhaps the most famous entrepreneurial case at HBS. It's one of the first cases that Howard Stevenson wrote when he returned to HBS and began to assemble the entrepreneurship curriculum. When Marla, Chris, and Marc attended HBS, the school didn't require students to take an entrepreneurship course, although perhaps 90 percent of them enrolled in second-year electives such as Entrepreneurial Finance and Entrepreneurial Management. Now, HBS requires that every student take a course called the Entrepreneurial Manager in the second semester of the first year. If you look at the syllabus for that course, almost all of the assigned cases are less than five years old, and none is older than a decade—with one exception. R&R, which Stevenson wrote in 1983, is the common thread that connects virtually everyone who has attended HBS and studied entrepreneurship in the past twenty-five or so years.

The case protagonist, Bob Reese, had been in the board game business for years, and at the height of the Trivial Pursuit craze in the early 1980s, he came up with the idea of designing a similar game that would focus on TV trivia. In a matter of months, Reese managed to get a wide range of stakeholders to cooperate and produce his product, including a game designer, *TV Guide* magazine, a department store, and others.

Stevenson outlined his approach to the case to me one day. "We ask the question, 'Is the game business risky?' Everybody says, 'Yes.' And then you analyze the case and you say, 'Well, who does Reese have to get to cooperate?' He only has about three months to launch the game, and you ask, 'What does he give, and what does he need to get from them? Who took the risk?' The designer spent two weeks designing the game, but he was paid $250,000, and since he normally made $30,000, he sure wasn't taking any risk. He didn't even have to design the game until orders were in place. I can go through each of these—the department store, for example, placed orders—but Reese arranged for *TV Guide* to give them free advertising that exceeded the amount of their order. So even if the game bombed and they never sold a single unit, they'd get these twelve pages in *TV Guide*, which was at that point in front of seventeen million subscribers. And since the stores were never going to reorder, they weren't taking an inventory risk. By the time we've finished our study of the case, I always say to the students, 'Well, where did the risk go? I thought you told me this was risky!' "

THE THING I DID WELL

As you begin to form a concrete plan to launch an entrepreneurial venture, think about value. Take an inventory of what you will bring to the venture and value your assets accordingly. Start with your idea: that's worth something. Your time is worth something, too, and so is your passion, your experience, and your contacts. We've seen how opportunity varies depending on who is considering it; similarly, the risk differs greatly depending on who thinks about taking those risks. The intelligent entrepreneur works hard to ensure that the people bearing each risk are the ones who perceive them as least risky.

Before this gets entirely bogged down in theory, let me give you a personal example. I mentioned in the introduction to this book that I had started or joined several entrepreneurial ventures over the years, and that looking back I think I'd made every possible mistake. One of these ventures was an edgy legal magazine that a classmate and I cofounded during law school in the late 1990s. In retrospect, I can see good reasons why the venture no longer exists. Among other things, we didn't know the ten rules that you're learning here.

For example, we came up with a solution before we looked for the problem. (We had previously run a smaller publication on campus, we both wanted to write professionally, and we wanted the creative freedom that would come from owning our own publication.) We didn't "think big" enough or "think new" enough. (A print magazine? Really? At the start of the Internet boom?) And we didn't assemble the right team. Although my cofounder in that venture is a great guy whom I'd recommend to anyone, in retrospect our backgrounds and skill sets were similar, not complementary. Furthermore, our approach to hiring was a mess, so it's no surprise that we didn't assemble the right team.

But the one thing we did do well was manage risk and stretch resources.

We couldn't afford graphic designers to work on our prototype, so we persuaded a professor at a local design college to have her class assemble it as a project. The work obviously didn't require her students to take any risks: they got real-world experience and good samples for their portfolios. (In fact, one of the better personnel decisions we made was to hire one of the students after graduation.)

We couldn't afford to rent an office, so we persuaded a nearby city's economic development committee to find one for us. There was no risk to the landlord, who gave us a few months of free rent; we occupied a couple of rooms in office space that was otherwise nearly empty, and having us working there made the building look a little more successful and vibrant.

We had little money to market the magazine to lawyers, or to ship the first prototype issue to them. So we decided to give it away to law students and professors. We rented a big yellow moving truck, drove to every law school between Boston and Washington, D.C., snuck into the schools' mail rooms, and hand delivered over twenty-five thousand free copies over a three-day period. There was very little risk to us, other than a few days' work that turned into a fun adventure.

The takeaway here is that we needed a number of "scarce assets" (as Chris Michel would have described them back in 1999), and virtually every one of them could have cost us a lot of money and thus substantially increased our risk. But the design work, the office space, the truck, and many of other assets that we "acquired" were not similarly valued by the people we brought into the endeavor. And although the company eventually faltered, we kept it running for a long time because we managed risk well.

Let that be your mantra as you try to assemble the resources you need (the part about managing risk, of course, not the part about eventually faltering). After all, whenever we make what we consider a rational choice, we are in some sense managing risk. When you decide to go to work for someone else rather than start your own business, you may well be making a decision not to take the risk that the venture you might otherwise start would one day disappear. Statistically, you'd be making the rational choice, because a prospective business almost certainly has less chance of surviving than an established one. But even taking a job with a well-known company is a risk—it's not by accident that I chose to highlight the recruiting advertisements displayed in the HBS student newspaper in the late 1990s for firms like Andersen Consulting, Lehman Brothers, and Enron. Just a decade later, none of these firms existed.

Here are some other issues to think about as you take inventory of your "scarce assets."

Do you have a financial background? The lifeblood of your business—of any business—is, of course, cash. Almost as important, though, is a good understanding of money and finance. Throughout this book, I've tried to avoid offering suggestions that would require you to make big outlays of money or time—such as going back to school—but in this case I'll make an exception. If you're committed to starting your own business (and by now I hope you are), you should either have some experience with finance and accounting or dedicate yourself to learning the basics in those fields. Practically speaking, understanding such things as cash flow and balance sheets will help you make critical decisions every day; in a more general sense, having a working understanding of finance will significantly reduce your risk. Even if you expect that a business partner or an outside firm will be managing your company's money, at the very least you need to be able to understand what they're doing.

Incorporate. If you're serious about starting a business, it's well worth the time and the minimal investment required to observe the formalities of incorporating. Do it early—from a risk-management perspective, you don't want to expose any personal assets unnecessarily. And if you have partners, cofounders, or equity investors, be sure your agreement with them is on paper. Frankly, I was surprised to find that several of the highly successful entrepreneurs I interviewed didn't incorporate their companies or enter into formal agreements with their cofounders until just before raising investment.

Have a Plan B. It's both comforting and sensible to have a backup plan, just in case it turns out that your entrepreneurial venture isn't quite as viable as you first believe it is. We've already seen that Marla, Chris, and Marc all managed the risks inherent in starting a company by having not only an MBA from Harvard, but also either a job offer in hand or the prospect of getting a job if their venture failed. And the list of entrepreneurs in our story who made sure to hold on to their day jobs until the last possible moment is long—not just Marla and Anne Dwane, but also Andrew Koch, Richard Safran, and many others. So although you should of course maintain an intense focus on your new venture, you also should keep an eye on what you'll do if things don't work out. That might mean working on your venture part-time at first, or maintaining as good a relationship as you can with former employers so that you have a place to land if you need it. And if you're not coming to an entrepreneurial enterprise from another job—or at least not one you could imagine ever returning to—it might mean working hard to keep networking in your field even after you've launched. It's much better to have some other offer and not need it than to need one and not have it.

Liquidity is your friend. If your goal is to minimize cash outlay and risk—and it certainly ought to be—you should rent assets instead of buying them, persuade suppliers to give you their products at a discount or for free, and do whatever you can to get paid quickly. And be sure you pay close attention to the current costs of goods and services. It's remarkable, for instance, how much the costs involved in starting an Internet-based business plummeted over the decade during which the stories in this book occurred. "Scarce resources" that cost Marla and Chris hundreds of thousands of dollars in the late 1990s cost Marc tens of thousands of dollars in 2003 and 2004. Today, the same products and services can often be had for much less money.

THE NEXT RULE

It's rare that you can completely mitigate risk, but you can often manage it down to a reasonable level. Once you've done so, you need to measure your appetite for risk. Many successful entrepreneurs are surprisingly risk averse, but keep in mind that too much caution opens the door to a different sort of risk: inaction. The old saying is old for a reason: nothing ventured, nothing gained. At some point you have to take the leap.

A good way to manage risk is to follow a version of one of the previous rules: don't manage it alone. If you've come this far, you've probably already brought in—or in some way involved—a team of people who can help you achieve your dream of starting and building a successful company. The assets that each member of your team brings to your venture will help you limit your exposure to risk; after all, you've brought them on board because you believe they can make a substantial contribution to your success. But once you've involved others in your new venture, you'll quickly come to realize that they are looking to you to set a course toward the beckoning horizon. Cofounders, partners, employees, even unpaid interns—they will all depend on you to motivate them, manage them, communicate with them, and lead them.

Which brings me to the next key point, one that I heard over and over from the truly intelligent entrepreneurs I came to know: whoever you are, whatever your personality, your success will likely turn on whether you learn to lead people effectively.

CHAPTER 15

If you start to take Vienna—take Vienna.

—NAPOLEON BONAPARTE

MARC: LEARNING TO LEAD

In early 2004, Michael Shafrir, a twenty-three-year-old University of Michigan graduate living in Philadelphia, was bored. He decided to make a change in his life—maybe he ought to live in New York. One afternoon, he came across a blind job ad on Craigslist. An unnamed company was looking for energetic, can-do people interested in working at a dynamic Internet startup in Manhattan. The ad stressed that investment banking experience was preferred.

Shafrir had been a psychology major in college, and he had no experience whatsoever in banking. He'd spent a year after college as a teacher's aide working with autistic children; for about the past six months, he'd been working for a nonprofit that promoted Philadelphia as a tourist destination. But he'd interned at an Internet career site called the Vault during college. He'd enjoyed the experience and thought it might be fun to work for an Internet company again. With nothing to lose, he sent his résumé to the anonymous e-mail address listed in the ad.

A day or two later, Shafrir got a phone call from Andrew Koch at TheLadders. Andrew described the company and explained the kinds of people they were looking for. TheLadders had expanded exponentially over the past few months—nearly one hundred thousand people now subscribed to the free version of the newsletter and service that Marc had dreamed up. They needed to hire people quickly.

Would the fact that he had no investment banking experience hurt his chances? Shafrir asked.

"Oh, that," Andrew replied. They didn't really need investment bankers, he explained. But they did want people who were willing to work investment-banker hours—eighty or ninety hours a week. And, Andrew hastened to add, not for very much pay.

Still, Shafrir was sufficiently interested. He headed to New York for an interview on a Friday afternoon in late March.

Marc Cenedella was wearing a polo shirt with a Grateful Dead logo on it when he met with Shafrir for the first time. Both men turned out to be big fans of the band, and before they exchanged a word about the company or discussed Shafrir's background, they spent ten minutes discussing the Dead and another band, Phish. The interview that followed was casual, but Shafrir was intrigued by Marc and his young company, and he spent much of the weekend thinking about the TheLadders and its charismatic founder.

On Monday, Shafrir called Andrew back.

"I really want to work for you guys," he said.

That's great news, Andrew replied, because we want you to work here as well.

But, he warned, the salary would be very low, and they weren't yet in a position to offer health insurance or other benefits. He made the offer: $30,000 a year.

"Can you do a little better?" Shafrir asked.

"No," Andrew replied. "Sorry."

Shafrir hadn't expected to get rich quickly working for this new venture. Besides, in his previous jobs as a teacher's aide and a low-level worker at a nonprofit, he hadn't exactly commanded huge salaries. More than anything, he wanted adventure and the chance to do something he believed in—the money would come eventually. "Okay," he said. "I'll join anyway."

A few weeks later he moved to New York and came aboard as Employee Number 11.

———

Seven months after launching, TheLadders was now doubling and tripling in size every few weeks. Marc had never been the ultimate leader of such a large group before, and though he knew he was doing some things well, he often felt as if he were feeling his way forward in the dark. Knowing the challenges involved in running his company would grow only more intense, he redoubled his business reading. He devoured management books, and at times he led his staff as if he were a novice teacher keeping just one textbook chapter ahead of his students. In *Made in America*, for example, the memoir of Wal-Mart founder Sam Walton, Marc read about the legendary Saturday morning meetings that Walton used to hold with all of his company's managers. Marc decided to imitate them as best he could, but since Saturday mornings probably didn't make sense, he began bringing the entire staff together every Friday afternoon. Each week, while their competition at HotJobs, Monster, Dice, and other job boards got ready for the weekend, Marc's staff would spend part of Friday afternoon developing the tactics they would use in the week ahead to scale TheLadders as fast as possible.

Hiring was a real challenge for Marc. Bringing in Michael Shafrir was an encouraging example of how things could go well. He'd had a good feeling about Shafrir right away, and if not for a sense of professional propriety he might well have offered him a job during the first interview—somewhere between "hello" and the first mention of Trey Anastasio, the lead singer of Phish. But when hiring went poorly, it could go very poorly. Marc faced a classic entrepreneur's dilemma: learning to both lead and empower the people he brought aboard. He was a demanding boss, he realized, and he had such a strong vision for the company's future that it was hard for him to relinquish any control of either its operation or its evolution.

Marc was now facing the same sorts of problems that Chris Michel had addressed years before. He needed people, and he needed them now. But he'd already brought on Alex, Andrew, and his friend Steve Higgins; he'd almost tapped out all of his personal contacts. Time was now his most valuable commodity. He could no longer interview every potential employee five or six times—as he'd done with Richard Safran—and he was finding it increasingly difficult to get to know each new person who did come aboard.

Safran, meanwhile, was working absurdly long hours as chief technology officer. The Web site was growing very fast, but there was only so much one man could do, and he finally asked Marc if he could hire two programmers. Marc granted the request, even though his first priority was adding people who focused on customer service and community building.

Safran knew that Marc wanted to keep close tabs on every communication that went out to his subscribers—it was critical, in Marc's view, that real, live people answer the phones and respond to subscribers' e-mails. Safran found this refreshing. In his experience, CEOs of Internet startups usually wanted to maximize automation in order to eliminate human involvement, thus saving money. Marc, by contrast, believed that one of Safran's most important jobs was to build the technological tools that would allow the company's customer service people to communicate more efficiently and effectively with its subscribers.

Marc's cofounders were as dedicated as ever, but after putting the company first for many months, they now had to take a little more time for their personal lives. Andrew was getting married; Alex's wife was pregnant with twins. And although Alex was very happy to be getting a regular paycheck, his salary was modest by New York standards. In Manhattan, $60,000 a year would not go far, especially now that he would soon be raising a family. The irony was thick: here, they had built a company devoted to $100,000-a-year jobs, but no one working for the company itself made anywhere near that much.

But they all understood that the only sure way to increase both their salaries and the value of their equity was to do everything possible to build TheLadders. By this point, Marc and Alex had a reasonably reliable formula worked out. If they listed a certain number of jobs and spent a certain number of marketing dollars, they could count on signing up a fairly predictable number of free subscribers. And for each hundred new subscribers, they could make a pretty accurate guess about how many would eventually sign up for the premium service.

Marc was very open with his employees about how much money they brought in. At each weekly meeting he emphasized that they were pouring every spare penny into building their subscriber base. The base continued to grow rapidly, but in March 2004 they hit a speed bump. They'd been advertising TheLadders on their competitors' sites, and the ads had essentially encouraged the competitors' users to take their business elsewhere. Nearly a quarter of the company's leads came from running ads on one competitor's site alone, and when that company abruptly banned TheLadders from its site, the loss of revenue dealt TheLadders a potentially crushing blow. The big job boards might not know how to compete with his company, Marc realized, but they were at least savvy enough to understand that it made no sense to make it so easy for Marc to target their customers.

Soon after getting the news, Marc called the entire company into the conference room. By now the staff comprised the largest company working out of the SOS offices.

"Guys," he said, "here's the deal. We just lost the mechanism that brings us a quarter of our clients. I don't know how you're going to do it, but I need you to do it: go find more clients!"

Alex, Andrew, Mike Shafrir—everyone pitched in, scrambling to find new places to run their ads. Marc was adamant about charting the return they got on each marketing dollar; happily, most of their dollars delivered a good return, and even after losing the big job board, they kept bringing in more subscribers. Each Friday, when all the employees gathered in the conference room, Marc would write two columns of numbers on a whiteboard. One column showed TheLadders' planned and actual numbers, and another listed historical data that Marc said represented the progress of giant companies like Wal-Mart or eBay back when they had been young companies.

Marc would announce, for example, that they were beating eBay: Today ends the forty-second week in the history of TheLadders.com and we have this many subscribers. At the end of its forty-second week, eBay had only this many users.

Nobody knew where Marc was getting these historical figures, but it didn't matter. The information was a great motivator; it set the bar high, and it suggested that Marc fully expected the company to play in a major-league arena.

Marc's business plan projected that TheLadders would be cash-flow negative for a year. But because the company was bringing in more paying customers than they'd planned, by April they were in the black. Determined to take advantage of being so far ahead of schedule, Marc ramped up their marketing and hiring yet again, pushing them back into the red. But the money spent on signing new subscribers continued to pay off, and by June they were cash-flow positive once more. The free version of the weekly newsletter passed the one-hundred-thousand-subscriber mark and Marc could hardly keep up with all the hiring he had to do. Finally he reached out to the best HR person he knew in New York City: Dave Carvajal, who had recruited both Marc and Alex to HotJobs four and five years earlier.

Dave had kept track of Marc and his exploits, but lately Dave's career had taken a backseat to his family life. Now he was looking for something new and exciting to do, and he agreed to come by Marc's office and help out for a few days. Dave began what he called "networking in real time." He made a list of the positions he needed to fill, searched online for people who held comparable positions at other firms, and then cold-called them and explained the opportunity. If they wanted to interview, great. If not, he'd ask for the names of two or three colleagues who might be interested.

Within a day or two, Dave had assembled a list of ten promising technical people and set up interviews. Within a week, three of them had joined the company. Dave couldn't work for free forever, but when he looked around he saw an office humming with ambition and talent. He remembered that in early 2003 Marc had wanted to bring him in as a partner and investor, but he'd declined.

Holy cow, he thought now. What have I missed?

Instead of leaving, Dave made one more hiring suggestion: himself. In July 2004 he signed on.

The next month, Marc decided that it was time to talk again with Warren Spar.

Should we think about raising some money? Marc asked him. Will the VCs take us seriously? "Of course, we have no idea what our annual revenue is," Marc acknowledged. "But that's okay, because we pay salaries with our weekly cash flow, not our annual revenue." By then, the company was bringing in between $20,000 and $25,000 a week.

Warren agreed that Marc should meet with a few potential investors. TheLadders didn't necessarily *need* venture capital now; clearly the business would continue to grow without it. But every time they funneled more of their revenue into their marketing budget—or, as Marc put it, every time they poured gasoline on the fire—their subscriber base grew bigger. Imagine what they could do with a few million dollars—dramatically ramp up their marketing, build a more robust Web site, and cement their position in this new market before their competitors knew what had happened.

Warren began setting up meetings with VCs, and Marc and Alex made their first pitch on the Tuesday after Labor Day. This time their presentation was received very enthusiastically, and within two weeks they had a term sheet in hand. But they decided to hold out and push for an even better deal. Besides, Marc was having fun. Pitching to VCs after you'd already been offered a deal was validating, and it also turned the tables: now the investors were competing for Marc's attention, not the other way around. It was also a way to get some great free advice about his business from some very smart people.

By the third week of September, he and Alex had made their presentation more than a dozen times, and some of the excitement was beginning to wear off. Then, on September 24, Marc got a call from a partner at a venture capital firm in Boston: Nick Beim, of Matrix Partners.

A Stanford- and Oxford-educated investor, Beim had been very taken with Marc and Alex when he'd met with them. He liked the look of the business model, but he was even more impressed by the quality of the management team Marc and assembled. Soon after the meeting began, Beim started checking off several mental boxes. This team had been working in the industry at high levels for several years before starting TheLadders. They brought obvious passion and commitment to their enterprise. They had developed a unique and counterintuitive business model—though no one had ever tried to charge job seekers for listings, it was clearly working. In addition, their argument that Monster and HotJobs wouldn't be able to compete on TheLadders' chosen playing field was persuasive. Finally, there was the idea itself, which put the company squarely in the pain business rather than the pleasure business. As Beim knew, finding a job trumps *everything* when you don't have one.

The Monday after that first phone call, Beim paid a visit to Marc in New York City. They had another very good conversation and quickly reached a deal.

Three weeks later, Marc and Andrew were working in the office on Twenty-third Street. Alex was by his wife's bedside at New York–Presbyterian Hospital on Sixty-eighth Street—their twins had arrived two months early.

Marc, Andrew, and Alex were in close contact throughout the day, constantly checking their BlackBerries for news of the deal.

Finally their lawyer sent them the e-mail they'd been waiting for: "Check your bank account. You should have $7.5 million."

CHRIS MICHEL: ALL ABOUT OUTCOMES

Chris Michel and Anne Dwane—along with James Currier and his cofounders—were now employees of Monster Worldwide. They continued to direct their respective companies, but they did so with the muscle and resources of a billion-dollar parent company behind them. If he'd thought about it before he sold, Chris realized, he might have been concerned about how running Military.com would be different under the auspices of a large corporation. But he and Anne felt they'd lucked out. Andy McKelvey, Jeff Taylor, and Brad Baker were entrepreneurs at heart, and they tried to infuse their whole company with that ethos. Military and Tickle were the only two Monster properties in San Francisco (Monster itself was based near Boston), and for the most part the Big Company left them alone. As long as Chris and Anne met their monthly revenue targets—and Military.com, which was now bringing in millions of dollars a year in profit, was doing that and more—Monster had no interest in meddling. But when they needed support, the Big Company was there.

Payroll? Monster handled it. Add a jobs board to the site? Monster got it done. And Chris and Anne also had a new and very effective way to solicit potential members: Monster let them troll the résumés in the company's database for current and former armed forces members.

With the financial pressure off, Military.com had a Washington office again, and Chris could once more stay at the Ritz-Carlton on business trips. He flew out to D.C. and called Brad Clark, who was now working at the Motley Fool. Chris and Brad had endured their share of hardship and bruised feelings during the darkest days at Military.com, but the passage of time and the clearing of checks proved to have a remarkably beneficial effect on their relationship. When they met for a drink at the Tombs, a forty-year-old Georgetown University bar, their conversation was relaxed and friendly. Chris was pleased to hear that Brad was thriving at the Motley Fool, and he remained grateful for the role Brad had played in launching Military.com.

But if Chris felt good about the way he treated Brad when selling his company to Monster, he was less happy about Anne's payoff, which had been considerably less than his own. Yes, he had come up with the original idea and quit Mercer when the venture was little more than a credit card and a dream. Yes, he had taken the leap and actually started the company. But Chris believed that it was Anne who had saved Military.com by figuring out how to sell qualified lead referrals on a grand scale. He told himself that they should have substantially increased her equity in the company way back when—except that the shares were worthless until near the very end, when suddenly they weren't. Chris wasn't sure how, but he promised himself he would find a way to ensure that Anne eventually got the credit—and the financial rewards—she deserved.

Though he was now a multimillionaire, very few of the external trappings of Chris's life had changed. He still didn't own a car. He still lived in the same studio apartment across the street from Anne and overlooking the bay. He also felt a little uncomfortable that James Currier insisted on giving him credit for managing Monster's acquisition of Tickle. But James was adamant about wanting to give him some sort of token of appreciation. For months, he and Chris had been talking about taking some kind of trip together, but things never worked out.

Finally, James and one of his cofounders came up with an idea. They took Chris for a weekend at the Esalen Institute, a humanistic retreat in Big Sur, California. Esalen, the birthplace of the Human Potential movement, was about as New Agey as anyplace in the country, and James had a lot of fun watching his straitlaced friend, the former navy man, trying to blend in with all the hip Californians trying to feel the energy in their toes.

"Don't laugh at these people," James had warned on the way in. "If you have to laugh at someone, laugh at me."

But Chris adapted as always, and by the end of the weekend he fit right in. He and James had a good laugh about how "all it had taken" for Chris to loosen up was to spend five years building and then selling a $40 million company.

As 2005 began, Chris felt a breeze of change blowing through his professional life. Since selling Military.com to Monster, he'd been reporting to Brad Baker; now, when Baker was given a promotion, Baker in turn offered one to Chris. The new position would be a significant step up: he'd be overseeing not just Military.com but several other Monster properties.

Chris thought about it hard, but in the end he decided to turn Baker down. For now, he was happy running Military.com; moreover, he realized that he had little interest in climbing the corporate ladder at Monster. He marveled at how much he'd changed in the course of a decade. During his time in the navy and throughout his early years in the business world, he absolutely would have judged his progress by how far up the ladder he moved.

That measure of success held little appeal for him now. Despite all the hard times at Military.com, all the worries and sleepless nights, Chris realized that he missed the idea of creating something out of nothing. Monster had treated him extremely well, but he was starting to feel the familiar hunger. One day he finally asked himself the question point-blank: was he ready to commit himself once again to starting a new venture?

He immediately realized that he already knew the answer. He really had no choice. Yes, he wanted to do this again.

While thinking about what his next opportunity might be, Chris decided to distill some of his experiences as an entrepreneur into an article for *Proceedings*, the monthly magazine of the U.S. Naval Institute. Although the piece was ostensibly written for a military audience, it had clear application to the topic of leadership in general.

Writing with remarkable candor, Chris admitted that he'd fallen into a dangerous trap while building Military.com. He had confused *activities* with *outcomes*, believing that both fell under the broader heading of accomplishments. In the early days, he and his team had thrown people and money at problems with little discrimination. They'd had those assets in abundance, and it seemed almost criminal *not* to spend them. But they often mistook the *feeling* of accomplishing something for actually doing so, and as time went on that confusion had nearly killed the company.

To illustrate his point, Chris used a frame of reference his audience would readily understand. Suppose you could get a look at the official records of two navy fighter squadrons, he wrote. Imagine that these hypothetical units flew the same airplanes, trained in the same way, and undertook the same missions. Further, imagine that the squadrons were made up of people with virtually similar backgrounds. Given these equivalences, you might think that the two squadrons would perform pretty much on a par. But the data showed that this wasn't the case at all. In fact, navy studies had revealed that strong squadrons outperformed weaker ones by a factor of ten.

What was the difference? Maybe luck played some part. Maybe one squadron happened to have more naturally gifted pilots or more dedicated officers. But scale it over time, analyze the data coming from dozens of different squadrons, and the most likely explanation for the striking differences in performance was leadership, culture, and a relentless focus on desired outcomes. Equipping and training the squadrons was important, but not nearly as important as the paramount goal— patrolling and deterring during peacetime, fighting and winning in times of war.

Understanding the distinction between activities and outcomes was a fundamental pillar of leadership, and yet, Chris wrote, it was something he was "embarrassed to say that it took me ten years to learn."

Writing the article led Chris to reflect further on these critical issues. In particular, he found himself revisiting the hiring decisions he'd made at Military.com. He'd hired a lot of people; some were terrific; some were horrible. But not until the company was all but out of money and he'd had to lay off almost the entire staff did he focus on the true value each person brought to the enterprise. With a cold eye, he looked at each employee and asked a question: could he or she help grow the company and make it profitable?

With the luxury of hindsight, Chris realized that only two characteristics really mattered when evaluating team members—competency and fit. He took out a pad one day and sketched out a 2×2 matrix.

Great fit. Low competency.	Great fit. High competency.
Lousy fit. Low competency.	Lousy fit. High competency.

↑ FIT ↓

← COMPETENCY →

At the outset, he had hired quickly, and almost inevitably he had hired people in all four categories. Once you realized that an employee fell into either the lower left or upper right quadrants, you had no trouble knowing how to respond. But how do you handle the highly proficient person who was nevertheless a complainer who hurt other employees' morale? Or the enthusiastic, nice person who just didn't have the skills or competencies to get the job done? When things were going well, you could cover up for poisonous or incompetent people— but when times got bad, they simply had to go. At great cost, Chris had come to understand that sooner or later the health of a company will be threatened unless everyone on the team is both passionate and effective. It was almost always better to have a hole in your lineup than to bring in or retain a marginal performer.

Looking back, Chris admitted that he hadn't focused on developing a culture of excellence until his company had reached the brink of extinction. Why had it taken a near death experience to learn this incredibly important lesson? Again he thought back to the navy. In a good unit, it didn't matter whether the commanding officer was present on any given day, because the lowest-ranking sailors would encourage one another to do the right thing and insist that everyone aspire to excellence. And they did so because they took pride in both their individual performance and the enterprise to which they belonged.

If he ever launched another business, Chris promised himself, he would do his best to lead, lead, lead, while at the same time doing everything possible to create a culture of excellence. From the start, he would focus relentlessly on outcomes.

MARLA: NOTHING'S GOOD FOREVER

By 2004, Marla's and Barry's lives had been completely transformed. Once they were married, Marla had added Barry's last name to hers, and before long they had two children and a house in the suburbs. Their company was remarkable not only because it had survived and grown, but also because it had escaped disaster when so many others around it had imploded. Marla and Barry could look back at the founding of E2Enet and take great satisfaction in the knowledge that five years later theirs was the only E2Enet-funded company that still existed.

Soon after Jon Ledecky sold E2Enet to U.S. Technologies—the prison-labor company turned new-economy investor run by Greg Earls—the company had gone down in flames. Then, plagued by accounting scandals, the firm had brought in William Webster, the former FBI director, to set the books straight. But it was too little, too late. By early 2004, Earls had been indicted for stock fraud, and Jon Ledecky wound up testifying against him in federal district court. Earls was convicted and sentenced to ten years in prison.

After U.S. Technologies disintegrated, the Carlyle Group acquired some of their investments—including the original Ledecky interest in bluemercury. Now Carlyle's managing director, Ed Mathias—who had helped both Ledecky and Marla countless times over the years—had an even bigger stake in Marla and Barry's success.

Bluemercury was opening stores at a fast pace now. By the middle of 2004, they had added a second store in the Philadelphia area and three stores in New Jersey, with two more scheduled to open before year's end. By the end of 2004, they projected annual revenues of about $9 million. Buoyed by their success and wanting to grow even bigger, they raised yet another round of funding. Attracting investors was comparatively easy now. Andrew Sachs, who had introduced them to the Dinner Club in 2001, had started a new fund with a real estate developer who built luxury homes on the Delaware Coast. This fund, called Bethany Partners, invested $500,000, and other investors came in as well, pushing the total influx of cash up over a million dollars.

Relative to her peers in retail, Marla's management style continued to be fairly unconventional. She still insisted on hiring only full-time employees, even though some of her investors encouraged her to switch to part-time staff so she could save on fringe benefits. Marla was convinced that the lower level of service her customers would receive wouldn't be worth it. She still used a store-based bonus structure, so that her employees were encouraged to work together rather than compete with one another. And Marla still personally interviewed every new employee in every store. She knew that her employees thought she could be exacting and tough to work for, but she made no apologies for that. She held herself to a very high standard and the stores reflected her ambition to be the best of the breed.

Meanwhile, Marla also continued to pour all of bluemercury's profits back into the company. For five years, almost since the start of bluemercury, two of Marla and Barry's most influential mentors had been urging them to "recapitalize"—to cash out at least some of their equity in the company. It was all very well to say you had succeeded financially because you had a large ownership stake in a growing chain of stores— but it was another thing entirely to be able to recap. Until now, though, Marla and Barry's focus had always been on building the chain, never on taking money out of it.

But by the start of 2005, Marla was pregnant with their third child. It was amazing how having children changed one's perspective: she and Barry were now responsible not just for themselves but for a young family.

Nearly every time they saw Jon Ledecky these days, he'd ask them when they were going to sell. He would come by Marla and Barry's house for a drink or a party, and whenever the conversation turned to business, he'd ask her: "So, have you taken any money off the table yet?"

Or Barry would run into Ledecky at the local CVS and his friend would say: "Hey, Bar, when are you going to pull out some of your money?"

Marla had also remained close with Dick Darman, her Kennedy

School professor. Invariably, he would say to her: "Remember, Marla, nothing is good forever."

MARC: BECOMING A CEO

Prior to the venture capital round of financing, Marc Cenedella had repeatedly told everyone attending the weekly meetings at TheLadders that he hoped to raise somewhere around $3.5 million. In the end, they had received more than double that amount, and now expectations were running very high. Everyone was still working extremely long hours, and as many as four or five people crammed into each of the growing number of offices they rented from SOS. Inevitably, perhaps, tempers grew short and tension mounted, especially when some of the newer hires complained that they should be making higher salaries now that the company was fully funded. Marc addressed this complaint directly at one of the Friday meetings. Speaking with evident heat, he told the staff that the company's revenues were to be used "for marketing and growth," not for padding the wallets of employees.

Space was another obvious issue, and Marc finally decided to do something about it. In April 2005, TheLadders moved out of the temporary office space that had been their home for eighteen months and into a 12,500-square-foot office in Soho. The larger quarters meant that they could hire even more people; one day, not long after moving into the new offices, Marc passed an odd milestone. He walked into the company he'd started and was greeted by an employee he was certain he'd never seen before.

As the company grew, Marc continued to make a concerted effort to improve his management skills. At the outset, his leadership style amounted to pushing the four guys working out of his apartment to match his ambition and his work ethic. He was completely clear about the results he wanted, and while he had been very good at predicting which result they would achieve and when they would achieve it, he was less able to recognize the psychological impact he could have on other people. Now, if he was serious about continuing to grow, he had to become a much more effective leader. He adjusted his approach to running the company in a number of ways. Among other changes, he began to dress differently. At the beginning, he had come to work dressed casually, sometimes wearing Hawaiian shirts and cargo pants. But now he started wearing suits every day. If he was going to be the CEO of a successful company, he reasoned, he ought to try to look the part.

But Marc had no desire to change some of the company's traditions. Though TheLadders had never paid especially well, it had always thrown fun parties and provided its staff with some great perks. This was just Marc's way; he believed in motivating people by promising to give them something special if they really performed. He liked to tell a story about the time, years ago, when HotJobs had signed a $250,000 advertising deal with another company, only to find that the ads weren't delivering even a fraction of the traffic they'd been promised. Marc challenged Alex Douzet to negotiate the company down to $200,000, and he told Alex that if he could pull it off, he'd take him anywhere in the city for dinner to celebrate. A few days later, Alex came into his office smiling; he'd driven the price all the way down to $175,000. He'd saved the company $75,000, and Marc was happy to spend $1,000 taking Alex and his wife out to celebrate.

Now, as the leader of his own company, Marc reasoned that even the most recently hired employee could understand the idea of setting a tangible goal, and then having a party or event of some sort to commemorate achieving it. From his first lunch with Steve Higgins—after subscribers number one, two, and three had signed up to receive his newsletter—to the much more extravagant cocktail parties and dinners at local bars and restaurants, Marc insisted on celebrating the company's wins. In Marc's view, the camaraderie and sense of pride that developed as a result of these kinds of celebrations were well worth the expense.

But as TheLadders grew, it was sometimes hard for Marc to explain the fundamentals of what he called "the ecosystem" to all the new employees—the delicate balance of new leads, subscribers, employers, and ads that drove the company's performance. They could practically measure their progress by the hour, and every week they were making more money than the week before. Success breeds yet more success, Marc would explain, and a scoreboard measuring performance was essential. In fact, very early on in the company's life, Marc insisted on installing a dashboard on every employee's computer that showed down to the minute how TheLadders was doing.

Still, it took a while before Marc could admit that he needed to develop CEO-level skills in order to run his company effectively. When he finally crossed that psychological bridge, he began meeting with a group of New York CEOs every month and exchanging tips and ideas about leadership. He also started working with an executive coach. Top athletes had coaches; why shouldn't CEOs?

One lesson Marc learned early on was that many of his employees were reluctant to deliver bad news. To get around this problem, Marc's coach suggested several techniques. One of them was to make his inquiries about performance progressively more specific. He might start by casually asking someone who worked for him how things were going.

Nine times out of ten, the person would answer: "Great. Fine."

Marc would follow up by asking a slightly different version of the question: "How's *work* going?"

Again, the answer would almost always be, "Great."

Then he'd move in for the kill. "Glad to hear it. But let's say work wasn't going well—what would you say to me in that case? What would that conversation sound like?"

Usually that would be enough to give the employee permission to open up, and finally Marc would get the information he needed.

Marc also started holding off-site meetings, which allowed his staff to step away from their daily responsibilities and reflect on some of the strategic issues they were facing. At these meetings, someone would almost always ask just how large they would have to grow to arrive at the point where he'd be willing to sell the company. Marc's answer never varied: it isn't going to happen. Grow revenue to a hundred million dollars a year, he'd say, or grow the company to the point that its market value reached a billion dollars—do that and then maybe we can talk about cashing out. But Marc loved what he was doing, and he'd seen what had happened at HotJobs when the company was acquired by Yahoo!—the spirit had been drained out of the place. No way was he going to let that happen to his company.

CHAPTER 16

LEARN TO LEAD

Leadership is getting someone to do what they don't want to do,
to achieve what they want to achieve.

—COACH TOM LANDRY

When the highly successful entrepreneurs I got to know talked about learning to lead, I kept hearing an odd echo. It took me a while to figure it out, but then it came to me: they were often using many of the same words and phrases that they used when they talked about learning to sell. They talked about integrity, clarity, and enthusiasm; about finding the right people; about giving them the power to make decisions even while shepherding them toward a particular goal. Over time, I realized that they used similar language because they were talking about two sides of the same coin. Learning to lead and learning to sell—which we'll get to shortly—are about making promises and then doing everything you can to keep them. The intelligent entrepreneur does both.

It was never my first question—in fact, I usually waited until fairly late in the process—but at some point I asked Marla, Chris, and Marc whether they thought they were good leaders and managers.

"I don't really see myself as a classic manager," Marla told me. Although she believed she was a very effective CEO, she acknowledged that she loved corporate strategy but hated the sort of detail work required of a chief operating officer. Fortunately, Barry was excellent at handling all the large and small operational issues that bluemercury faced every day.

In her heart, Marla said, she thought of herself as more of a leader and an entrepreneur than a manager. "When I think and behave like an entrepreneur, I make really good decisions. It's kind of a counterintuitive lesson: I have to put blinders on. If I listen too much to other people, I make mistakes."

Here's one example of what Marla means. The managers and salespeople at bluemercury never know which of the company's brands are selling especially well or especially poorly, or what kinds of margins bluemercury makes on each item. "We're giving our customers much better service, because it's based on what's right for them, not for us. Our staffers don't even know what our sales are by brand. They often ask, but I never tell them."

When I asked Barry Beck about his leadership style, he was typically blunt. "I'm a total micromanager," he said. "If you don't want to be micromanaged, then we're not a good fit. It doesn't mean I don't trust you. It's just my style."

And how about Chris Michel: did he think he was a good CEO?

"I think I was a competent CEO," he replied. "I don't think I was a crazy iconoclast who didn't know what he was doing. I felt like a pretty reasonable guy. We were organized, prepared, and thoughtful. But there were some leadership challenges, and there were certainly some credibility challenges."

What made him better, Chris said, is that he nearly failed.

"My advantage was that I experienced real adversity. I'd been tempered by that—the same way you temper steel. And that was the greatest management gift that I've ever been given. If I had not walked through the fires of adversity, I would never have the kind of confidence—and a sort of visceral sense for the right way to do things—that I do today.

"I did not know what I did not know," Chris continued. "I made a lot of mistakes. One was not keeping a well-balanced, mutually supportive team, and that becomes a huge liability when the environment is challenging. Particularly when the going got rough, I was not the most popular guy in the world—far from it. After three rounds of layoffs, people distrusted me. And team dynamics is the hardest and most personal challenge of all. Getting that wrong really hurts. Fundamentally, it's all about leadership."

As a CEO, he said, he learned that his most important responsibility was being completely honest in his dealings with people. He learned this lesson the hard way, and it took time. Looking back, Chris said that although he didn't stretch the truth when running Military.com, he was sometimes not sufficiently conscientious about how he communicated with people, especially early on. Over time, he learned to pay closer attention to his shorthand and to think harder about who his audience was.

"In the navy you tell everybody that you fly for the navy," Chris said by way of example. "That's just what you say in flight school: 'I fly for the navy.' But if you think about it, you realize that people could misinterpret this—they might assume that I'm saying that I am the pilot, instead of the navigator or mission commander. When I was running Military.com, I sometimes said that I flew for the navy, and once, much to my surprise, I found myself challenged on this point. The response shocked me, but after I got past feeling defensive, I felt badly, like I had let this person down. But it was a really important lesson. I recognized that people were paying very close attention to what I was saying, and that I needed to pay close attention to my words and actions."

Speaking about a venture he founded after selling Military.com to Monster, Chris also talked about the importance of setting high standards when communicating with employees. "I like to think of our company as a meritocracy—that's how we approach the often difficult issue of raises and promotions. I always try to be very blunt and very direct with people; I talk to them about how this is a culture of people, passion, and performance, and passion is a critical part of your job. If you are not passionate, let me either help you become passionate or help you find something else that you're truly passionate about. If people actually believe that you have their best interests in mind, you can have great conversations with them, even if they're sometimes pretty tough. You can have a real impact, not just on their work but on their lives."

Marc Cenedella seemed to understand the importance of this focus on integrity and communication from the beginning. But he enjoyed a significant advantage over many entrepreneurs: because he'd worked as a senior vice president at HotJobs, he'd had to hire, fire, and manage a number of people. Marla and Chris, by comparison, had worked in consulting, so when they launched their companies they had had no first-hand experience operating a business.

When I talked to Marc's employees, I noticed that most of them eventually brought the conversation around to the weekly Friday meetings. In those meetings and others, they said, Marc was very candid about how the company was doing, and he spoke in specific terms about where they were spending their money and why it mattered. But his employees also consistently mentioned how much they enjoyed his parties.

In the early days, when the company had just a few employees, Marc took everyone to a New Orleans–style bar for crawfish and beer when they hit one thousand paid subscribers. Later, when they reached $100,000 in cash collected per week—and then $200,000 and $300,000—he threw big celebrations. When the company reached the $1-million-a-week milestone, Marc threw a black-tie ball. Now, with so many employees, they've had to cut back a bit. "We're so big now," he said, "that it would cost us $250,000 to have a party."

Marc said he also believes that a bash is about more than having fun: they're a good way to show both his passion for the company and his appreciation for the contributions of others.

"A party says, 'I appreciate your efforts—please do more,'" Marc told me. "This is why it makes good business sense. But also, on the human side, you have to get people fired up and excited; you have to get them to realize in their heart and their gut that we're winning."

Of course, every enterprise is different, and Marc's company grew much faster than either Marla's or Chris's. Moreover, whereas bluemercury's staff was spread across several cities, almost all of Marc's employees were based in one place, New York City. Fairly early on, Marc recognized that the size and central location of the company's rapidly growing staff required that he adapt his management style accordingly.

"At the point where you have eighteen employees, you can bark at everyone and tell them what to do. It's not much more complicated than simply exerting personal willpower—'Okay, team, let's go!' But as you grow larger, you can't see all your people every day. You can't literally tell them what to do every day. You have to hire more talented and capable people, and you have to manage them using different skills."

As his company continued to grow, Marc held regular off-site meetings, worked with his executive coach, and read a lot of books about management. "You read Jack Welch and others, and you see that leadership and management demand a whole new set of skills. The more that gets beat into your head, the more open you are to changing the way you lead."

It wasn't always easy for Marc to hear about what he needed to improve. Early on, his coach did a so-called 360-degree evaluation—she interviewed a number of Marc's friends, along with key employees and several members of the board of directors. Hearing the results was not a pleasant experience.

"When you first get 360 feedback," Marc recalled, "your first-time reaction is 'That's so unfair,' or 'That's not what I meant to do, not how I should be perceived.' There's always an element of hurt involved when you really see yourself in the mirror for the first time. But it is the reality, and now you face a choice: What are you going to do with it? Deny it? Or say okay, this is what they think and I'd better pay attention."

Whenever I spoke with academics and researchers about the topic of leadership, they invariably said that for anyone who wants to become a better leader, there's simply no substitute for experience.

"Most entrepreneurs are the idea people," said Ed Zschau. "But when you start out as an idea person and then over time learn how to manage the company, lead the company, and then bring it to a successful outcome—when you've done that, you've developed some essential skills that make it possible for you to be a capable CEO. That doesn't necessarily mean that you want to be the day-to-day, get-stuff-done person, but at least you've become reasonably good at it. Then you can decide whether you want to hire a CEO to run your company day-to-day, or whether really want to be both the idea person and the operations person. Sure, the ideal is that you can do both, but that isn't right for everybody."

"Leadership is without question a huge issue," agreed Noam Wasserman. "Innovators who don't know how to lead people or operate businesses can flame out very fast. The most successful entrepreneurs can work alone *and* be a team player; they can make a critical individual contribution to their venture *and* make that transition to leading others. To use a sales example, it can be very tough to make the transition from being a salesman to being a manager of salesmen. In some very prominent cases, new ventures have promoted their best salesman to manager and as a consequence killed their company."

One lesson that's especially difficult to learn is that no good leader will be universally liked. Go online, search for bluemercury or TheLadders, and deep down in the search results you'll find the disgruntled musings of a few former employees. And as Chris Michel freely admits, he was sometimes very unpopular when he led Military.com. But complaints about a company's management are par for the course—and for every disgruntled former employee of these three companies, I found many more who respect and even like those responsible for leading them. The more important point is that Marla, Chris, and Marc all built thriving companies that continue to employ hundreds of people. That simply wouldn't have happened if they had failed to learn how to be effective managers and leaders—or failed to understand that it's far less important to be friends with your employees than it is to lead them to build great companies.

The key to becoming a good leader is not about having greater intellectual horsepower or better skills than your employees. "Most applied business problems are incredibly mundane," said Stig Leschly. "General management is almost anti-intellectual. True, some strategy problems are hard, but most aren't impossible. And in some disciplines—manufacturing science, engineering science, and life sciences, for instance—specialists are critical to the success of a company. But general managers don't need to have a specialized skill set. When it comes to effective leadership, what really matters is what transpires among human beings—whether you can hire and fire, whether you can run a meeting with two or seven or twenty-five people, whether you can relate to people, motivate them, connect with them."

Some entrepreneurs, however, struggle to learn this essential lesson. In these cases, says Noam Wasserman, "it's usually a combination of ignorance and ego. The techie, for instance, has no idea how tough it is to sell, or how tough it is to manage." And as Wasserman points out, many entrepreneurs think that management must be easier than developing innovative solutions to compelling problems. "After coming up with an ingenious idea, these founders are thinking, 'Hey, I've conquered rocket science. This business stuff should be simple.'"

During a venture's early days, of course, every intelligent entrepreneur has to be both the Big Idea Guy and the Get Stuff Done Guy. But Wasserman's research demonstrated that when successful companies finish their initial product development, or when they've raised a significant new round of outside investment, it's often time for the founding CEO to step aside. In many cases, he or she simply doesn't have the management and leadership ability needed to run a larger organization. One venture capitalist Wasserman interviewed told him that success hits the CEOs of the fastest-growing companies so quickly that they hardly have time to react, which is why he often tries to push a founding CEO out early. "It's best to add a professional CEO before the scale of operations might logically justify it," said this partner in a VC. "You've got to stay ahead of the curve to drive momentum."

You might well find the prospect of being forced out of your own company nothing short of horrifying. But stop and think about it: if you launch your venture successfully, there may well come a day when it has grown beyond your ability to lead it. As the CEO of an ever-expanding enterprise, you have to worry not only about your product, but also about such things as building a sales force, distributing and supporting your product, managing finances, and leading bigger and bigger teams. Maybe you can do all those things and more, but what if you reach such a pinnacle of success that one day you take a look at your competition and realize that your new, innovative, game-changing company has become the status quo? Are you really the right person to reinvent your own enterprise?

After interviewing many successful entrepreneurs, I came to understand that what motivates people to launch companies is often incompatible with what motivates someone to lead a large firm over the long term. Are there exceptions? Of course. But is it surprising that in 2005 and 2006, Chris Michel decided that he didn't want to run a bigger division of Monster and climb the corporate ladder? Hardly. Instead, despite all the trials and tribulations, he so enjoyed the experience of building a company from scratch that he wanted to do it all over again. As I heard more than once, winning the entrepreneurial game can be addictive—and for many entrepreneurs, once they've experienced that rush of success, nothing else quite compares to it.

HOW DO YOU LEARN TO LEAD?

It ought to be clear by now that becoming an intelligent entrepreneur requires a curious sort of humility. It's humbling but absolutely necessary to look at yourself with a pitiless eye and regard your strengths and weaknesses with equal clarity. As a leader, you owe it to both yourself and those you lead to conduct this sort of honest self-appraisal. So take a good, hard look at yourself in the mirror and ask the following questions:

How well do you communicate? When speaking with colleagues or employees, can you get your point across clearly? When someone on your staff speaks, are you a good listener, even when you may not like what he or she has to say? And do you make a conscious effort to deal with people openly and honestly? In any entrepreneurial venture, passive-aggressive leadership will almost certainly lead to disaster.

How clear is your vision? Can you point to a destination on the horizon and explain to those who work for you why it's important to sail toward and ultimately reach that destination? If so, you'll have to make promises to your employees about how the company will get there— can you fulfill those promises? If you can't articulate a vision for your enterprise or if you doubt your ability to make and keep promises to your people, you are almost certainly not ready to make your dream of becoming an entrepreneur a reality.

Can you put ego aside? Begin with a basic test: are you a Big Idea Guy or a Get Stuff Done Guy? (You may think you're both, but at the very least you're probably better at one of these roles.) Are you willing to step aside and delegate when necessary? Can you empower other people? And when evidence of a weakness in your own management style becomes blindingly apparent, can you admit the truth and then do something about it?

What do you truly want to do? As we've seen, starting a company and running it are two very different things that require very different skills. Do you want to start or run? Think about what you wanted from the experience of being an entrepreneur in the first place. And ask yourself Noam Wasserman's question: do you want to be rich or be king?

THE NEXT RULE

To put it as simply as possible, leadership is about organizing people and motivating them to work together toward a common goal. But since that sounds a little dry, let me put it in more personal terms. When it's your baby and your idea, it's up to you to provide the shining vision around which your company will revolve, but it's also up to you to motivate everyone you hire to work like hell to achieve the goals you set for them. And if you can learn how to provide this sort of leadership, you will substantially improve your odds of become a successful entrepreneur.

As I suggested at the outset of this chapter, this lesson about leadership happens to be closely related to another rule. I didn't see this right away, but the more I talked to successful entrepreneurs, the more apparent it became that the flip side of good leadership is the ability to sell. You may think that launching a company is all about innovation, but the real truth is that it's equally important to learn how to persuade people that your idea is as ingenious and invaluable as you think it is. As every intelligent entrepreneur will tell you, your venture is only as good as its best salesperson.

CHAPTER 17

When does a marketer become a salesperson? When he needs to make payroll.

—ANNE DWANE

MARLA: TAKE THE MONEY?

Marla Malcolm and Barry Beck got an out-of-the-blue phone call from a senior executive at a Fortune 500 company in the fashion and apparel industry in early 2005. The executive made an unsolicited offer for bluemercury, and it was substantial enough to get Marla and Barry's full attention. The terms weren't quite what they were looking for, but the offer—the first serious solicitation they'd ever received—forced them to step back and think hard about whether it was time to sell. Their company had pulled down $9 million in revenue in 2004 and was still growing. Maybe, Marla thought, they should at least take some money off the table.

Deciding that it made sense to take the next step, Marla and Barry interviewed half a dozen investment banks about possibly serving as their adviser if they entered formal negotiations. Each firm was eager to move quickly, and all wanted to introduce Marla and Barry to other potential buyers, meet with the CEO of their current suitor, and use that opening offer to start a bidding war. But Barry's brother, with whom Barry had started the commercial maintenance company, was in the middle of a similar negotiation, and he'd had a positive experience with a

Chicago-based bank called William Blair & Company. Barry called the partner his brother knew at Blair.

In their first phone conversation, Barry was again typically blunt. "So, are you guys any good?" he asked.

In reply, Barry told Marla later, the partner had said, "With this phone call, the value of your company just increased thirty percent."

That kind of bravado convinced Barry that he should at least sit down with William Blair & Company. The partner he'd talked to obviously knew how to make a promise—now it was time to see if the bank could back it up.

Barry flew to Chicago for a meeting, and as he walked into the room he realized he recognized one of the bankers. Chris Spahr, the head of the bank's specialty retail group, had been a fraternity brother at Cornell. Graduating two years ahead of Barry, Spahr had worked at Goldman Sachs before getting his MBA at Northwestern, and he'd been with Blair ever since. Not that Barry was about to hire a bank because an old fraternity brother worked there, but it was nice to see a familiar face.

As the meeting got under way, it immediately became clear to Barry that the bank was unimpressed by the Fortune 500 company's interest in bluemercury. Spahr had sat through hundreds of meetings with potential retail clients, and he was quick to see that the formula Marla and Barry had developed for bluemercury worked. They opened stores, marketed them aggressively, and consistently grew revenues and profits. They could also project the likely return on their investment in each store with confidence and unusual precision.

Barry explained the very specific objectives he and Marla had settled on after receiving the unsolicited bid—how much capital they wanted to raise to fund the continued expansion of the company, but also how much money they wanted to take off the table. The other banks Barry had talked to didn't want to set specific price objectives—they all advised him to shop the company right away and see what the market would bear.

But Spahr didn't want to do that.

"You aren't big enough yet," he told them. "You guys need to wait a couple of quarters."

With eight stores operating by the end of 2004, bluemercury

projected to have twelve by the end of 2005. Four new stores wasn't a big deal in the mergers and acquisitions arena, but it was significant that the company was expecting to grow by 50 percent in a single year. And the idea of a young company, with only a small number of stores, growing as fast as they were and making money? That was very unusual. But Spahr's view was that this was still an early chapter in bluemercury's story; he felt strongly that it needed to turn a few more pages before going to market.

Soon after this initial meeting, Marla and Barry met with Spahr in Philadelphia, where they walked him through one of their newer stores. After talking further with Spahr, they decided to sign with his bank, hold off on any talk of selling, and continue with their plan to keep opening stores over the next twelve months. Assuming all went well, by early 2006 the company would have enough stores and sales to justify the numbers they wanted.

As 2005 went on, Marla and Barry opened two bluemercury stores in Chicago and began developing plans to open yet another in New Jersey early in 2006. They spent much of the summer working with Chris Spahr's team at William Blair & Company, putting together a 112-page book about the company, referred to as simply "the memo." A pure sales document—very glossy, lots of pictures—it provided an overview of the company, spelled out their investment thesis, and offered a cursory examination of the financial model behind it. In October, William Blair held its annual, invitation-only private equity conference in Chicago. Marla presented the company to the conference, but only as a sort of buzz-generating sneak preview for an expected offering the following spring. She made a great impression, but then—exactly as planned—they put the pitch on ice for four months.

They would finish out 2005, audit their books, and then be ready to take the company to market in the spring of 2006.

MARC: FREE IS THE WRONG PRICE

Marc Cenedella thought of himself as an autodidact. When he encountered a problem, he would research it online or read a book addressing the issue. In late 2004, for instance, he'd read a book called *Death by Meeting*, by Patrick Lencioni. One of the big takeaways was that if you scheduled meetings too often, you would inevitably cover the same shallow pool of items over and over. He'd liked the book so much that he bought fifty copies and handed them out throughout the company.

As TheLadders grew, Marc took that lesson to heart. Instead of short, frequent meetings, he began holding what he called Deep Dives, quarterly three-hour meetings with each of his company's various teams. This seemed to be the best way to find out what was happening deep inside each team and thus put himself in a position to offer his help and direction.

One muggy day in July 2006, Marc had a Deep Dive scheduled with the company's employer relations team—the folks in charge of persuading companies to keep posting the free $100,000 job listings that enticed TheLadders' paying customers (the job seekers) to keep coming back. In practice this meant Marc would be meeting with two people: Dwane Martin, the vice president of business development, and Michael Shafrir, the former Philadelphia teacher's aide who had joined the company from a Craigslist ad in early 2004. Shafrir had been one of Marc's best hires, and in his two years with TheLadders he had risen to become the head of the recruiter group.

Preparing for the meeting with Marc, Shafrir recognized that his group was facing a serious and growing problem. While they were attracting a large quantity of ads for jobs, the quality of the jobs was not what it should be. The issue was that the job listings were coming from headhunters and other middlemen, rather than from the employers themselves.

Shafrir had an idea about how to solve this problem, but he knew it would be controversial. He'd also worked with Marc long enough to know that he couldn't just toss out an opinion at a Deep Dive—he had to have the hard data to back it up. To put it in business-speak, he couldn't go into the meeting with a qualitative deck—a "deck" was the preferred shorthand for a presentation—based on his hunches. It had to be a quantitative deck, or a presentation that would rely on hard numbers to tell the story and therefore allow Marc to draw his own conclusions. Ideally, Shafrir wouldn't have to say a word about his proposed solution until Marc came to it on his own.

The three men walked into a small, windowless conference room near Marc's office, which Marc had named after "Ophelia," a Grateful

Dead song. Shafrir had prepared a PowerPoint presentation that topped out at nearly one hundred pages, and he handed printed copies of it to Marc and Dwane Martin. The deck contained chart after chart, laying out data that had to do with where their job leads came from, which segments and cities generated the most responses, and the reasons given by corporate recruiters when Shafrir's team asked what prevented them from using TheLadders more often. (It was especially frustrating to Shafrir that several recruiters told him that although they'd had great success using TheLadders to recruit good candidates, they'd simply forgotten about the company the next time they'd had jobs to post.)

Roughly forty minutes into the meeting, Shafrir dropped an anecdote that he knew would get Marc's attention. Recently he had spoken with Marc's cousin Jen Cenedella, who—with Marc's other cousin Loraine—had lunched with him when he was dreaming up the idea for the company in summer 2003. If anyone would be inclined to use TheLadders when it came time to hire people for her company, Jen would.

But she can't, Shafrir explained, because her company had a contract with one of the other big job boards. Its corporate policy was that everyone who worked there had to use TheLadders' competitor—even though listing jobs with TheLadders was free.

Shafrir went on to break their employer-users down into categories. Executive headhunters who weren't associated with any one employer, and who would receive a referral fee if they found the right candidate, used the site constantly. But the site was cluttered with ads from these kinds of middlemen. The companies themselves—who did the actual hiring, after all—resisted.

By now, Marc was working on his second iced tea from the small refrigerator in the corner of the conference room. He sensed where this was going.

Overall, Shafrir explained, even though TheLadders succeeded in getting large companies to use the free service, closing the deal took a lot more work than it should. To prove the point, Shafrir had written a couple of detailed case studies. In one case, it had taken his team two months and a total of eighty-seven phone calls—to sixteen different people—just to get a company to post its first job ad. And the ad was free!

I know it seems like this should be the easiest sale in the world,

Shafrir told Marc. But we're just not getting it done, and we're not getting nearly enough ads directly from the big companies.

Part of the problem, Shafrir continued, was that at the beginning of too many conversations with recruiters they had to explain what The-Ladders was and who was behind it. If Marc could do more media and become a recognized expert in the $100,000-a-year-and-up job market, that would undoubtedly help.

But the deeper problem was that since they had set the price for employers to post ads at zero, they had sent a clear message that their service wasn't worth anything. To make his point, Shafrir offered another anecdote, this one about a corporate recruiter who worked for a Fortune 500 firm and who had become a big booster of TheLadders. Whenever a job was open in her corporate division, she would submit it to TheLadders. She'd had great luck with their service and told her colleagues that they should use it as well. But almost no other recruiter within the company had followed suit.

We have an evangelist inside the company, and even she can't sell it! Shafrir said.

The meeting was supposed to run three hours. At around the fourth hour, they took a break. Marc and Shafrir went up to the roof for some air.

"Free just isn't working," Marc thought as he looked out over the city. "My God, though—we've been saying for three years that we're not going to charge the recruiters."

But Shafrir had made their problem plain as day. Finally Marc said it aloud: "Free is the wrong price."

These were Fortune 500 companies they were targeting. They had money to spend on recruiting. The decision makers in these companies weren't looking for a way to save their bosses a few hundred dollars. They were looking for whatever service worked the best.

All three men went back into the conference room and continued working the problem. By the time they were done, six hours had passed and they had completely covered the white board hanging on the wall.

TheLadders' business model had taken them this far. It had gotten the company off the ground and protected them from the bigger job sites. But now the model was broken. They had to find a way to fix it.

A month or so later, Marc took over one of the company's Friday after-noon meetings in dramatic fashion. He began by playing a few minutes from President Kennedy's 1961 speech challenging Americans to send a man to the moon and return him safely to Earth before the end of the decade. Once Marc had everyone's attention, Shafrir stepped up and gave an abbreviated version of the presentation he'd made to Marc in July. He explained the problem they'd found in their business model, and summarized three short case studies to illustrate the point. Then he turned things back over to Marc.

"Folks," Marc said, his voice rising. "We're going to the moon."

After three years of promising they'd never charge employers or recruiters to post jobs with TheLadders, they were going to completely change course and do precisely that. After explaining his audacious goal—a complete revision of their business model—he was quick to acknowledge the enormity of the challenge.

"John F. Kennedy stood in front of the nation and said we'll send a man to the moon. He didn't know how to do it, but he set the goal. Folks, I have no idea how we're going to build a system to charge recruit-ers and employers. But this company is amazing, and you guys are great. And we will succeed."

Delivering an inspirational message was about all Marc could do for now. His employees' reaction was mixed at best, as he'd known it prob-ably would be. But he was certain they had no choice—they had to find a new way forward

MARLA: PUTTING A PRICE TAG ON IT

Bluemercury was becoming a hot commodity. In early 2006, Pricewater-houseCoopers (PwC) audited the company's books for 2005 and con-firmed that it had generated $17 million in revenue—nearly twice what it had done the year before. Chris Spahr had seen retail firms sell for six times annual revenues or higher and, as the weeks went by, he, Marla, and Barry were increasingly confident. By the end of March, they had identified about thirty potential acquirers and investors—Fortune 500 companies, private equity investors, and the like—and they were ready to make the formal pitch. Although Spahr routinely sent out solicitations to sixty or more possible investors when looking for a deal, he had decided to keep the number small, which would signal that this opportunity was exclusive and rare.

"The book" was now a slick forty-page document, full of photographs and images intended to evoke the clean, modern environment of the bluemercury stores. Besides putting the prospectus together, identifying investors, and running interference, William Blair & Company's additional contribution was to position bluemercury in the luxury personal care segment. Even to a cosmetics industry neophyte, the business made sense—selling high-margin, disposable products to people with high levels of disposable income. And, as Marla had understood when she first envisioned the company, bluemercury's good relationships with dozens of high-end cosmetics manufacturers were also enormously valuable.

With the PwC seal of approval, no one reviewing the book would get bogged down in the financial information; after all, the would-be suitors knew that they'd get more than enough financial information once they indicated their firm interest and signed a nondisclosure agreement. For now, the photos of Marla radiating confidence, the images of the crisp, light-filled stores, the promise of a cosmetics cash machine—all created a sense of alchemy and magic around the company.

By late spring, Spahr had received letters from just under a dozen companies and private equity funds expressing serious interest. The valuations of bluemercury were coming in at $50 million or more. Several of the proposals were very interesting, but one stood out: an offer from an investment fund called Invus, which also happened to be the majority owner of Weight Watchers. Invus was headed by Ray Debbane, a French-born, Stanford-educated MBA whom Spahr knew from a previous deal.

Over the next few weeks, Spahr held meeting after meeting with Debbane and others from Invus, trying to work out the fine points of the deal. One day, with the two sides now very close, Marla and Barry met with Spahr at the Nassau Inn in Princeton, New Jersey, just a block or so from the local bluemercury store. As he had before, Spahr warned them that no deal was ever done until the wire transfer went through and the money landed in the client's bank account. But after their conversation, the three of them walked across the college campus. It was a beautiful spring day—shining sun, singing birds. Marla and Barry knew, just knew, that this deal was going to come together.

MARC: JAPAN

Marc Cenedella had been planning for a while to take his company's senior leadership on a management training trip to Japan. He'd been fascinated by the country since before his Forbes Pacifica days and had visited many times over the years. One of his favorite management books was *Made in Japan*, the autobiography of Akio Morita, the cofounder and former CEO of Sony, and Marc was especially intrigued by the Japanese approach to customer service. Even TheLadders' motto—"Love the Customer. Our Team Wins."—was based on a Japanese business saying, "Okyaku-sama wa kami-sama desu," which meant, most precisely translated, "the customer is a god." The best way to teach his top employees about Japanese customer service practices, Marc decided, was to take them to Japan. Finally, in September 2006, he and about a dozen other members of TheLadders' senior management team flew to Tokyo.

Marc's Japanese was still passable—good enough to get around the city and have simple conversations with people in restaurants and the like. For ten days, they worked with Japanese management trainers and visited hotels, department stores, and restaurants, all to learn how a culture that put customer service first treated the people who paid for their goods.

The trip wasn't all business—in typical Marc fashion, everyone worked hard and played hard. Karaoke restaurants and sake bars were the order of the evenings. But they spent their days with a pair of trainers whose usual clients were much larger companies—Apple, for example. They took on a full curriculum, eight a.m. to six p.m. every day, with mornings in a hotel classroom and afternoons on field trips to talk with the leaders of different businesses—everyone from the general manager of the hotel where they were staying to the president of an Internet company and several executives of Tokyo department stores.

On one such field trip, Marc became fascinated with the level of detail involved in one employee's job—that of an "elevator girl," who directed customers to the next available elevators. Dressed in a formal, conservative uniform, she stood ramrod straight and used an elaborate series of subtle hand gestures to indicate which of a number of cars in an elevator bank clients should use.

Does anyone want to try to perform this job? the store's general manager asked after the elevator girl finished her demonstration. Marc jumped up and stood right next to her. He parroted her hand gestures intently, working hard to get his arm at the precise angle that suggested rigor and professionalism, as if he were delivering a sequence of military salutes. He enjoyed himself enormously.

For months after returning from Japan, he told his elevator story at company meetings. In Japan an employee might work in the same department store for thirty years, Marc explained, and he or she could spend the first two years doing nothing but directing customers to the correct elevator. But these employees took great pride in their work, doing their best to perform everything exactly as described in the company manual.

Imagine, Marc would say, a manual to teach you how to direct someone to the proper elevator, with practice every day! Then Marc would quickly add: But, of course, that's why Tokyo is so expensive. They hire three people to do a job where in America one person might do it. So although you can't directly translate this approach to the way we do business in the United States, the attitude is what's important.

Soon after his trip to Japan, Marc traveled to Washington, D.C., for a meeting with Donald Graham, the chairman and former publisher of the Washington Post Company. Afterward, he took a cab to Georgetown and paid a visit to his friend from Section A at HBS Marla Malcolm Beck. Barry joined them as they sat at the large brown table in bluemercury's conference room.

Talk soon turned to Marla and Barry's effort to "recapitalize" their company. Barry, caught up in the heat of their efforts to sell bluemercury, made a passionate case for why it made sense for Marc to sell TheLadders as well.

No, Marc replied, he wasn't interested. He had big plans for the company, and he was absolutely convinced that it could become a billion-dollar firm.

But you don't need a billion dollars! Barry insisted. He had been down this road with many entrepreneurs over the years. He was a firm believer in the Ledecky-Darman theory of entrepreneurship: start and build, but take your win! Take some money off the table. So few entrepreneurs ever had the opportunity to recapitalize, Barry said. And of those who did, too few actually seized the moment.

"Don't fall in love with your business," Barry said.

Barry then turned to his favorite metaphor—Icarus, the character in Greek mythology who flew too close to the sun. "Don't be Icarus," Barry implored Marc. Be Daedalus, who flies a little lower and survives.

Marc started to reply but Barry was on a roll.

"Sell that business and you can walk away with $20 million or more." He scribbled some calculations on a napkin—that was the magic number: $20 million. "You're set for life! Why do you need to go to the moon?" he asked.

"Yeah, I know I *could* sell it now," Marc began, "but—"

"Recap!" Barry interrupted.

"Yes, but what I'm thinking—"

"Recap!"

"But—"

"Recap! Recap! Recap!"

Marla left the room. Her husband and her business school friend could have it out on their own.

MARLA: THE RECAP

Barry and Marla had held court with group after group of investors during late spring, trying to decide which firm would be the best fit. Within just a few weeks, they had settled on Invus as the most interesting suitor, and Marla and Barry agreed to negotiate exclusively with the firm. It had done well with its previous investments and, just as important, it had a history of leaving the founding management teams in place.

Marla found she was handling much of the back-and-forth from home. One evening she sat in the master bedroom of the house she and Barry had bought in the Washington suburbs, talking over several important points with Ray Debbane. By the time she looked at the clock, three hours had gone by.

Finally they reached an agreement in principle: Invus would invest in the firm at a pre-money valuation of $62 million. Together, Marla and Barry owned just over 70 percent of bluemercury's stock; after the deal they'd hold on to 24 percent, and so they would be walking away with well above Barry's goal of $20 million in cash. Moreover, there would be $10 million available to fund the expansion of more stores, and Marla and Barry would stay in place as the CEO and COO of the company.

They reached a deal and waited for it to close. On June 15, a hot, humid late spring day, Marla and Barry stood, talking, in the gravel driveway outside their home. Their elder daughter would be turning three in mid-June 2006, and Barry's and Marla's parents had come to stay with them in the Washington suburbs, traveling from Philadelphia and Oakland. Something could always happen at the last minute, as Chris Spahr had emphasized—no deal was ever done until the check cleared. Marla called their bank on her cell phone. She hung up and found herself speechless.

The clerk at BB&T had the news they had been waiting for: the eight-figure wire transfer had arrived. The money was sitting in their account. Seven years, one month, and fifteen days from the day Marla had left Jon Ledecky's company, she had done it. She had started and built bluemercury—and she had taken money off the table.

CHRIS: STARTUP, THE SEQUEL

Chris Michel loved what he and Anne Dwane had created at Military .com, but now that the company was part of Monster he was beginning to feel that it was suffering from what he called "the success penalty." Throughout 2005 and 2006, Military.com enjoyed healthy cash flow and its year-on-year growth numbers were strong. But in a public company there was no such thing as doing well enough. Each month, each quarter, you had to beat your sales numbers from the month and quarter before. Although Military.com always achieved those goals, Chris grew concerned that pushing short-term growth too hard carried with it some risk—both because they would always feel pressure to package more and more Military.com members to sell to their lead-generation clients, and because the strict focus on monthly numbers might stifle innovation.

Lately Chris had begun to sketch out what he hoped was another way to grow. Rather than keep pushing around the edges, trying to squeeze a few more points and a few more dollars out of the companies that wanted to reach the membership of Military.com each month, why not replicate the model and build communities focused on other affinity groups? For example, why not take the concept behind Military.com and start a new Web site for law enforcement officers called something like Police.com? Assuming that site worked, they could follow it up with others like it—Firefighters.com, Teachers.com, Nurses.com.

Chris's first thought was that he could graft all of these new communities on to Military.com's organization. But then he began to wonder if that was really the best option. In one sense, he realized, he was now paying his own success penalty. Having built one company, he wasn't satisfied. Like any true entrepreneur, he wanted to build another company, have a bigger impact, and sell the new one for more than he got for the last one.

Besides, Chris missed the creativity and adventure that was so much a part of launching a new venture. He wanted to take that joy ride all over again.

One afternoon, Chris sat down with Andy McKelvey. "I think it's time for me to leave," Chris told him. Then, by way of explanation, he described his new idea. Of all people, he figured, McKelvey would understand his desire to move on.

But McKelvey countered with a surprising proposal. "Don't leave," he said. "If you really want to do this, I will support you. Monster will fund it."

Chris immediately understood that he couldn't possibly refuse McKelvey's offer. Monster would put up the money for his new venture. Chris would be able to leverage the company's technology, sales force, and users, to say nothing of the more pedestrian parts of its huge infrastructure.

He and McKelvey quickly worked out the basic terms of their deal. At any point, Chris would have the right to sell his interest in the venture to Monster for a guaranteed minimum of $5 million; meanwhile, Monster would have the right to purchase the entire company after a certain number of years. Other terms of their deal established the formula for determining the purchase price if and when Monster did buy Chris's new company—in essence, Monster would pay an amount equal to that year's sales.

Chris thought McKelvey's proposal was brilliant. It was virtually a risk-free deal for him, of course, but he also understood that for a relatively small investment, McKelvey was putting Monster in a position to reap enormous benefits if the company launched and did well.

Though he had just a handshake deal with McKelvey at this point, Chris started making plans to launch his new venture. Anne Dwane would stay behind and take over as the head of Military.com, so Chris would have to recruit a whole new team, starting with his right-hand man or woman.

Chris began interviewing aggressively. With his article about outcomes and activities still fresh in his mind and the chance to build a new company from the ground up, he was determined to replicate what had worked at Military.com but avoid every mistake. For example, although Brad Clark had been an important partner at Military.com, Chris reflected now that bringing in the first person to express any interest in his idea and offer investment as a cofounder was not exactly a well-thought-out strategy. He needed to cast his net wide in order to find the right team.

A friend who was a partner in a major venture capital firm suggested Chris meet with a young entrepreneur and programmer named Will Harbin, who had just moved to Silicon Valley after a stint working for AOL. Harbin had been programming since he was eight years old and had started a slew of companies—he was an Internet veteran even before he'd graduated from college. He had only just begun working at Yahoo! but he was already beginning to wonder if it was a good fit. Google seemed to hire away their best people, and a lot of his new colleagues felt disillusioned. Harbin was a smart guy, Chris's friend told him, and he had begun looking around for something better.

Harbin had arrived in California so recently that he and his wife were living in a nearly empty apartment while they waited for their furniture to catch up. Not wanting to worry his wife, Harbin didn't tell her where he was going when he left especially early one morning to meet Chris.

Military.com was on the seventh floor at 799 Market Street now, near Union Square, and they met in Chris's windowless office. Sort of an unusual spot for an Internet company, Harbin thought as he sat down, right smack in the middle of tourist-land San Francisco.

They talked for about an hour. This time around, Chris was intensely focused on revenue growth, and he talked to Harbin in detail about how his new company would identify likely affinity groups that could be banded together, Military.com-style. Chris explained how much he'd learned about qualified-lead generation in the higher education market, and why he was sure the concept would fuel rapid growth in this venture as well. And he broadly described the deal he'd worked out with McKelvey.

Harbin was interested, but he wasn't quite as eager as Brad Clark had been six years before when Chris first pitched the idea of Military.com to him. Now thirty, Harbin had been through several startups already and he had no illusions about how hard it was to launch a new company successfully. Still, Chris had made this model work once, and Harbin recognized that Chris was essentially proposing to run the same play he'd used to build Military.com.

As their conversation continued, Chris cautioned Harbin that two unknowns—both out of his control—could doom the venture before it got off the ground. First, he still had to work out a formal agreement with Monster acknowledging that he, not Monster, owned the intellectual property he had created while working on this new idea, which he was now calling Affinity Labs. Second, if anything happened to Andy McKelvey, the whole venture would be off. Chris believed that McKelvey still had the curiosity and stamina of a kid, but he recognized that his boss was now in his seventies and had already battled pancreatic cancer. Besides, Chris told Harbin, this was an unusual deal, based as much on his nearly two years of knowing and working with McKelvey as on the business model itself. Probably no other CEO of a similar-sized company would have agreed to it.

Over the next couple of weeks, Chris and Harbin kept talking. Chris was impressed by Harbin, but since he now understood that the most important thing any leader could do was to recruit and retain the best possible people, he asked a lot of tough questions. He also called several people who had worked with Harbin—all the reports were very favorable.

Finally, convinced that he had found the partner he needed, Chris offered to bring him in as a cofounder.

Harbin, meanwhile, did his own due diligence, interviewing people who'd worked with Chris in the past and learning all he could about the history of Military.com. He, too, heard only positive reports. The only unanswered question was how many "verticals" could really be exploited—in other words, how many so-called affinity groups would react as the military community had? But even if they turned up only a few, Harbin realized, that could easily be enough to make the company viable. After all, Military.com had become very successful with only one vertical. He signed on.

Besides Will Harbin, Chris recruited Curtis Atkisson, a Stanford MBA who would be coming in as chief financial officer. He also began recruiting an IT director and several key engineers. Increasingly excited about his new enterprise, Chris talked constantly about the culture he wanted to create this time around.

"Passion is a critical part of your job," he emphasized during virtually every job interview. He recognized that at this point his primary role was to be an evangelist for the new company. Everything he did involved some form of selling—selling his own track record as an entrepreneur, selling the value behind the model, selling potential employees on the notion of working for him. One way he liked to test people during the interview process was to sell them on the idea that working for Affinity Labs was simply too challenging for most people.

"This is a tough place," he would say to a candidate. "It's more than likely that the worst possible outcome of this interview is that you actually get this job."

To the best candidates, of course, this made Chris's new company all the more appealing.

Andy McKelvey had slipped off the *Forbes* list of the four hundred richest Americans, but that was primarily because other people were now making even more money than he was. In 2005, he'd bought a very expensive toy—the *Aurora*, one of the largest privately owned boats in the world. In August 2006, McKelvey took the 160-foot yacht on a cruise in the Aegean Sea, off the coast of Turkey. Just before Chris was to leave Monster and officially start Affinity Labs, McKelvey invited him and Anne Dwane to spend a few days on the yacht with him. The Aegean was gorgeous during the summer, and Chris and Anne enthusiastically accepted the invitation.

Just as they were flying across the Atlantic Ocean in McKelvey's private jet, the online magazine *Slate* ran a sardonic story headlined, THE CEO BOUGHT A YACHT? TIME TO SELL. The article posited that when CEOs of public companies bought big boats, it was a reliable indicator that either their company's stock price was about to plummet (Revlon's stock fell 90 percent after the CEO bought the world's twenty-sixth-largest yacht) or the CEO was about to experience a major personal misfortune (two years after Tyco CEO Dennis Kozlowski bought an enormous yacht, he was convicted of tax fraud and sentenced to prison). *Slate* called this phenomenon the "Yacht of Doom Rule"—and then singled out McKelvey as one of its few exceptions.

The article proved to be eerily prescient. Not long after McKelvey welcomed Chris and Anne aboard the *Aurora*, he informed them that he had some bad news. In fact, he had invited them to the Aegean to tell them in person that he would soon be leaving Monster. The company was about to go through a very rough patch, he said—recently, he'd become aware of allegations that the company had improperly backdated stock options for several key executives, himself among them. McKelvey was adamant that he'd done nothing illegal, but he was going to have to resign.

Worse was to come. "I'm sorry, Chris, but the company isn't going to go for the deal on Affinity Labs," McKelvey said. He was sure that Chris could keep his job at Military.com, but their plan for his risk-free startup was dead.

Chris was shocked, disappointed, and disturbed. It was the last thing he'd expected to hear.

A few days later, back in the States, he called Will Harbin and Curtis Atkisson.

"Remember when I said only two things could kill this deal?" he asked. "One of the two has happened. Andy McKelvey is leaving Monster."

Without McKelvey, he explained, the agreement with Monster was now off, and the risks inherent in the company's launch were dramatically higher. Chris told them that he believed they had little choice but to abandon the venture immediately.

Harbin and Atkisson pushed back, and hard.

"There's no reason why we can't do this on our own," Harbin argued. He had successfully pitched his first company to VCs when he was only twenty-one. If Monster had seen the value in it and was willing to put up resources, he was confident that other investors would as well. Atkisson agreed.

Chris took a couple of days to wander around San Francisco and think it over. It meant a lot that Harbin and Atkisson believed so strongly in the idea and believed in him. But going it alone required a much bigger leap, and in the end it would be his call. He asked himself the hard question: do I really want to do this again?

He thought of the advice he always gave to young entrepreneurs. It's about timing and tenacity, Chris would say. And yet here he was, wavering. His thoughts returned to the early days of Military.com; even before they'd raised their first round of venture capital, he'd thought seriously about calling it quits and going back to Mercer. It had taken people like Steve Echikson to set him straight then, and now Harbin and Atkisson were playing the same role.

The choice was really no choice at all. Chris believed in his idea. He believed in his team. He had done this once, and he was certain he could do it again.

He pulled out his cell phone and dialed Harbin. The game was on.

CHAPTER 18

LEARN TO SELL

I have never worked a day in my life without selling. If I believe in something, I sell it, and I sell it hard.

—ESTÉE LAUDER

A confession: maybe I should have talked about the importance of selling earlier in the book. In fact, I thought about making it the second rule, right after "Make the Commitment." As soon as you decide to become an entrepreneur, you become a salesperson. Even before you've decided which problem you're going to solve—and thus which business you're going to launch—you've got to sell yourself as someone who can innovate, lead, and execute. If you can't or won't do that, sorry, but your venture will simply never get off the ground. So get used to it: sell today, sell tomorrow, sell all the damn time. First and last, you're an entrepreneur. But in between, you're all about selling.

Anne Dwane is right: anyone who has ever had to make a payroll can give you plenty of examples of why sales is the lifeblood of any business. Stories that speak to the importance of selling run throughout my narrative about Marla, Chris, and Marc, from the very first moments when Marc started Forbes Pacifica right through to the final pages of this book. And believe me, every other successful entrepreneur you ever talk to will agree—you must learn to sell.

Before we dive in, though, some advice: when somebody suggests that they can teach you to "sell anything to anybody," run—don't walk—away. For one thing, anyone who tells you this is almost assuredly full of baloney or worse. For another, cultivating a talent for selling just about anything would be a complete waste of time for any true entrepreneur. You don't want to sell *any* thing, after all; you want to sell *your* thing. You want to sell an effective solution to a real problem. You want to sell your idea and your venture. *That* is what you need to learn how to sell.

PASSION

As an entrepreneurial salesperson, you're always balancing your passion and your credibility. Both are crucial—and that's why we spent so much time in the beginning of this book looking at how Marla, Chris, and Marc developed business ideas that were both compelling and real to them.

The mistaken impression many people have about sales, Ed Zschau believes, is that it's all about convincing people to do things they don't want to do. Despite what cynics and bad salespeople seem to think, as a salesperson, it's never your job to "put one over" on your customers.

"A good salesperson," Zschau told me, "is somebody who can understand the values and the objectives of the customer, and then make a proposition that resonates with those values and objectives. He's also got to convey a sense of credibility and integrity."

Zschau knows Chris Michel and admires his ability to sell. "Chris is really good at understanding other people. He's a real person, not a phony or a fraud. He's also tenacious. Salespeople encounter so many situations where a customer says no, no, no way—and the good salesperson will say, 'Okay, I'll put you down as uncertain/undecided.' You have to be persistent in the appropriate way, because you will of course get turned down a lot. But if you know how to bring a customer back to the table and say something that really makes sense, you'll get business."

When I asked Chris Michel where he learned to sell, he immediately thought back to his time in the navy. "The first job I ever interviewed for was the position of admiral's aide. I had to convince a lot of people of my skills and value before the navy offered me that job. I remember sitting there in an interview and realizing that I really had to sell myself."

Chris acknowledges that selling comes to him naturally. "I think one advantage I have is that I've always been a passionate and enthusiastic person." Military.com struggled to get off the ground for a long time, but despite all the setbacks and hardships, Chris never lost his passion for selling his concept to potential customers and investors. In his case, an unwavering belief in his vision—and a never-say-die commitment to selling that vision—was the difference between survival and oblivion.

Recalling the early days of Military.com, Chris said: "One of the most important things to understand about a startup, particularly in the early stages, is that you have to sell a promise. People want to believe. They want to believe in you. They want to believe in your company. And your job is simply to give them the opportunity to believe. This is especially true of investors and employees. Investors don't want to spend hours each day turning people down—they want to find the next big thing. And employees want to work for a great company. When you help them make that connection, you're doing something important—both for you and for them."

CREDIBILITY

Marc Cenedella's passion for sales was contagious from the moment he started TheLadders. He sold employees, customers, and investors on his company. He chose a motto—"Love the Customer. Our Team Wins."— that spoke directly about the importance of a selling attitude. He even sold his idea to people who were unlikely ever to be involved in his enterprise. Early on, he made time each week to e-mail updates about his progress to people he hoped might someday invest in his company. He didn't send out those updates because he had to; he sent them because he enjoyed telling people about his efforts. Quite simply, he loved what he was doing—his updates, for instance, would invariably include at least one mention of how much he loved the job seeker and rooted for his or her success.

To my way of thinking, Marc's success grew directly out of both his passion and his credibility. I wish I could tell you that every HBS alumnus and young entrepreneur I interviewed said they believed that credibility and integrity were as important as passion in sales. But, in truth,

I heard a number of statements suggesting that an entrepreneur "has to be comfortable with selling a lie," or at least that entrepreneurs inevitably have to bend the truth by saying they've already achieved things that in fact they only hope to achieve. As one person told me, when you're at Step A trying to get to Step B, you have to tell them you're at Step B, and you want their help to get to Step C.

That approach may work in the short term, but I am convinced that it sets up the aspiring entrepreneur for long-term failure. The most effective entrepreneurs I got to know believed that credibility—a combination of integrity and competence—is just as important as passion. They knew—sometimes from hard experience—that in the end making a hollow promise just to close a sale often comes back to haunt you.

When integrity is combined with competence, a person earns real credibility. Marla Malcolm Beck is a superb example of what I mean. From the start, she chose to sell beauty products she personally believed in, and then she became very good at finding effective ways to sell those products to her customers. Long before I met Marla, my wife was a bluemercury customer. Soon after I began interviewing Marla, I asked my wife why she liked the company so much. It's the salespeople, she answered immediately. They took the time to work with her and even steered her away from a number of more expensive products they believed weren't right for her. They seemed to have her best interests at heart, and because she trusted them, she enjoyed buying what they had to sell. Their passion was contagious and their credibility closed the deal.

Chris Michel knows—now—how important credibility is. "I don't think I am a traditional salesperson," he commented. "I don't use a particular technique. I just try to be honest with people. I care a lot about making my partners successful—I don't want to sell somebody a bag of goods. I mean, I know I'm going to hear from them if it doesn't work out later."

It must be said, however, that when Chris first began selling Military .com to investors, he wasn't entirely credible. Initially, he simply didn't have a sufficiently detailed and convincing strategy for making money via the Internet. He knew that the U.S. military was a powerful affinity group, and that if he could collect enough of its members, he could potentially deliver a lot of buying power. But the crucial piece of the puzzle that he was missing was who, exactly, would pay for that information. Chris was hardly the only founder who hadn't figured out how his company would generate substantial revenue; in those days, after all, many would-be Internet entrepreneurs were selling completely untested and far less workable business models.

Chris was remarkably candid when we spoke about this issue one day. "This is kind of a sensitive subject for me," he told me. "But I will be honest with you. We were really, really scrappy as a young company. And maybe we did tend to oversell our business a bit. We say things like, 'we have almost ten million members.' Well, what does that actually mean? Early on, I think I was doing a lot of what you might call 'puffer fish stuff.' In fact, I had a couple of people call me out on it, and it really bothered me to have my integrity questioned. But they were right, and I learned a valuable lesson. It's like burning your hand on the stove—that kind of pain is a pretty good teacher."

Marc Cenedella still sends out a weekly e-mail, but it now goes out to more than four million people—to everyone, in other words, who has signed up for either a free or a paid membership to TheLadders. He is, of course, hoping that his newsletter will help bring in new members, but he says that his larger purpose is to help job seekers find the right opportunity, whether his company benefits or not. He knows that if those who receive his e-mail believe that making money is his only goal, they will tend to respond cynically. But he hopes that by now he's earned their trust, and that most of the readers of his newsletter are convinced that he's legitimately trying to help them reach their goals.

To make his point about the larger purpose of these newsletters, Marc told me a story about the most successful e-mail he'd ever sent, at least when measured by the number of people who opened it and clicked through to read the full message.

The subject was "Man, I Hate American Airlines," and it told the story of Katherine, a flight attendant on an American Airlines flight Marc had taken from Miami to New York. He'd been shocked to see that Katherine was wearing a button on her uniform that read, I HAVE NO IDEA WHY I WORK HERE.

In his e-mail, Marc wrote:

> I have to tell you, that was just about the most deflating, disheartening, dispiriting, depressing thing to read after a relaxing weekend. Katherine and her type stand for everything that's bad in the world. For every one of us trying to achieve great things, there's a Katherine standing nearby ready to tear it down. For each of us trying to make the world a better place today, this hour, this minute, there's a Katherine in the wings sticking her tongue out. And not only is there a Katherine, but there's a company willing to hire her. Like American Airlines. . . .
>
> So don't be a Katherine! As you go about this job hunt, don't waste your talents or fall into the trap of working for a company that doesn't respect you, in a job where you stop respecting yourself. You're too talented, forward-looking, and capable to waste your years away inside a rotting body like American Airlines. . . .
>
> Whatever you do, don't sell yourself short, and don't let the Katherines of this world bring you down.
>
> I'll be rooting for you!
>
> Warmest Regards,
> Marc Cenedella,
> Founder & CEO
> TheLadders.com, Inc.

Marc sent out this e-mail early one morning. By 7:35 a.m. he got a call from one of the company's sales directors, pleading with him not to write anything like that ever again. American Airlines, for all its foibles, was still roughly the one hundredth biggest company in America; it was exactly the sort of firm they hoped would pay to run job ads on TheLadders. Not only will this e-mail alienate American Airlines, the sales director told Marc, it will also make other companies hesitate to post their jobs with TheLadders.

That may be true, Marc conceded. But he also recognized that his willingness to criticize a company like American Airlines gave him a certain credibility—and credibility was an important reason why job seekers would consider becoming members.

"We don't sell out our good name to anybody in exchange for sales," Marc told the sales director. "We simply don't do that. American Airlines is a bad company. I want to see it out of business, and I don't want our subscribers working for them."

Of all the stories about selling in this book, my favorite may be the one about Michael Shafrir's meeting with Marc Cenedella in July 2006, when Shafrir had to sell the idea that the company had to change its business model. Shafrir faced a daunting challenge, and only by putting his credibility and competence on the line did he have a hope of succeeding. He knew he had to lead Marc to the counterintuitive idea that they could sell more ads than they could give away for free. It was risky. What if Marc concluded that the problem wasn't the business model, but Shafrir's execution of the model?

The only way to prepare for this difficult conversation, Shafrir realized, was to be sure that everything he told Marc was backed up by extensive data. If he nailed the data, and then found a way to lay out the numbers so that they told a story, Marc would understand what had to be done. But if he didn't present a watertight case—if he wasn't credible, in other words—Marc might well be tempted to shoot the messenger.

Shafrir deserves to be credited with more than just being a great salesman. Though not a cofounder, he'd joined TheLadders when it was still very young. He was immediately struck by the company's entrepreneurial spirit, and that spirit encouraged him to act like an entrepreneur himself. That ethic informed the way he prepared for his meeting with Marc about the challenges the employer relations team was facing, and to his credit Shafrir approached the meeting as an intelligent entrepreneur would. He saw a problem that badly needed fixing and offered a bold new solution.

That's a good lesson for any founder about why it's so important to foster an entrepreneurial culture. But it's also an important lesson for anyone who imagines becoming an entrepreneur someday. Until you launch your own venture, you will of course work for other people. But that doesn't mean you can't or shouldn't act entrepreneurially. Seek out employers who encourage creative thinking and risk taking. You'll be happier working for this sort of person, and you'll also develop the mind-set and reflexes that will serve you well when you're finally ready to found your own company.

WHAT THEY DON'T TEACH AT HBS

Every entrepreneur talks about how learning to sell is absolutely crucial to success. But if you ask HBS alumni what they don't teach you at Harvard Business School, do you know what they invariably say?

Sales.

Check out the course catalog even now. There are a number of courses on marketing, several on negotiations, but just as there wasn't a single course title at HBS that used any conjugation of the word *entrepreneurship* in the 1940s, now not a single course uses the word *sales*. (A few electives do include sales in the course descriptions, but not in the course title—and these courses aren't required in any case.)

When I mentioned this to Stig Leschly he protested mildly. "Actually," he said, "I think we accidentally teach sales in the entrepreneurial course." But he agreed that selling is a skill that a lot of HBS students simply don't have. By and large, he said, the school's students are not good at "walking up to somebody and convincing them of something."

Even so, Leschly agreed that for an entrepreneur learning to sell is critical. "It's overwhelmingly true that you're selling all the time. It's all you ever do—you're persuading people to give you money, to join your company, to buy your product."

Noam Wasserman made the same point a different way. "When some of my founders came to speak to my class," he told me, "I videotaped interviews with them afterward. I would almost always ask them, What's the most important skill for an entrepreneur to have? But finally I got so tired of hearing the same answer—sales, they would say—that I stopped asking that question."

One of the founders who visited Wasserman's class encouraged the students to watch movies about salespeople, like *Glengarry Glen Ross* or *The Pursuit of Happyness*. Another went to lunch with Wasserman and several of his students afterward, and explained that he had started out as a technology expert, but later switched gears completely and moved over to sales and marketing. That, he told them, had made all the difference in the success of his company.

Wasserman remembered the lunch vividly. "He vehemently pushed the students who wanted to be entrepreneurs to go out and carry a bag. Go out and sell something door-to-door, and do it as early in your career as possible. And then he said, 'That's the most critical difference between me and lot of other entrepreneurs. There's no question that I have a big advantage over the people who have really never sold anything.'"

HOW TO LEARN TO SELL

I heard over and over that if you want to become an effective salesperson, there is no substitute for experience. At one HBS panel, a group of successful entrepreneurs who were emphasizing the importance of learning to sell were asked, If sales are so important and there's no substitute for experience, then how do you find a good sales job?

"Take a job where you will learn the ropes from people who are good teachers," one founder said, "and put compensation last on your list of priorities." It also helps, another founder said, if you're selling products you understand and have a feeling for. Ideally, you'll get the sales experience you need by selling something not unlike what you would sell if you had already launched a company of your own.

Does getting a sales job sound a bit like starting at the bottom? If so, banish the thought. In fact, selling is crucial at every step up the ladder. And though you may imagine that as CEO you'll finally be able to delegate sales and selling to subordinates or a professional sales force, you're only partly right. The CEO is often responsible for many of a new company's earliest and most important sales, and as your company grows, the need to sell becomes ever more important—even if what you're selling and who you're selling it to changes. It's also worth keeping in mind an excellent comment by Noam Wasserman. His research, he told me, has shown that the ability to sell is one of the few things that can inoculate a founding CEO from being forced out over time.

THE NEXT RULE

Have I sold you yet?

I hope so. After following and studying the three stories I've been telling, I hope you understand how important it is to learn to sell—and how often this crucial skill is undervalued.

But if I've convinced you that selling is essential to successful entrepreneurship, notice that I've never said that selling is easy. Even the best salespeople fail more often than they succeed, and for a lot of people, closing a sale is a relatively rare event. So don't expect to come up a winner every time. Celebrate your successes when they do come, but don't beat up on yourself when they don't. You're likely to hear "No thanks" or "No" or "NO!" far more often than you're going to hear "Yes."

Which might prompt you to ask: how can I possibly handle the constant rejection?

To which I will answer: perfect timing, because it's just the right moment to learn the next rule. And that rule is: persist, persevere, prevail.

CHAPTER 19

Never give in. Never give in. Never, never, never, never—in nothing, great or small, large or petty—never give in, except to convictions of honor and good sense.

—WINSTON CHURCHILL

CHRIS: MAKING IT LOOK EASY

Raising money was a comparative breeze this time for Chris Michel. Miltary.com projected nearly $10 million in pretax profit for 2006, and the company was now considered a great success. He departed from Monster Worldwide in September, leaving his first creation, Military. com, in the capable hands of Anne Dwane. With his track record—among other pluses, he was unusual for being a dot-com survivor—and with a promising business plan built on his previous success, he was something of a hot commodity, and he received an offer for capital after only one pitch. Soon several venture capitalists were fighting over the opportunity to invest in Affinity Labs. By November 2006, Chris came to terms on a $6.5 million venture capital deal led by Trinity Ventures and another firm, the Mayfield Fund, which had been the initial investor in Military.com.

With Will Harbin and Curtis Atkisson beside him, Chris moved faster and smarter on every front. No longer was he an inexperienced entrepreneur starting his first company. Technology expenses had continued to fall; even elaborate Web sites cost much less to design now than when he had started Military.com. And Chris was now much savvier about how to keep his operating costs to a minimum. At first he tried to outsource the development of the company's Web site infrastructure to eastern Europe, but when this turned out to be more expensive and more difficult to manage than expected, they pivoted quickly, hired engineers, and brought the project back in-house.

That's what entrepreneurship is all about, Chris told a friend at the time. Try something. If it doesn't work, try something else—but just keep trying.

Even though his new venture wasn't affiliated with Monster, Chris worked out marketing and development deals with the company, which in turn made it possible for him to use Monster's sales force and marketing acumen. And the business model for Affinity's various Web sites provided a resilient template. Joining the sites would be free for users, just as it had been at Military.com, and each site would offer the same mix of news, career information, community, and camaraderie that had worked so well at Military.com.

The first big question Chris faced was which career fields to target. He and Will Harbin began looking for the answer by combing through freely available government data from the U.S. Bureau of Labor Statistics. They looked for professions with the largest populations, highest incomes, biggest percentage of Internet use, and—perhaps most important—the intangible notion of their affinity for one another. Cops were right at the top of the list, much as Chris thought they'd be. By and large, police considered themselves to be part of a "thin blue line" protecting the rest of America. And just as members of the military often did, cops identified themselves as much by who *wasn't* in the group as who was. In addition to police officers, nurses, teachers, and firefighters made up the initial batch of professions that Affinity would target. They would continue to look for other promising professions as they went forward, but for now the idea was to begin by identifying the stickiest groups and then locking them up.

The next question was how to find general managers who would do a first-rate job of running each site. Chris had known the armed forces inside and out when he started Military.com, but what did he know about being a police officer or a teacher? He and his partners needed to find skilled managers who had deep ties in the fields they were targeting, and they began by approaching well-known bloggers, editors, and organizers who already had huge lists of contacts within the four professions. Soon they had identified a number of strong candidates, hired several of them, and begun working on the design and functionality of the four sites. By spring 2007, the first new Affinity Labs community was ready to launch: PoliceLink.com.

PoliceLink immediately attracted heavy traffic, as did the other sites when they went up. Affinity Labs rolled out new communities far faster than the partners had anticipated; by the end of that summer, barely nine months into the company's life, they had launched seven successful sites. Besides the original four, they created ArtBistro for artists, GovCentral for government workers, and TechCommunity for people working in information technology. Anticipating yet more sites, Chris snapped up domain names, registering a few that hadn't been purchased by anyone and paying at most $5,000 to $10,000 for a few others. Affinity began rolling out a new site every couple of months, and although not every community lasted, that was okay. In 1999, Chris had spent millions of dollars developing the original Military.com site; now each new portal cost a tiny fraction of that amount. They would start a channel, push it hard, and quickly determine whether it could become one of the top two communities for that particular profession. If that wasn't possible, they would shut the site down and funnel their resources into other affinity groups.

Everything that had taken so much work at Military.com came together almost effortlessly this time. They built the sites, signed up partners, and sold qualified leads. By the end of 2007, Affinity Labs had generated over $2 million in revenue for the year, and Chris projected that they would achieve four times that amount in 2008. The company was a sterling example of intelligent entrepreneurship. They'd developed an excellent business plan, hired well, and executed smartly. Morale was high and their direction was clear. Chris and his partners had every reason to believe that they'd built the foundation of a company with dazzling potential.

MARC: THE SWITCH

Marc Cenedella unquestionably had a way with words—had he not been an entrepreneur, he might well have written for a living. He still wrote the newsletter that was e-mailed to more than 3.5 million addresses each week. He savored the replies he got from people who'd found jobs through his company, and many of them thanked him for starting it. Marc also prided himself on writing great recommendations; he was especially pleased to write one for Andrew Koch, who applied for admission to the Harvard Business School class of 2010. Andrew had first worked for Marc at HotJobs in the summer of 2000; looking back, Marc felt as if Andrew's decision to follow in his footsteps and apply to HBS was practically predestined.

Though TheLadders continued to thrive, it was clearly a company in transition. Turning the business model 180 degrees and charging employers for ads was the most delicate move Marc had ever had to make. As always, he researched the issue intensively, gathering all the data he could find on how other companies fared when they switched from a free to a paid model. Of course, he had his own experience to draw on as well: in January 2004, TheLadders had "flipped the switch" and for the first time begun charging job seekers. Although Marc's company had made that transition look easy, other Web sites often struggled or failed. Only a few had been able to hold on to even one in ten subscribers when they moved to a paid model.

TheLadders faced another problem, too, in that it had always marketed its service as "free for employers." The company's ecosystem was fragile, as Marc always liked to say, and converting it to a new model without completely destroying what they had so painstakingly built would require both a huge commitment of resources and meticulous execution. And since all of its competitors already charged employers to list jobs, TheLadders would be giving up one of the characteristics that had set it apart in the recruiting field. The company faced the possibility that as soon as it announced the change, it might face the equivalent of a revolt. If a lot of the employers who currently listed with the site abruptly stopped advertising on their site, it could potentially lose a large number of their subscribers. But Marc was undaunted by these difficult problems. This was a challenge to be overcome, not an excuse for inaction.

The solution Marc's team came up with, after many months of analysis and discussion, was to roll things out gradually. They went through the records of all the recruiters who had used the site and assigned each one a score based on twelve criteria—how often they posted, how often they logged in and searched for applicants, and the like. Based on these scores, they offered each recruiter between one and twelve months of free service before requiring that they begin paying to list jobs. The more active and desirable a client had been, the longer the client could list its jobs for free.

The existing business, meanwhile, continued to move ahead aggressively, and the company extended its reach by launching a European version of TheLadders. In early 2007, Marc took another group of employees to Japan. Despite the tricky challenges involved in changing their business model, Marc was increasingly convinced that TheLadders could indeed become a billion-dollar company with active and profitable sites all over the world. He had a team of capable executives working for him, a buoyant company culture, and a healthy balance sheet. They would figure out how to make this crucial change, and they'd been even stronger on the other side of it.

Besides, this wasn't the first time Marc had undertaken this process of reinvention. He knew that entrepreneurs almost never get things right the first time around: you just had to keep plugging away, trying first one approach to finding a solution to your problem, and then another and another, until at last you found one that worked. He'd learned that lesson years ago, soon after starting Forbes Pacifica. That company's launch had been wobbly at best; if he hadn't buckled down and begun thinking more creatively, working harder and flying to Japan more often, who knew how his life might have been different? If he hadn't persevered and made that company a success, he might not have gone to Harvard, worked at Hot-Jobs, or started TheLadders.

Maybe the new business model would work. But if it didn't, he would experiment with another model—and keep experimenting until he found one that worked. The solution was out there; it was only a matter of time and persistence before he found it.

Sounding a lot like Chris Michel—who was making a similar point at virtually the same time—Marc told a friend, "You try great things, you take a bit of a risk, and you get smacked. All sorts of bad stuff hits you, but you learn to roll with it and you keep going."

CHRIS: TWO-FOR-TWO

By the fall of 2007, Affinity Labs was operating eight thriving online communities—eight mini-Military.coms, in essence—with a total of six hundred thousand members. It was a diversified collection of sites, and in a few cases the company had discovered unexpected affinity groups: IndiaOn, for example, was a bustling site for expatriate Indian nationals in the United States. The venture was now so far ahead of schedule that Chris started putting out feelers for a second round of venture capital. He was confident that with more funding Affinity could generate explosive growth.

As focused as Chris was on building his company, he also continually looked for an opportunity to sell Affinity Labs, take it public, or at least get some kind of recapitalization. Recalling the experience of selling Military.com, he felt that Anne Dwane hadn't received as big a payout as she should have, and he decided that this time he would take an early, careful look at how much equity had been distributed to his cofounders and core team members. Chris concluded that Will Harbin, Curtis Atkisson, and a handful of others didn't own enough of the venture; if the company were acquired or "recapped," they would receive less than he thought they deserved. Gradually, he began giving them bits of his own equity. This was so unusual that the company had to hire a law firm to figure out how Chris could give away equity without creating serious tax problems for the recipients.

Later, when a magazine writer asked him about this unorthodox decision, Chris said it was "easy for me to do. I don't think you can ever overincentivize the truly great people on your team."

When he began to pitch his company to VC firms for a second round of investment, the reception was enthusiastic. Almost immediately, Chris had a term sheet from Reed Elsevier ventures; its so-called pre-money valuation was nearly four times the amount of the company's estimated value just a few months earlier, and the firm wanted to pump tens of millions of additional dollars into Affinity Labs. Chris found it hard to believe how quickly things had come together. Only a little more than a year after he had visited Andy McKelvey on his yacht in the Aegean Sea, Affinity Labs was poised to dwarf the success of Military.com.

Word got out that Chris was looking for a second round of venture capital and, in November, Monster Worldwide called to say that it wanted to be in on it. McKelvey had been replaced by Salvatore Iannuzzi, an outsider and career executive who had held senior positions with Motorola and Symbol Technologies. Though Chris didn't know the new CEO, he flew east to meet with Iannuzzi and the company's CFO at Monster's headquarters in Massachusetts.

They talked for a while about all that Chris had accomplished in such a short time, and about the great synergy between Military.com and Monster's core business. Monster wanted to build on that relationship, Iannuzzi told Chris, by investing in Affinity. Though he appreciated the vote of confidence, Chris turned him down. There were simply too many other potential investors, he explained, and he was also concerned that an investment by Monster might lock out other potential acquirers and so limit their eventual exit options.

"Okay," Iannuzzi responded. "Would you be open to an acquisition?"

Suddenly the conversation had become much more interesting. Flying home after the meeting, Chris concluded that Iannuzzi had intended to pitch the idea of an outright purchase to him all along. Monster's initial offer was in the mid–$50 million range, and as the negotiations proceeded over the next several weeks, Chris talked through several options with Will Harbin and Curtis Atkisson. All three believed that Affinity Labs had the potential to become a billion-dollar company, but Chris was concerned about how long the economy could stay healthy. Recently he'd begun moving his own money out of stocks and into safer, more conservative investments like treasury bills. As he told his partners, his guess was that if they didn't sell now, the next opportunity would probably be far down the road. Besides, it was awfully hard to imagine leaving the kind of money Monster was offering on the table.

Monster, meanwhile, stepped up its efforts to close the deal. Military.com, which now had ten million members, was arguably worth fifteen to twenty times what Monster had paid for it a few years earlier. Clearly Iannuzzi had a strong sense that Affinity Labs could also grow to a similar scale.

Chris and Iannuzzi talked the money back and forth, and finally settled on a number: Monster would acquire Affinity Labs for $61 million. About 40 percent of that amount would go to Chris. In just eighteen months, he had started, built, and sold his second significant company.

Not bad for a self-described "state school guy" and former navy officer, Chris thought to himself. Not bad at all.

The sale of Affinity Labs to Monster closed in January 2008. By deciding to give away some of his equity before the deal closed, Chris had forfeited a little under half a million dollars, but given the size of his own windfall he hardly minded. Chris's desire to be an entrepreneur had never had much to do with money anyway. He still lived in the same one-room apartment on Davis Court that he'd moved into almost ten years ago. Since selling most of his possessions after leaving the navy, he had never purchased much—he still didn't own a car, for instance. He traveled, took pictures, and bought nicer sports jackets and blue jeans. That was about it.

After the deal with Monster was announced, the accolades poured in. Even Marc Cenedella noted the sale on his personal blog. Chris found it amusing that some people thought Military.com had been a mixed success and that Affinity Labs was a much bigger win. He did understand their point of view: Military.com had struggled, survived, and been acquired, but it was not all that remarkable in the context of early 2000 Internet startups. A lot of other entrepreneurs had built companies, sold them, and received personal paydays in the single-digit million-dollar range. Affinity Labs, on the other hand, was not only a bigger payout in a much shorter time, but Chris had made it look easy. What a lot of people didn't understand, though, was that Affinity Labs would never have existed if he hadn't found a way to make Military.com work. And with his second venture, Chris had proved that his first entrepreneurial success was no fluke.

The success of Affinity Labs was sweet, but it was his experience with Military.com that had truly made him an entrepreneur. He had spent far more time building his first company—it had taken him seven years, versus a year and a half in the case of Affinity. And he had grown so much while running Military.com, in large part because he had nearly lost everything. His first venture had been his magnum opus, the company he'd created with nothing at the start but a blank sheet of paper. He understood its members as well as he understood his closest friends. He had set out to solve questions that bothered him personally—the whole company, in fact, could trace its origin back to one simple question: how does a former member of the military make his or her way in civilian society? He'd built a number of tools that had helped solve that problem and a number of others, not just for Military.com's members, but for himself as well. What gave him greatest satisfaction was knowing that his company had made a real difference in a lot of people's lives.

In the wake of Affinity's sale, Chris finally began to enjoy both a few of the things money could buy and the psychological advantage of having a sizable bank account. He finally bought a car (he splurged on a Porsche); he also purchased a much bigger loft apartment in San Francisco's SOMA neighborhood. He gave some money to his parents. Life was good.

But there was one note of disappointment. After so many years together, Chris and Anne were no longer romantically involved. Melancholy as this was, they remained the best of friends. They'd spent years undertaking one exciting, stressful adventure after another—HBS, the move to San Francisco, and of course the five-year odyssey that was the launch, near death, recovery, and eventual sale of Military .com—but now they had decided to chart their own courses.

At almost precisely the same time that Chris was planning to step down from the helm at Affinity Labs, their old booster at Mayfield, Mike Levinthal, was trying to recruit Anne away from Military.com and Monster to become the CEO of a fledgling new startup called Zinch. Founded by two twenty-something college students, Zinch's business model was similar to that of Military.com and Affinity Labs—the company provided highly qualified lead referrals to colleges and universities. Instead of focusing on retiring veterans or other nontraditional students, Zinch went straight to the largest source of college applicants: high school students.

When Anne decided to take the leap, Chris saw an opportunity as well; he stepped up and became a significant angel investor in her new company. Helping to make Anne and Zinch successful were now among his top priorities.

Chris left Affinity Labs officially in September 2008. On his recommendation, Will Harbin succeeded him as the new company's general manager. With the transfer of responsibility complete, Chris walked out of his office and entered a brave new world—one where, for the first time in his adult life, his identity would not be defined by his work, his career, or what he did to make money.

MARLA: DROOM, REDUX

Marla and Barry traveled to Paris and London, and they took a vacation in Saint-Tropez. Eventually they bought a beach house in New Jersey. But otherwise they didn't do very much to celebrate their recap. In truth, Marla felt that the amount of money they had made was so staggering that she almost couldn't get her arms around it. You heard about bankers who got giant end-of-the-year bonuses of a few hundred thousand dollars, who sometimes went out and spent all the money at once. But she and Barry had made so much money that it was surreal, and therefore they didn't really change their behavior much. When they ran into Marc Cenedella's housemate, Steve Perricone, at a social gathering he was startled when they began asking him for informal financial advice.

"Damn it," Steve thought, as he recalled that in the summer of 1999 Marla had practically begged him and Marc to invest in her company. (He'd followed Marc's lead and declined.) Marla and Barry knew that much of his business involved investing on behalf of very wealthy individuals; if they were asking his advice, he reasoned, they must be doing very well now.

But then, just when all the cards seemed to be coming up aces, Marla saw trouble ahead. Week by week, she became more convinced that the economy was due for a significant fall. Their new, postinvestment strategy called for opening as many as three hundred bluemercury stores throughout the United States within the next few years. But even as the first round of new stores began coming on line, she worried that they had chosen a very bad time for a major expansion.

Every two hours, she received updates on the current retail sales in each of the bluemercury stores. In late 2006 and early 2007, she watched as the numbers grew increasingly volatile. Her gut told her that a recession was more than possible, but it was hard to be sure—economists and business leaders expressed fears that the economy might be trending downward, but no real consensus had emerged as to how bad things might get.

According to their expansion strategy, bluemercury was supposed to open thirty new stores in 2007 alone. But as the year went on and the growth of her same-store sales numbers started slowing down, Marla's skittishness only increased. She believed that virtually every good decision she'd ever made about the direction of bluemercury had been based on her instincts—and her instincts were telling her not to go full throttle at this particular moment.

She and Barry reviewed the entire business, made their best guess about where it was going, and then made a hard, unpopular call. In November and December 2007, they canceled all their plans to open more stores; where they could, they also backed out of contracts they'd already signed.

DROOM had been Marla's mantra for nearly a decade, and she swore she was not going to overextend herself or her company. By late spring 2008, she was forced to consider the possibility that she would have to lay off employees; by the end of July, she had closed her two weakest stores—one near Boston, the other in Boca Raton. They were the first two closures in the company's history, and Marla felt sick about it. Ironically, she'd described precisely this scenario in her HBS applications a decade before. Contemplating the prospect of advising a McKinsey client who wanted to cut costs, Marla had written, "I wondered how I could be responsible for eliminating people's livelihoods."

Meanwhile, bluemercury's investors and board of directors were understandably disturbed. Invus had just invested tens of millions of dollars, and now Marla was telling them that the company would shrink in the short term. Marla had been through one difficult period before: in 1999 and 2000, she'd had to cut payroll in the company's earliest days. But that had been a completely different situation. They had been a new startup, and volatility was to be expected. Now bluemercury was an established, well-capitalized company; retrenching so soon after she and Barry had taken their "recap" was a bitter pill for everyone to swallow.

But Marla had known since she was young that she wanted to be a

CEO, and making tough decisions came with the territory. Besides, ignoring an unpleasant reality now would only open the door to much more dangerous problems later on. Despite pressure from her investors and her board, she hunkered down and prepared to wait out the coming storm.

MARC: CASE IN POINT

Predictably, as soon as Marc announced that TheLadders would be charging recruiters and employers to list jobs on their Web site, some recruiters who had long been using the site peppered them with the e-mails. A lot of people apparently never cleaned out their in-boxes— Marc was amazed when the company was flooded with copies of solicitations they'd made over the years, promising that the service would always be free for recruiters. The vitriol troubled him, but he couldn't let old marketing strategies define their future.

The transition to a paid model was painful, but by December 2008 it was complete. Only about 14 percent of the original recruiter-users remained, but Marc was convinced that they were now booking ads from the better class of job posters they badly needed. Although they still had trouble attracting ads from Fortune 1000 companies, that was hardly unexpected, given that they were now competing directly with the older job boards. By selling hard and encouraging existing companies to run more ads, however, they managed to maintain a volume of advertisements roughly comparable to what they'd had before they made the switch. More important, what Marc called the site's ecosystem had changed very little. They still listed just as many jobs for each applicant; the difference was that the person posting the job was more often directly involved in the hiring decision, rather than a headhunter or other middleman.

TheLadders was now more than five years old, and by just about every measure it was thriving. One business publication, the *Business Insider*, ranked the company as the sixteenth most valuable privately held tech startup in the world as of March 2008, estimating their revenue at $50 million a year and projecting a valuation of as much as $500 million if they ever came to market. Even Marc's alma mater was paying close attention to his company's burgeoning success. Throughout

2008, a team of HBS researchers stayed in close touch with him, working on a case about TheLadders that focused on the challenge the company faced when making the switch to their new business model.

Marc's personal life was also going well. After living with Steve Perricone for ten years, he'd recently moved into his own place—although he persisted in renting because he didn't trust the volatility of the New York City real estate market. But that wasn't the only big change Marc was making.

Two years earlier, he had called Steve at work one day with an out-of-the-blue question. Steve was on the boards of a couple of New York City charities—the Lower East Side Girls' Club, for example, and a cancer charity called Fertile Hope.

"That charity thing you're doing," Marc began. "Is that a good way to meet women?"

Steve found Marc's question hilarious, but he knew almost immediately what it meant. Marc had obviously decided that it was time to start looking for someone to share his life with. And having reached this conclusion, he would approach the issue the same way he approached everything else: methodically, intelligently, efficiently. As usual, his friend had a plan.

Soon Marc was going to every charitable event he could get invited to. Just as he'd hoped, a lot of smart, sophisticated women also attended these events, and he met as many as he could.

A few months after his talk with Steve, Marc phoned his cousin Loraine. He'd been asking for her advice on dating and relationships since his HBS days, and he frequently reminded her that since he'd introduced her to her husband, it was her job to find him the woman of his dreams. Now he was calling her to say that she was off the hook. He'd gone to a fund-raiser for the Metropolitan Museum of Art and found the woman he was looking for: a twenty-five-year-old Harvard-educated lawyer named Angela Kim. Now, in March 2009, they were engaged.

CHAPTER 20

PERSIST, PERSEVERE, PREVAIL

Nothing in this world can take the place of persistence. Talent will not; nothing is more common than unsuccessful people with talent. Genius will not; unrewarded genius is almost a proverb. Education will not; the world is full of educated derelicts. Persistence and determination alone are omnipotent. The slogan "press on" has solved and always will solve the problems of the human race.

—CALVIN COOLIDGE

At the outset of this project, I aspired to write a book that would take the luck out of entrepreneurship. But as I went along, I learned that you really can't do that. Over time, with the benefit of experience, some of us can improve our predictive abilities and make smarter bets about what's going to happen. But there will always be luck, both good and bad. The key is persisting long enough to take advantage of the good fortune that does come your way.

Nevertheless, I was struck by how many entrepreneurs told me that they believed they were lucky, or even "just lucky." In a few instances, this was probably true. More often, I suspect that those entrepreneurs who gave a lot of credit to luck simply hadn't reflected in a serious way on what they'd accomplished and how they'd become successful.

The best comment I heard on this subject came from an entrepreneur from the HBS class of 1999, who told me that luck is "always a necessary ingredient, but never a sufficient one." Woody Allen famously said that 80 percent of success is just showing up. But the highly successful entrepreneurs I got to know would disagree. As the subjects of my three narratives suggest, showing up just gets you started. The truly crucial ingredient is the determination to persist, persevere, and prevail.

This rule about persistence applies both to a particular venture and to the larger objective of becoming a successful entrepreneur. Earlier in the book, we talked about the importance of managing risk, and to my way of thinking, persistence is an excellent hedge against risk. You can't ever know for sure what is just over the horizon. Maybe someone else is about to launch a better-executed version of exactly the product you're working on. Perhaps a natural disaster will affect your suppliers or your customers' demand for your product. But whatever the future holds, you have a much better chance of surviving a run of bad luck if you've cultivated the habit of persistence. If you genuinely believe that you will persevere—if you've proven to yourself over and over that you simply will not quit—the likelihood that you'll eventually achieve your goals is high.

If persistence improves your odds of surviving, it also allows you to take advantage of opportunity when it does come along. Sometimes, after all, an unexpected event can affect you positively. Academics at business schools like HBS call this a "shift in the context." A classic example of this phenomenon—often cited by Professor Bill Sahlman—is the case of a packaging company that was doing poorly in the early 1980s. One of its products was a cheap mechanism for making consumer goods tamper-resistant. The owners were on the verge of selling their struggling business when a tragic event turned their fortunes around completely. In fall 1982, seven people died after consuming Tylenol capsules that had been laced with potassium cyanide. Sales of Tylenol plummeted, and the company's manufacturer, Johnson & Johnson—as well as every other manufacturer of consumable goods in the United States—clamored for a way to package their products so they would be tamper-resistant. The ailing packaging company was suddenly flooded with orders and quickly became profitable again. Persistence paid a huge dividend: the company had survived long enough to take advantage of a completely unforeseen change in the business landscape.

I am of course not advocating that you should pursue a venture that depends to a great extent on events outside your control. Luck is not a strategy, after all. But if you've been intelligent about launching your entrepreneurial venture—if you've started with a problem rather than a solution, assembled a quality team, hedged your risk, and taken to heart all the other lessons we've talked about—then persistence may well be your salvation.

The data support this point. The longer a business endures, the better its chances of surviving over the long term. Studies show that a company that makes it to its second anniversary has better odds of lasting for ten or more years than a company that is still operating on its first anniversary. And with each passing year, the odds of long-term survival improve. Although we have to be careful about confusing correlation with causation, it makes intuitive sense that a company with a fatally flawed business model or a weak executive team will fail early, whereas a company that is structurally sound has a better chance of celebrating the tenth anniversary of its founding.

The three stories we've been following consistently illustrate the importance of persistence. What was the key to Chris Michel's successful effort to lead Military.com to safe harbor? Above all, it was his ability to persevere despite many setbacks and disappointments.

Chris, unlike a number of entrepreneurs, is very thoughtful about the reasons for his success. As he told me one day, "I love the Louis Pasteur quote, 'Chance favors the prepared mind.' Work ethic matters. We did everything we could think of to improve our chances of succeeding, and we never stopped looking for opportunity. Because you never want to run the regrets analysis and realize that there was something you could've done that you didn't do."

Marla Malcolm Beck is also a believer in persistence. "In a lot of businesses, the idea just gets you started," she commented. "Once you get in the game, you've got to work at it until you figure it out. And no matter what we do, no matter how much success we have in a given year, the game is always about survival. Nothing stays the same for ten years. We've had to change our strategy year after year after year. If you can survive through all the tough times, you'll be that much stronger when the good times finally come."

PERSISTENCE IN SUCCESSIVE VENTURES

Some people argue that failure is an even better teacher than success. If an entrepreneur's first venture doesn't succeed, this thinking goes, he or she is more likely to succeed the next time around. But one HBS study, published in 2009, denied any correlation. Successful entrepreneurs "had a 34 percent chance of succeeding in their next venture-backed firm," according to HBS professors Josh Lerner and Paul Gompers, whereas only 23 percent of founders who failed in their first attempt succeeded the next time around. By comparison, 22 percent of entrepreneurs who had never launched a business succeeded on their first try.

When Lerner and Gompers's results were summarized in a *New York Times* article, they got fifty or so angry e-mails from failed first-time entrepreneurs who insisted that their chances of succeeding with their next venture had significantly improved. But, Lerner told me, "We didn't have an agenda. We're like Fox News: we report, you decide."

He offered three possible explanations for this seemingly illogical result. First, it's possible that the successful entrepreneurs simply had the right stuff to begin with. Second, perhaps success really is a better teacher than failure—Chris Michel, for instance, benefited enormously from his success with Military.com. Third, entrepreneurs who succeed the first time may enjoy an "attribution effect," meaning that they have better luck in later ventures because they can recruit better people based on their earlier success.

Perhaps it makes most sense that all experience—both good and bad—can be valuable, but only if you take the time to reflect on it and learn the lessons it teaches. A failure can indeed be a necessary proving ground, and if you're willing to take a hard and honest look at your own mistakes, you can substantially improve your chances of succeeding the next time around. Moreover, most serial entrepreneurs seem driven at least in part by a desire to incorporate the lessons they've learned in succesive ventures. Part of being persistent is understanding that you can never know enough, learn enough, or manage risk down to zero.

This is why graduates of a case-based MBA program like the one at HBS may have an advantage over those who haven't attended a good business school. The entire program is built around the belief that a student of business and entrepreneurship can learn a great deal from other people's successes and failures.

As Noam Wasserman explained in one interview, HBS uses a pedagogical model built around case studies for two reasons. "First, we want our students to learn from other people's experiences—studying the R&R case, seeing all these founders who encounter problems, and learning from them so it's less likely that you will someday run aground on the rocks. That's the content side." HBS's second objective, he explained, is to teach its students how to learn. "I have a recurring theme," Wasserman continued. "We study at least one serial entrepreneur case in each module of my course, where we see what an entrepreneur learned from his earlier ventures, and what he changed in the second venture as a result of that learning. That's one of the critical things that entrepreneurs have to do, because in high-growth ventures and those that focus on new technologies, the imperative to learn is even greater. It's critical that my students see that continuous learning is essential. Learning how to learn is, I think, one of the most important lessons that students take away."

Stig Leschly is especially thoughtful about why the rule of persistence—and its association with learning—is so important. In part, that's because his wisdom is hard-won: it comes out of his own experiences as an entrepreneur, and a story about a spectacular success that was made possible by his refusal to accept failure as a final outcome.

Leschly entered HBS in 1994, but he didn't graduate until 1998 because he studied both law and business and so received a joint JD/MBA degree. In the summer before his final year, he borrowed $100,000 from his parents and spent the entire amount trying to create an online auction engine that ultimately didn't work. Discouraged but unwilling to give up on his idea, Leschly went back for his final year at HBS, rewrote the business plan, found a technical cofounder, and then took advantage of the VC boom, raising $16 million during late 1999 and early 2000. He built his site and bought out all of his competitors, including a company called Bibliofind, which was the first Web site for people who collected rare books. This second go-round was much more successful, and Leschly's venture (which he renamed exchange.com) now seemed to be coming to market at the perfect moment. By spring

1999, Leschly heard that Barnes & Noble wanted to make an offer to buy his company. He "dodged the negotiation," as he put it to me, and flew to Seattle. There, he pitched the venture to Jeff Bezos at Amazon.com. He was scheduled to meet with Yahoo! a few days later, but when Bezos learned that Leschly planned to sit down with Yahoo! he made an offer to buy Leschly's company, and ultimately the deal went through.

"They bought us for $200 million, and at that point we had thirty employees and a million in revenue," Leschly explained. "We were tiny. We were very lucky. We settled on the deal in March 1999—if you look back, that was literally the month, the peak of the first wave. Believe it or not, I went through a lot of anguish and pain before conceding to sell this enterprise for $200 million. But when the deal was done and the money was in the bank, I was like, Wow—this is crazy."

Unlike Marla, Chris, and Marc, Leschly didn't spend five or ten years building a successful company. But his story still carries a valuable lesson about perseverance. The key to his ultimate success was his willingness to revamp a failed strategy and persist long enough for the market to catch up to him. He had no idea—none—when he launched exchange.com that he would build a business that could be sold for a huge amount of money.

"What first-time entrepreneurs need to know," Leschly explained to me, "is that they will encounter successful entrepreneurs who are both competent and lucky. But they probably won't understand how little these entrepreneurs knew about their futures when they began. You won't succeed because you have one good idea. You'll succeed because you work your ass off, because you never give up, because you reinvent yourself constantly. You've got to be paranoid all the time; you've got to readjust based on every little piece of meaningful data. And, even after you've done all that, you still have to get lucky!"

Luck—and success—may not come for a long while, but the intelligent entrepreneur understands that it's okay. "Here's the comforting thing," Leschly continued. "I believe that although you may have to start five or six ventures, eventually something's going to work. So take it easy on yourself—just because you didn't succeed the first or second time doesn't mean you won't get there in the end. I had a venture guy say to me, 'If you act with integrity, you have nothing to lose here. If you burn through your investment and the company implodes, but you come out of it with your reputation for integrity intact, you're still going to get your calls returned when the next opportunity comes along.' So however hard it is psychologically, you have to be willing to fail and keep failing until you finally find your own way to success."

HOW CAN YOU IMPROVE YOUR LUCK?

Luck is such a rich subject that HBS professor Howard Stevenson wrote an entire book about it called *Make Your Own Luck*, a fairly complex, mathematical tome about trying to improve predictive abilities. Others have also written books on the topic, and if you believe that fortune will smile on you more often because you've read a lot about how to attract her attentions, more power to you. For my money, though, you'll be much better off if you cultivate your ability to persist and persevere, learn as much as you can from both success and failure, and prepare yourself for the day when good luck comes your way so you can take full advantage of it. Meanwhile, here are a few practical things you can do to help you achieve that goal.

Keep a record of what you do. If you're serious about improving your entrepreneurial skills, you should make a concerted effort to think about what you've done well and what you've done poorly. Marc Cenedella blogs about both his company's history and what he's learned from his mistakes. Chris Michel wrote his article about outcomes and activities; he also kept a diary at times. If I were your lawyer I'd advise you not to keep a journal (only because it could wind up in court if there's ever a legal dispute involving your company). But as someone who wants you to succeed as an entrepreneur, I strongly encourage you to keep some kind of journal—just don't *tell* anyone that you're doing it!

Be a student of business. Follow Marc's example. He constantly reads books about management, leadership, and other business issues. And don't forget that the eureka moment that convinced him that TheLadders would work came while watching a videotaped speech by an HBS professor. Read magazines and books about business and entrepreneurship, and share what you've learned with your team. (I promised my publisher that I would remind you of Marc's response when he read a book that he thought was especially valuable—he bought fifty copies and gave them to colleagues. Just a thought. . . .)

Go to the well. You will find a wealth of valuable information and advice about entrepreneurship just by browsing the Web sites of schools and organizations such as HBS, Stanford, Babson, and the Kauffman Foundation in Kansas City. More important, take full advantage of your relationships with your mentors; they can almost certainly save you heartburn and hardship by passing on some of the wisdom they've accumulated during their own careers as entrepreneurs. And do as Marc, Chris, and Marla have done: as your business grows, reach out to other entrepreneurs, develop new relationships, and learn as much as you can about how they've handled the challenges they've faced.

When you can't move forward, move on. Persistence doesn't mean you should stay with one venture until the cause is utterly lost. Maybe you'll discover that you're ahead of the market, or maybe you misjudged the amount of competition you're facing. Maybe the product you're selling doesn't solve an essential problem or the team you've built simply isn't strong enough. Maybe you've legitimately encountered a run of really bad luck. (It does happen, though not as often as people think.) Whatever the reason, there sometimes comes a point when the smartest thing you can do is walk away. As virtually all of the highly successful entrepreneurs I talked with made clear, a committed entrepreneur will find a way to get back in the game. One roll of the dice might be the beginning—but don't let it be the end of your entrepreneurial story.

THE NEXT RULE

Here's a test for you. HBS professors who studied entrepreneurial success found that any firm that becomes viable enough to attract venture capital has between a one-fifth and a one-third chance of surviving. The question you should ask yourself is: Do I look at these odds and conclude they're so long that it isn't even worth trying to start my own company? Or do you look at it the way Stig Leschly does and say,

Well, I guess I'll have to plan on attempting this at least three to five times?

If you are serious about becoming a highly successful entrepreneur, understand that you'll be committing a significant chunk of your life to achieving this goal. Maybe your objective is to start something, cash out quickly, and then start something else; maybe it's to build the business that you'll lead until your dying day. Regardless, recognize that you're choosing a way of life that very few others have the guts to pursue—and that even attempting to do so will change you and set you apart. You've chosen the red pill, so to speak, and there's no going back to the cubicle. As all successful founders know, when you play the entrepreneurial game, you're playing the game for life.

CHAPTER 21

The reasonable man adapts himself to the world; the unreasonable man persists in trying to adapt the world to himself. Therefore all progress depends on the unreasonable man.

—GEORGE BERNARD SHAW

MARC: THE TOUGHEST DECISION

When he made up his mind to do something, Marc Cenedella rarely hesitated or second-guessed himself. After he and Angela Kim became engaged in March 2009, they immediately began planning their wedding, and when Marc discovered that the Plaza Hotel in New York City had a couple of cancellations in June—casualties, he presumed, of a sour economy rather than broken romances—they locked in on a date. Their plan was to follow the wedding with a two-month honeymoon, during which they would travel throughout Europe and Asia. At some point during their trip, Marc would spend a week working out of TheLadders' office in London. But aside from that week and his promise to check in occasionally via e-mail, Marc would be leaving his company alone for the first time since he had started it.

Though the global economy was in bad shape, TheLadders was a counter-cyclical business, and in the wake of the financial meltdown in September and October 2008, the company had seen a strong uptick in the number of people using the site. A lot of people were either out of work or afraid of being out of work, and many of them were more than willing to consider using a paid service to look for new jobs. By this point, TheLadders had pretty much overcome the challenge of converting to a business model that depended on payments from both employers and job seekers. TheLadders was also hiring aggressively, and to accommodate all the additional employees, it had recently signed a lease for the third floor of a new office building.

The company unveiled its first television commercials, including one that ran immediately after the 2009 Super Bowl. Suddenly its brand seemed to be everywhere. Moreover, the overseas expansion had continued to go well; TheLadders.co.uk, for instance, already had one hundred thousand subscribers. And the HBS case study that the school had been working on was almost finished. In April, Marc was due to visit Harvard and attend a class during which the case would be discussed for the first time.

But then, days before he was scheduled to fly to Boston, Marc received some news that shook the foundation of his company.

He was at home one Friday evening—it was Good Friday, in fact—when he got an alarming weekly report. The number of TheLadders' customers whose credit cards had been declined had taken a sharp turn for the worse. This was completely unprecedented. Given that their job-seeking subscribers either made at least $100,000 a year or were within shouting distance of that milestone, it simply hadn't occurred to them that a large number of reliable customers would suddenly be unable to pay for their service.

Marc and Alex dug through their records, going back as far as February. Though still in the single digits, the percentage of declined credit cards had tripled during the past few weeks. Initially, Marc had little sense for whether the problem would moderate or soon become very serious. He knew credit was tight and that some of his customers were undoubtedly overextended, but he soon realized that another factor was also coming into play. Congress was considering a bill that would make it harder for consumer credit companies to raise interest rates and fees, and the companies were reacting to the possible change preemptively by reducing credit limits and even canceling cards. Add to that the fact that there had been so many recent mergers in the banking industry; customers were often receiving new credit cards but forgetting to update their information with TheLadders. The company was facing a critical and unexpected threat.

Marc had been sitting at his computer and analyzing the data since seven p.m.; before he knew it, it was after midnight. He went to lunch the next day with his fiancée and his future in-laws and returned home around four p.m. The more he thought about the problem, the more convinced he was that it posed a dire threat to his company. They lived on cash flow, and if the amount of money coming in every week diminished significantly, they would have to cut costs immediately. As with many companies, their biggest cost was payroll. Marc dreaded the prospect of laying people off, but given the coming contraction he didn't see how he could keep everyone he had on staff.

The timing was terrible, too. TheLadders had hired new employees as recently as a few days before, and they had just signed the lease for their new office space. The need for the additional space had seemed obvious— after all, just a few weeks ago they had forecast that the company's revenue would nearly double in 2009. Clearly, they couldn't count on that now.

The hardest question was how many people the company could still employ. For as long as he had been in business, Marc had made almost every important decision based on extensive data, or at the very least by getting the counsel of people whose opinions he trusted. But in this case, he decided, he simply didn't have time. He would have to rely on his instincts. As the hours ticked by, he sketched out several different models, trying to determine how bad their situation would get and how many employees of TheLadders would have to lose their jobs.

He stayed up all Saturday night analyzing the numbers, trying to settle on a plan that would cause pain to as few people as possible, but also ensure that the company would survive this challenge. Marc knew he had to get the number right. The layoffs would do serious damage to the company's morale, but it would be devastating if he miscalculated and found himself forced to announce a second round of cuts a few weeks later.

"If we're going to lay off people," he told himself, "we'll do it once, and we'll cut deep enough to ensure that we don't have to do it again."

Finally, Marc made his decision. He e-mailed Alex Douzet with the number just as dawn was breaking over New York City. It was 6:03 a.m. on Easter Sunday.

Andrew Koch was in his first year at HBS now, and he felt great about his decision to go there. During the coming summer, he would be working for Matrix Partners, the lead investor in TheLadders, and he was sure he wanted to start a new company of his own after graduation. While attending business school, he'd also been working part-time for TheLadders, putting in maybe twelve hours a week, much as Marc had once run Forbes Pacifica on the side. But much of his work involved straightforward operational matters; he was no longer in the loop on strategic issues.

Over the school's Easter break, Andrew had flown down to Florida for a brief vacation. He expected to see Marc soon after his return to Boston, when his former boss was due to come to HBS to attend the discussion of the case on TheLadders. On Easter Sunday, he was surprised to answer his cell phone and find Marc on the line.

"Bad news," Marc said, and then he explained the credit card problem, the deteriorating financial picture, and the plan for layoffs.

Andrew was stunned. He'd thought the company was thriving—but then again, so had Marc until a few days ago.

Although he could do little to provide hands-on help, Andrew could serve as an important sounding board. He had been present at the company's creation, so he understood as few others could how hard it was for Marc to take these drastic measures. But Andrew was also removed from the current circumstances and objective enough to see that the layoffs were necessary. Marc had already made the hard call, but he wanted to talk through the decision, and it meant a lot to him that his friend agreed with it. He also wanted to get Andrew's thoughts on how best to explain the cuts to the staff.

Later the same day, Marc met with Alex and worked up a plan for rolling out the cuts. Then they called the company's dozen or so top-level decision makers, telling them to get to the office early and come to an emergency meeting at 8:00 a.m.

The next morning, Marc made sure that all his team leaders were present, then shut the door to the conference room and immediately delivered the bad news.

"Guys, we're cutting," he said, and then he specified the exact number of positions that each group had to shed. The room was utterly silent: the total cuts represented more than a quarter of the workforce.

We'll be making the announcement on Wednesday, Marc added. "You have until five p.m. today to give me your cuts."

Everyone around the table was stunned. Those who had been with the company since before it had received venture funding had never heard anything but good news from Marc. And no one from any department had seen this coming—especially with the recent hires and the new office space, it seemed as if the company was getting stronger every month. Slowly his executives began speaking up, asking him the same questions he'd asked himself over and over during his weekend deliberations. What had happened? Were the layoffs really necessary? Was it likely that there would be more than one round of cuts?

On Tuesday night, Marc called an emergency meeting of his board of directors, explained the situation, and received its endorsement of his plan. The next morning, he split the company into two groups—those who would be staying were sent to one of the offices leased by TheLadders, while those who were getting laid off were sent to another.

"The lawyers will tell someone in my position to say as little as possible in a situation like this, " Marc began, as he addressed the employees who had just learned they would be losing their jobs. "But we've always had two rules: Love the Customer, and Our Team Wins. And I have not led you to a win today. I've led you to a loss, so I owe you more than just thank you and good-bye."

He took them through a twenty-minute presentation, laying out exactly what had gone wrong financially and why the company simply couldn't keep everyone. Delivering that speech was the hardest thing Marc had ever done. He was letting go of some people whose contributions he deeply valued. Even Dave Carvajal, who had introduced Marc to HotJobs so many years ago and had finally decided to come aboard, would be leaving. (Dave's job was to recruit new employees, and it was clear they wouldn't be doing much recruiting for a while.)

His marriage to Angela, the rush of recognition that the TV commercials and the HBS case about TheLadders brought with them—this was supposed to have been Marc's moment in the sun. But now, as summer 2009 approached, Marc and Alex found themselves faced with a series of hard strategic choices that could make the difference between TheLadders' long-term success or failure. They revamped their revenue targets for the rest of the year and told the company's slimmed-down staff that they should focus on growing by 15 percent during 2009, rather than the 80 percent or so they'd originally hoped for. Marc felt confident that they could hit this figure, and doing so would not only move the company in the right direction but also restore his employees' confidence that they would be successful—credit crunch be damned.

Steve Perricone came into the office to visit in early June. TheLadders had always been a crowded place, marked by constant growth, with people sitting almost on top of one another—hence the near-continuous need to keep adding new office space—and at first Steve was struck by an eerie silence. But as he walked around the company and talked with people, including men and women he'd known for years now, he was struck by something else: a note of defiance. The people Marc had recruited and held on to believed deeply in the company. They were not about to let the down times they'd just experienced define their future.

By the time Steve stood next to Marc as the best man at his friend's wedding at Grace Episcopal Church in mid-June, it looked as if the company had stabilized. The cuts Marc had made proved to be deep enough, and the credit card crisis eased. TheLadders was on track to meet its revised goals, and it was once again drawing up much bigger plans for the future.

Marc and Angela left for their two-month honeymoon as planned, and when Marc took a week off from his vacation to work out of The-Ladders' London office, he realized that both he and his company had passed an important test. Marc and TheLadders could survive without each other—at least for a little while.

MARLA: THE LEGACY

Summer 2009 marked the official ten-year anniversary of bluemercury. To Marla Malcolm Beck, it was a momentous milestone, and she spent a lot of time thinking about what she'd accomplished and what she wanted to do next. She had another two years on her contract, and she loved the company and all she had built. She was especially proud of the impact she'd had in the beauty industry. Other stores were now trying to copy her model, which was the sincerest form of flattery. She was also glad to know that her three children would grow up in greater comfort than she and Barry had; equally important, she wanted to nurture their inborn desire to grow and build. She didn't necessarily imagine that they would become entrepreneurs someday, but she did hope that they would, in the best sense, set unreasonable expectations for themselves.

Meanwhile, Marla's gutsy decision not to go forward with bluemercury's national expansion had been vindicated. Her instincts had been right: the economy had indeed taken a dive. And because she had reduced costs and taken such a conservative approach to growth, the company had escaped most of the pain suffered by its competitors. The lone exception was the last few months of 2008; when the company's sales faltered, Marla deduced that her wealthy clientele had suddenly realized how big a hit their investment portfolios had taken as a result of the global financial crisis.

Even when the future looked especially bleak, Marla had been confident that bluemercury would bounce back fairly quickly. She'd long since realized that she was truly in the self-esteem business, because her clientele's happiness depended on looking good and feeling good about themselves. Even in difficult economic times, women were going to buy beauty products like mascara. And they used up their supplies quickly; a tube of mascara might last three months, and then they'd have to buy another. For that matter, Marla had a sense that many of her customers considered bluemercury a pick-me-up. When times were hard, makeup could provide a kind of entertainment, a way to put troubles aside. Proving the point, one of bluemercury's vendors introduced a new skin cream that cost $295 a jar. When Marla learned that she had sold out her entire supply the first day, she was sure her company would be okay.

A year had passed since she had decided to put the brakes on their plan to expand. Now, as much of the rest of the business world continued to suffer, she and Barry began taking advantage of lower real estate prices. They started expanding again, opening stores in tony suburbs like Bethesda, Maryland; Westport, Connecticut; and Lake Forest, Illinois. The business model that had served them so well from the start continued to deliver great returns.

Marla also had plans for expanding bluemercury beyond its roots in retail. She had a catalog business now, and she was considering the possibility of developing a TV show for one of the home shopping channels. She and Barry decided to launch their own line of cosmetics. There was a gap in the marketplace, Marla concluded—a place for high-end, eco-friendly products. They planned to spend much of the summer assembling the necessary resources, interviewing chemists, and determining which products would be included in their introductory line. They settled on a name—M-61—after a blue-hued galaxy some 2.3 million light-years from Earth.

Marla had been so busy that for several years she had fallen out of touch with HBS. Recently she had decided to get more involved as an alumna, primarily because she felt that it was important for successful entrepreneurs to encourage those coming along behind them. In particular, as a female entrepreneur she felt an obligation to serve as a guide and mentor for other women. In 2008, she had been invited to join the board of advisers to the business school's Arthur Rock Center for Entrepreneurship, and she accepted with pride.

Now, in spring 2009, she was invited to address the HBS Luxury Goods and Design Business Club. She was delighted for the opportunity to do for others what Jonathan Ledecky had done ten years ago for her—stand in front of a crowd of would-be entrepreneurs and try to inspire them with her presence and example.

Marla's presentation narrated the bluemercury story—and hers—in thirteen slides. She told the tale well, and it clearly captivated her audience. She described the highs and lows, and how she and Barry had found not only business success but also love and a family. At the end of her talk, she presented a final slide that offered her Top 10 Lessons for Harvard MBAs.

1. Experiment with your summer job.
2. Get in the game.
3. DROOM. (Don't Run Out of Money—Jon Ledecky, HBS '83)
4. Do something you love.

5. The first year is the hardest.

6. Avoid the GBF* mentality. (*"Get big fast")

7. Angels are your friends.

8. Competition makes you stronger.

9. "Nothing's good forever." (Dick Darman, HBS '67)

10. You CAN have it all.

Afterward, she was surrounded by students, and they were as eager to pepper her with questions as she had been after Jon Ledecky's talk at HBS a decade before. They were curious about all sorts of things—from how she had managed bluemercury's financial challenges to how she had made key strategic decisions; from how she had integrated her business with her personal life to what she thought truly made an entrepreneur. Marla was only too happy to answer their queries. It was gratifying to give speeches like this one, but she also believed that doing so was her responsibility. So many people had helped her at so many points along the way, and she knew she never would have become a successful entrepreneur without them. Now it was her chance to pass along some of what she'd learned.

CHRIS: IF I CAN DO THIS, YOU CAN, TOO

After Chris Michel left Affinity Labs in late 2008, he found he was having a hard time answering the question "What do you do?" when he met new people. Surprisingly, not having a full-time job became almost a full-time calling, if not an easily defined one. He served on a few corporate and charitable boards. He spent a lot of time staying in touch with people from all facets of his life. He traveled the world, visiting places such as Antarctica, Cambodia, and the former Soviet Union. And he took photographs by the thousands. Anne had given him his first serious camera just before they'd driven from Massachusetts to California together in 1998, and over the years Chris had taught himself the art of shooting a striking and well-composed picture. Now that he had freedom and time, photography became one of his main passions.

He was passionate about something else as well: sharing his experiences as an entrepreneur and helping others to take the leap. Chris found that between board meetings and photography sessions, he spent two or three hours each morning answering e-mails and phone calls from would-be entrepreneurs, offering his thoughts about their ideas and often encouraging them to give it a shot.

During most of 2008, Harvard Business School professor Joseph Lassiter and a senior HBS researcher named Liz Kind had been working on a case study featuring Chris and his companies. Chris was invited to come to HBS and join Lassiter's class, where the case would be taught for the first time, and he leapt at the chance. Lassiter and Kind's work represented a kind of affirmation that Chris had never dreamed possible, nor did he realize that it would be so important to him. In moments of excitement, he would insist that having the case written about him and being invited to its unveiling at HBS mattered more than successfully starting both companies.

In ten years, Chris had come a long way. The insecure navy officer who was convinced that his presence on campus was the result of an admissions office mistake was now being held up as a role model for a new generation of HBS students. Increasingly, Chris found himself looking back and reflecting on all that had happened in the past decade. On two recent occasions, he had almost felt as if his entire life were passing before his eyes.

First, a few months before the sale of Affinity Labs, Chris had flown to Hawaii for a retirement ceremony honoring Ernie Phillips, one of his best friends from his navy days. Ernie had been Chris's sponsor in their squadron in Maine, and he was the navigator whose place Chris had taken on the ill-fated Orion flight that had almost crashed. Chris had even introduced Ernie to his wife, Stephanie. Now they had two teenaged daughters.

Ernie had been a few years ahead of Chris in the military, and in the decade since Chris left the military Ernie had followed a career path that might well have been Chris's had he not left for HBS. But after two full decades in the navy he had decided that it was time to put his family first and do something else with his professional life.

Traditionally, a retiring officer would ask an admiral or his commanding officer to be the guest of honor and keynote speaker at his farewell ceremony. But Ernie asked Chris Michel to do the honors, and his friend proudly accepted. Chris still loved the navy, and as he stood at a podium on the deck of the battleship USS *Missouri* at Pearl Harbor and made his speech, he could imagine an alternate universe in which he would soon be in Ernie's shoes, wrestling with the decision about whether to retire. It was a deeply sentimental moment.

A few months later, Chris had turned forty, and his old HBS friend and study group partner Tom Goundrey flew out to San Francisco to throw a surprise party for him. More than two dozen people gathered in a private room at the back of a trendy restaurant, people from all parts of his life—James Currier, Abigail Johnson, a number of HBS classmates, and, of course, Anne Dwane. Everyone took the opportunity to roast their friend, but when the toasts turned serious Chris couldn't keep the tears from welling up. Tom and a friend of Chris's named Ben Sebel presented him with a vintage nautical spyglass, similar to those used by the contemporaries of Captain Jack Aubrey, the nineteenth-century British sailor in Patrick O'Brian's Master and Commander novels. In its day, the glass was technologically advanced because it was designed for use both day and night. That made the gift especially appropriate, Tom said in his speech, because Chris was a man who continually scanned the horizon, always looking for the next far-off goal, even if it was barely perceptible. And Chris, Tom told the gathering, could always be counted on to make every effort to reach that distant destination.

Chris and Anne returned to Harvard Business School together for the unveiling of the case study about Military.com and Affinity Labs. After meeting up with Professor Lassiter, they walked over to Aldrich Hall and took the stairs up to room 207, the same room in which Section H had met during the years when they had attended the school. Eager young students filled the classroom; some of them approached Chris as if he were a rock star, and a few asked him to sign their copies of the case study.

Although the twelve-page case was entitled "Affinity Labs," its first half traced the story of Chris and Anne from their first meeting through the rise, fall, and rebirth of Military.com. Then the case challenged the students to figure out how to estimate a dollar value for Affinity Labs, and it put them in Chris's shoes as he faced the decision about whether to sell his company to Monster. Admittedly, the case suggested that the decision was more difficult than it had been in real life, but that served its purpose as a teaching tool. (Most HBS cases, in fact, included a disclaimer stating that certain details had been changed or disguised.) The events described in the case ended in December 2007, and the final paragraph of the narrative read like a cliffhanger, with Chris taking a walk around San Francisco and pondering Monster's offer to buy the company. Unless the students did some independent research, they wouldn't learn whether Chris had decided to sell until the final few minutes of class.

The students tore apart the case, politely but sharply second-guessing Chris's and Anne's decision making at every point. Chris didn't mind the critical comments at all. He vividly remembered that precisely this kind of role playing had instilled in him the confidence that he could launch his own company and helped him take the first steps toward intelligent entrepreneurship. And as he listened to the students eagerly analyzing the case from every angle, he was also reminded that HBS had provided him with both the beginnings of an invaluable network and a wonderful community of peers.

Even so, Chris had often reflected that the one thing HBS hadn't taught him was just how lonely the entrepreneurial process could be. Until you actually did it—until you created something entirely your own and so achieved the unreasonable goal that few other people considered worthwhile—you couldn't possibly know what the experience actually felt like. Only people like Anne Dwane and James Currier, who had also taken that exhilarating but lonely entrepreneurial journey, could truly understand. They knew how it felt to wake up afraid in the middle of the night, worrying about how much money, how many careers, how many hopes and dreams had been bet on you and your ability to deliver on a promise. They knew what it was like to fear that what they had to accomplish could not be done—and also know that it simply *must* be done. And, happily, some of them also knew what it felt like to play the entrepreneurial game and win.

He still sometimes wondered why he had been successful whereas others had not. How had he learned to act like an intelligent entrepreneur? He had made many good decisions and usually learned from his mistakes; he had also had the good fortune to meet a number of people who had encouraged him to make the most of his opportunities—and he had been savvy enough to listen. Most important, he had come to believe in himself. Now, he wanted to help others do the same. And not just here at HBS—he wanted to share what he had learned with anyone bold enough to pursue the dream.

Toward the end of the class, he and Anne stood up to address the students and describe what they'd achieved over the decade—what it had been like to start Military.com, to work for Monster, and in the end for Chris to start, build, and sell Affinity Labs.

As his presentation came to a close, Chris pointed to his old seat, right in the center of Worm Deck at the front of the room. "I sat right there," he told the class. "I was just some navy guy who wondered whether he even belonged here. Believe me when I tell you, if I can start something like this and be successful, you can, too."

CHAPTER 22

PLAY THE GAME FOR LIFE

We need 100,000 people in 100,000 garages trying 100,000 things—in the hope that five of them break through.

—TOM FRIEDMAN

At the start of my reporting on this project, I was looking for entrepreneurs who had achieved genuine success. I wanted to find role models who had learned the lessons that would help anyone—or at least a person who had the creativity and courage to try—to become an intelligent entrepreneur. But then, at a point when I was already well into my research, I realized I'd forgotten to do something very important. And maybe it's something you haven't done either.

I had neglected to define "success."

In an effort to do so, we can of course use quantitative metrics. We can look at companies like TheLadders, bluemercury, Military.com, and Affinity Labs, and ask, How much money do they make? How many people do they employ? Have they truly solved problems and somehow added to the common good?

Those are all useful questions, but I believe that understanding success requires that we dig a little deeper.

Let's face it: for most of us, an important part of any good definition of success is about money. As you've probably noticed, it can sound pretty hollow when people say otherwise—especially when the people saying so have already made lots of money.

But honestly? After spending months talking with and getting to know people like Marla, Chris, and Marc, I came to believe that the freedom and security provided by a high income or a significant windfall are much more important to highly successful entrepreneurs than the money itself. At the deepest level, what matters most is finding a true measure of fulfillment—one that leaves you feeling that you have used all your talents to accomplish something worthwhile, make a difference in people's lives, and leave a legacy for those who follow.

Entrepreneurship, as I discovered, isn't just about solving a problem, building a venture, managing risk, or making money. It's about having a positive impact on the world, making the most of the gifts you've been given, and realizing your full potential as a human being. An intelligent entrepreneur, in short, plays this game for life.

WHY AM I HERE?

Although I chose to end the three narratives I've presented in this book in mid-2009, Marla's, Chris's and Marc's stories continue to unfold. Following is a brief report on their further adventures.

Marc and Angela had a honeymoon for the ages, and Marc came home to find that his company was more vital than ever. Morale was good, and they hit the revised growth targets that they'd set for themselves after the layoffs. Meanwhile, the European version of TheLadders continued to thrive, with plans to expand into even more international markets. Marc's weekly e-mail reached more than 3.6 million subscribers as of early 2010, and he spent a good deal of time giving speeches all over the world now, too. He remained an evangelist for his company, of course, but he was also passionate about encouraging people to take charge of their careers and find fulfillment in life, wherever it might lead them.

Marla Malcolm Beck's bluemercury grew still larger throughout 2009 and into 2010. Increasingly, her competitors mimicked some of her most successful tactics. A number of them began instituting team-based bonuses and focusing much more intensely on providing first-class customer service. She was proud to report that her vision of helping her employees attain careers, as opposed to simply jobs, was working, and that many of her salespeople and managers were now celebrating their tenth year of working for bluemercury. She and Barry spent much of the second half of 2009 meeting with chemists and planning the launch of the bluemercury line of cosmetics, currently scheduled for fall 2010. "I love working on this new project," Marla told me. "It's like being an entrepreneur all over again."

Both of the companies Chris Michel started—Military.com and Affinity Labs—continued to flourish. By early 2010 both were worth far more than they had been when he sold them to Monster and, just before this book went to press, Chris accepted an invitation to return to HBS as an entrepreneur-in-residence. In 2009, Chris visited ten countries and traveled to almost every continent. He took thousands of photographs, many of them breathtakingly beautiful. He felt that one photo in particular—a sensational shot of a killer whale jumping out of the water—symbolized much of his life. He'd had to spend years developing his skill with a camera and then had traveled to Alaska to get the photograph, but the crucial point was that when he'd found himself in precisely the right place at the right time, he'd been fully prepared "To get that picture," he said, "you need to be on that boat. That's really the story of my life—you know what I mean?" I did: to become a *successful* entrepreneur, you've got to make a total commitment to the goal and then spend years working toward that moment when it all comes together.

All three of this book's protagonists turned forty between the time I started researching it and the time it was due to arrive in bookstores. That milestone provided a natural opportunity to take stock of what they'd accomplished in life. They had all begun the process even before I began asking them an endless series of questions. A recent conversation with Marc—one that began when he described the way he greets new employees on their first day at TheLadders—provided an especially good example of the sort of soul-searching that my trio of entrepreneurs were undertaking.

"We're here to solve a mystery," Marc Cenedella says to each new employee he meets. "And that mystery is, 'Why am I here?'"

He knows why the new employee is there, of course. He or she needs a job, and all of them hope they've found an interesting and exciting place to work—maybe even a place where they can have some kind of impact. But as Marc's greeting suggests, he is constantly asking himself the same question.

"When you start an Internet company," he explained to me when I asked him to answer his own question, "a lot of people will tell you to achieve a decent measure of success and then sell. That's a typical path followed by a lot of entrepreneurs, and not just those who launch Internet ventures. TheLadders has now enjoyed more than a modest success, and sure enough some people have come along and offered a fancy price for the company. So in a strange sense—but a very true sense—I am a volunteer here. Most of the other people who work here—well, if they didn't have a job at TheLadders, they would probably have a job someplace else. I, on the other hand, could spend the rest of my life on a beautiful beach. So as I say, the mystery we're here to solve is, Why am I here?"

He leaves the question unanswered when he talks with new employees, but in the conversation with me he was happy to provide his own answer. It's simple: he believes he has truly found his calling. Further, he believes that he never would have found it if he hadn't taken the leap and started TheLadders.

"I find it tremendously interesting to watch people take their skills, talents, and abilities, and find a way to use them to become productive in the world. I find that awesome. But almost everything people think they know about hunting for a job is wrong. My goal is to help these very talented, successful people by showing them the right way to hunt for a job. Not having the right job often causes people genuine pain. I want to help them end the pain. I want to help them get the right job and answer that question: why are they here?

"This is the work I was put here to do, so that's why I've never been interested in selling the company. Look, you know the motto here: Number one, Love the Customer. Number two, Our Team Wins. There's no number three that says Make a Bunch of Dough and Cash Out. I *do* love my customer, and I love my work. And TheLadders will win in this market, win in North America, and win in the world."

Of course, none of us can ever provide a definitive answer to Marc's favorite question. But I am persuaded that most people—my three entrepreneurs included—hope that they will somehow find a way to make a difference in the world. Chris started Military.com because he wanted to help military veterans make a smoother transition to civilian life. Marla believes that her company helps women feel good about themselves. And Marc helps people match their jobs with their larger aspirations. I think it's also true, by the way, that all three of them spent countless hours talking with me about their experiences in part because they hope that their stories might help others learn how to be successful entrepreneurs.

As it happens, Harvard Business School also asks their own version of "Why are you here?" For a long time HBS didn't teach entrepreneurship, and it still don't teach its students how to sell. But, perhaps surprisingly, they do teach—or at least try to teach—more than a little bit about how to live a fulfilling life.

Professor Howard Stevenson, for instance, designed a class to specifically address the sorts of questions. His course—called Building a Business in the Context of a Life—is built around small group sessions that, as the official description puts it, "focus on key steps in the life plan development process." In addition to offering the course, Stevenson and a senior research fellow, Laura Nash, wrote a book entitled *Just Enough*, which attempts to show readers how to juggle what they believe are the four key elements to success in work and life: happiness, achievement, significance, and legacy.

"It turns out that there's little correlation among the four elements," Stevenson told me in an interview. "You can achieve greatly without being happy. You can probably be significant without great achievement. You can leave a legacy without achieving it in your own lifetime—think of Edgar Allan Poe and Karl Marx, for example. And I think you can be happy without experiencing any of the other elements."

Moreover, Stevenson pointed out, acquiring one or more of the four elements sometimes precludes acquiring the others. You might aspire to be happy, he said by way of illustration, but if you're happy, you might not have the drive to achieve. Or you might focus on achieving a legacy, but because doing so arises to some degree from an altruistic impulse, you may not be able to maximize your own achievements.

"I don't like to think of it as striking a balance," Stevenson said, "because I prefer to think of it as juggling. In fact, if you think about juggling, you think about how hard it is to keep your eye on all the balls. And the most important ball is the ball that's about to fall. It's not the ball in your hand—it's the one that's about to fall."

Professor Joseph Lassiter is another HBS professor who is very thoughtful about what HBS students and graduates are looking for in life. "Students usually come back to see me. Most of them are happy and content, and I enjoy hearing about their successes and their lives. The minority who aren't satisfied, though? In almost every case, they're unhappy either because they don't feel intensely involved with their work or because they haven't fallen in love. More to the point, they're either working in a profession that someone else thought would be a good fit but is in fact of no particular interest to them, or they have no one to share their life with and they're fundamentally lonely. They never—ever—come to me and say, Gee, I'm not making enough money."

THE NEXT RULE?

So now it's your turn: Why are you here? How do you define success? Why, finally, do you want to become an entrepreneur?

I've identified what I consider the ten essential rules of successful entrepreneurship. But there are always new lessons to learn about entrepreneurship in particular and life in general, and I have no doubt that you will discover a number of key rules of your own. If this book has value for you, I hope that the stories of how Marla, Chris, and Marc launched and built their companies will inspire you to follow your own entrepreneurial dream. I hope you'll experience the tremendous excitement that comes from starting and building your own venture—and that you'll receive not only a substantial monetary reward but also the deep satisfaction of solving an important problem and making an impact that derives from your unique solution. When you do succeed, promise yourself that you'll take the time to reflect on what you've learned and to pass it along to others. Our world needs more people like you—men and women who are committed to becoming intelligent entrepreneurs.

NOTES

2   *But the truth is quite different*: The rates and characteristics of failure in entrepreneurship are well documented in Scott A. Shane, *The Illusions of Entrepreneurship* (New Haven: Yale University Press, 2008), beginning p. 7.

32   *Let's go back to the mid-1940s*: Jeffrey L. Cruikshank's *Shaping the Waves: A History of Entrepreneurship at Harvard Business School* (Boston: Harvard Business School Press, 2005) was invaluable in helping me understand the evolution of the entrepreneurship curriculum at Harvard.

51   *In one speech given*: A lengthy account of Professor Sahlman's speech was included in an October 14, 1997, *Harbus* article by Vikas Tuteja headlined "Sahlman Educates, Warns Prospective Entrepreneurs."

60   *The day before graduation*: The average starting salaries and other information about the career prospects of the Harvard Business School class of 1998 were found in the 1999 edition of *BusinessWeek* magazine's "Best B-Schools" feature, still available online as of this writing at http://www.businessweek.com/ bschools/98/top25/profile48.htm. Moreover, descriptions of the festivities surrounding graduation day 1998 come largely from

a June 15, 1998, *Harbus* article by Andrew Farquharson head-lined "Robert Rubin Shares Insights into Success with HBS." (Farquharson, a member of the HBS class of 1999, went on to become a very successful entrepreneur in his own right.)

81   *In the first weeks of 1999*: This reminiscence of the insane valu-ations of Internet stocks comes courtesy of Kimberly Blanton and Ross Kerber, "Internet Stocks Defying Wall Street's Grav-ity," *Boston Globe*, January 13, 1999, accessed online March 15, 2010, at http://www.highbeam.com/doc/1P2-8529099.html.

99   *Finish school, because startups founded*: Shane's book *The Illu-sions of Entrepreneurship* devotes study to the question of whether more education predicts better success as an entrepreneur, see especially pp. 45–47.

132   The quotes from Evan Williams were compiled from two news articles: "For Twitter C.E.O., Well-Orchestrated Accidents," in a *New York Times* blog, March 7, 2009, accessed online at http://www.nytimes.com/2009/03/08/jobs/08bosses.html; and Scott Kirsner, "60 Seconds with Evan Williams," *Fast Company*, December 19, 2007, accessed online at http://www.fastcompany.com/magazine/96/q-a.html.

161   *"I invest in people, not ideas"*: Arthur Rock's quote comes from: William A. Sahlman, "How to Write a Great Business Plan," *Harvard Business Review*, July/August 1997, p. 101.

162   *As the debate grows heated*: This possibly apocryphal story is included in Philip Delves Broughton, *Ahead of the Curve* (New York: Penguin Press, 2008), p. 27.

163   *Some of the academic research*: See, for example, Phillip H. Kim and Howard E. Aldrich, "Social Capital and Entrepreneurship," *Foundations and Trends in Entrepreneurship*, vol. 1, no. 2, p. 64, July 2005, accessed online at http://ssrn.com/abstract=939776.

191   *Look at the two HBS classes*: Data on the percentage of HBS alumni who immediately (or close to immediately) tried to become entrepreneurs come from Josh Lerner and Ulrike Mal-mendier's paper, "With a Little Help from My Friends: Success and Failure in Post-Business School Entrepreneurship," pre-sented at the University of Southern California on February 15, 2008. It can be found online at http://www.usc.edu/schools/

business/FBE/seminars/papers/AE_2-15-08_MALMEDIER.
pdf.

232   *While thinking about*: Chris Michel's *Proceedings* article, "Outcomes Versus Activity," March 1, 2006, is available online at http://www.military.com/opinion/0,15202,89647,00.html.

293   *But one HBS study*: Paul A. Gompers, Anna Kovner, Josh Lerner, and David S. Scharfstein, "Performance Persistence in Entrepreneurship," *Harvard Business School Working Paper* 09-028 (2008). The professors' results were summarized in "Try, Try Again, or Maybe Not," *New York Times*, March 21, 2009, available online at http://www.nytimes.com/2009/03/22/business/22proto.html.

ACKNOWLEDGMENTS

At the start of this project, I told my editor that I hoped to do three things. First, find an elite, cooperative group of entrepreneurs who weren't yet household names. Second, get to know them and their stories inside and out. And, finally, break down the lessons they learned about methodical, dynamic entrepreneurship. In truth, this proved more difficult than I had anticipated, but I hope I succeeded in the end. If so, the lion's share of the credit belongs to a legion of impressive people who shared their time with me.

At the outset, I am indebted to the people whose experiences formed the backbone of this book: Marla Malcolm Beck, Chris Michel, and Marc Cenedella, along with Barry Beck, Anne Dwane, Brad Clark, Alex Douzet, and Andrew Koch. I'm grateful to have been able to recruit this group of extraordinary entrepreneurs as characters—and even more grateful for the opportunity to have learned from them in the process.

Additionally, at least one hundred other entrepreneurs worked with me, helping me over time to organize, understand, and ultimately write this book. Most of them appear only rarely, if at all, within these pages. I cannot possibly list everyone who deserves credit here, but I especially want to thank a group of men and women from the Harvard Business

School class of 1999—the class after Marla, Chris, and Marc's—for their help. This incomplete list includes: Brian Backus, Jon Burgstone, James Currier, Owen Culligan, Andrew Farquharson, Kathy Korman Frey, Brad Keith, Shelia Lirio Marcelo, Patrick Mullane, and Farquan Nazeeri.

I would have been stuck in neutral at the starting line were it not for several Harvard Business School professors who sat down with me for interviews. Joseph Lassiter, Howard Stevenson, and Noam Wasserman, especially, have my thanks. Also, although Stig Leschly and Ed Zschau have moved on from HBS, I couldn't have written this book if they hadn't been willing to spend time talking with me. I greatly appreciate the help that Brian Kenny, HBS's chief marketing and communications officer, and Jim Aisner, director of media relations, provided. Additionally, HBS alumni Jon Ledecky and Ed Mathias helped me not only to better understand Marla Malcolm Beck's story but also to learn a bit about that "whole other level" of entrepreneurship that Barry Beck told me about.

My agent, Esther Newberg, listened patiently and offered great advice as I came up with several ideas for books before this one. My editor at Holt, John Sterling, improved the manuscript with every draft, and he deserves special note for figuring out how to organize the book. I also want to thank Holt publisher Steve Rubin for his support.

And two personal notes.

I'd like to thank my wife, Melissa, for her encouragement and love. Keeping up my custom of coming clean to her in author's notes, I hereby acknowledge that there might possibly have been a few, rare moments when the challenges of writing *The Intelligent Entrepreneur* threatened my otherwise uniformly cheerful, optimistic, positive nature. So she gets credit and thanks for her patience, too.

Finally, I'd like to thank Jamie Diaferia, my law school friend and my cofounder in the first for-real entrepreneurial venture I ever launched: Mercury American Publishing Company. If we hadn't launched that company, I probably never would have written this book. Neither Jamie nor I went to Harvard Business School, but we earned our MBA degrees together at the School of Hard Knocks.

INDEX

ABOUT THE AUTHOR

BILL MURPHY JR. is the author of *In a Time of War: The Proud and Perilous Journey of West Point's Class of 2002*. Previously, he worked as Bob Woodward's research assistant on the bestselling *State of Denial*. An inveterate entrepreneur who was on the founding teams of three separate startups, he is also a former military officer, lawyer, and *Washington Post* reporter.